WORKING BELOW THE SURFACE

Tavistock Clinic Series
Margot Waddell (Series Editor)
Published and distributed by Karnac Books

Other titles in the Tavistock Clinic Series:

Acquainted with the Night: Psychoanalysis and the Poetic Imagination
Hamish Canham and Carole Satyamurti (editors)

Assessment in Child Psychotherapy
Margaret Rustin and Emanuela Quagliata (editors)

Facing it Out: Clinical Perspectives on Adolescent Disturbance
Robin Anderson and Anna Dartington (editors)

Inside Lives: Psychoanalysis and the Growth of the Personality
Margot Waddell

Internal Landscapes and Foreign Bodies: Eating Disorders and Other Pathologies
Gianna Williams

Mirror to Nature: Drama, Psychoanalysis and Society
Margaret Rustin and Michael Rustin

Multiple Voices: Narrative in Systemic Family Psychotherapy
Renos K. Papadopoulos and John Byng-Hall (editors)

Psychoanalysis and Culture: A Kleinian Perspective
David Bell (editor)

Psychotic States in Children
Margaret Rustin, Maria Rhode, Alex Dubinsky, Hélène Dubinsky (editors)

Reason and Passion: A Celebration of the Work of Hanna Segal
David Bell (editor)

Sent Before My Time: A Child Psychotherapist's View of Life on a Neonatal Intensive Care Unit
Margaret Cohen

Surviving Space: Papers on Infant Observation
Andrew Briggs (editor)

Therapeutic Care for Refugees: No Place Like Home
Renos K. Papadopoulos (editor)

The Many Faces of Asperger's Syndrome
Maria Rhode and Trudy Klauber (editors)

Understanding Trauma: A Psychoanalytic Approach
Caroline Garland (editor)

Unexpected Gains: Psychotherapy with People with Learning Disabilities
David Simpson and Linda Miller (editors)

Orders: Tel: +44 (0)20 8969 4454; Fax: +44 (0)20 8969 5585
Email: shop@karnacbooks.com; Internet: www.karnacbooks.com

WORKING BELOW THE SURFACE

The emotional life of
contemporary organizations

Editors

*Clare Huffington, David Armstrong,
William Halton, Linda Hoyle,
and Jane Pooley*

KARNAC

LONDON   NEW YORK

First published in 2004 by
H. Karnac (Books) Ltd.
6 Pembroke Buildings, London NW10 6RE

British Library Cataloguing in Publication Data

A C.I.P. for this book is available from the British Library

ISBN 1 85575 294 8

Edited, designed and produced by The Studio Publishing Services Ltd, Exeter EX4 8JN

Printed in Great Britain

10 9 8 7 6 5 4 3 2 1

www.karnacbooks.com

CONTENTS

ACKNOWLEDGEMENTS   ix

CONTRIBUTORS   xi

SERIES EDITOR'S PREFACE   xv

FOREWORD   xvii
   Nick Temple

Introduction   1
   David Armstrong and Clare Huffington

CHAPTER ONE
Emotions in organizations: disturbance or intelligence?   11
   David Armstrong

SECTION I: PERSPECTIVES ON LEADERSHIP

Introduction   31
   Clare Huffington

CHAPTER TWO
Leadership, followership, and facilitating   33
the creative workplace
    Anton Obholzer with Sarah Miller

CHAPTER THREE
What women leaders can tell us   49
    Clare Huffington

CHAPTER FOUR
What is the emotional cost of distributed leadership?   67
    Clare Huffington, Kim James, and David Armstrong

SECTION II: CHANGE AND CREATIVITY

Introduction   85
    William Halton and Linda Hoyle

CHAPTER FIVE
From sycophant to saboteur—responses to   87
organizational change
    Linda Hoyle

CHAPTER SIX
By what authority? Psychoanalytical reflections on   107
creativity and change in relation to organizational life
    William Halton

SECTION III: WORKING RELATIONS IN A NEW
ORGANIZATIONAL ORDER

Introduction   125
    David Armstrong

CHAPTER SEVEN
The vanishing organization: organizational containment   127
in a networked world
    Andrew Cooper and Tim Dartington

CHAPTER EIGHT

The discovery and loss of a "compelling space".   151
A case study in adapting to a new organizational order
    Sharon A. Horowitz

SECTION IV: WORKING WITH THE EXPERIENCE
OF VULNERABILITY

Introduction   167
    Linda Hoyle and Jane Pooley

CHAPTER NINE

Layers of meaning: a coaching journey   171
    Jane Pooley

CHAPTER TEN

Clash of the Titans—conflict resolution using a   191
contextualized mediation process
    Linda Hoyle

Endword
    Clare Huffington   205

APPENDIX I: Notes on consultancy approach and techniques   209

APPENDIX II: Glossary   223

REFERENCES   231

INDEX   241

ACKNOWLEDGEMENTS

Our primary debt is to the clients with whom we have worked and from whom we have learned. We have also benefited much from our colleagues and associates, some of whom are contributors to the book. We are indebted to Jon Stokes, the first director of TCS, whose initiative brought us together in a shared enterprise and helped to shape much of our early experience and thinking. We are equally indebted to our parent organization, the Tavistock and Portman NHS Trust, to those who have supported and championed us directly, and to colleagues in other disciplines, whose work and ideas have on occasion served as a stimulus to new insight, unexpected links across a professional boundary. Finally, we owe gratitude to Janet Wint-Johnson, our business manager, and Baya Kapaya, our administrator, for the care, support and encouragement that has enabled us to bring so much of what we do to fruition, including this book.

CONTRIBUTORS

David Armstrong is Principal Consultant at the Tavistock Consultancy Service. An organizational psychologist, he worked in action research and consultancy at the Tavistock Institute, the University of London, and the Grubb Institute before joining TCS in 1994. His particular interests are in the dynamics of leadership and the significance of emotional experience as a source of organizational intelligence.

Andrew Cooper is Professor of Social Work at the Tavistock Clinic and the University of East London and Dean of Postgraduate Studies for the Tavistock and Portman NHS Trust. He is presently completing a book about the changing nature of modern health and welfare systems understood from a psychoanalytic perspective. Over the past five years he has led a large consultancy and evaluation project in a social services department, and draws upon this experience in his contribution to the present volume.

Tim Dartington is a social scientist and organizational consultant. He is a member of OPUS—an Organization for Promoting Understanding of Society—and associate at the Group Relations

Programme of the Tavistock Institute, London. Tim is also a visiting lecturer on organizational theory at the Tavistock and Portman NHS Trust.

William Halton is Principal Consultant at the Tavistock Consultancy Service and chair of the Consulting to Institutions Workshop. He has consultation and coaching experience in the public and private sectors and a special interest in mediation work, development programmes and group relations conferences. He has a background in child and adult psychotherapy.

Sharon Horowitz, PhD, is an organizational consultant, teacher, and executive coach specializing in the financial services, medical, and technology industries and is based in New York. Her primary focus is on the dynamic interplay between corporate culture, personal cultural influences, and work behaviour. She is clinical instructor at the Albert Einstein College of Medicine, where she teaches group dynamics and ways in which individual behaviour is shaped by the broader social and economic context in which one works. She is also an Associate Consultant of the Tavistock Consultancy Service.

Linda Hoyle is Principal Consultant at the Tavistock Consultancy Service. Linda is a chartered organizational psychologist with a PhD in organizational change and consultancy. She is Director of Development Programmes at TCS and has a special interest in organizational development, mediation, and executive coaching.

Clare Huffington was a founder member of the Tavistock Consultancy Service and has been its Director since 1999. She has worked as a teacher, educational psychologist, and chartered clinical psychologist before becoming an organizational consultant. She is also a qualified family psychotherapist. She is on the board of the International Society for the Psychoanalytic Study of Organizations. Clare is particularly interested in women's leadership development.

Kim James is a chartered psychologist and Member of the International Society for Psychoanalytic Study of Organizations. She is a member of the faculty at Cranfield School of Management, where she is director of the Cranfield Executive Doctorate. Kim directs and tutors leadership development programmes and undertakes team consulting and executive coaching assignments. Her special interests and publications include organizational stress, organizational politics, and leadership development.

Sarah Miller is Consultant at the Tavistock Consultancy Service. Her approach is based on her significant general management experience in one of the most complex and demanding sectors. She is the director of the TCS leadership programme—Mastering Leadership—and is involved in a number of other change management and development programmes. Sarah works with senior executives from leading international organizations and is a visiting consultant on psychodynamic leadership development programmes at IMD business school in Lausanne.

Anton Obholzer is a psychiatrist and a fellow of the Royal College of Psychiatry, and a psychoanalyst who trained with both the Tavistock Clinic and The Institute of Psychoanalysis. He is the former chairman of the Consulting to Institutions Workshop and Principal Consultant at the Tavistock Consultancy Service, as well as having been Chief Executive of the Tavistock and Portman NHS Trust. He consults and lectures widely on organizational change, and is responsible for organization development projects in Madrid, Turin, and Austria. He is co-editor and author of several papers in *The Unconscious at Work* (Routledge, 1994). Anton's special interests are unconscious factors that interfere with interpersonal and intra-institutional communication and change.

Jane Pooley is Principal Consultant at the Tavistock Consultancy Service and runs her own organizational consultancy practice. Jane is Director of the executive coaching training programme at TCS. She is a qualified family psychotherapist. Her publications and work reflect her interest in social development initiatives and she specializes in executive coaching and team and organizational development programmes.

Nick Temple is the Chief Executive of the Tavistock and Portman NHS Trust. He is a psychoanalyst and consultant psychiatrist in psychotherapy at the Tavistock Clinic. He is a Fellow of the Royal College of Psychiatrists and a former chair of the psychotherapy faculty at the college. He has clinical interests in psychoanalytic approaches to psychosomatic disorders, violence and guilt in clinical disorders, transference and counter-transference, and publishes and lectures in these areas. He is active in managing mental health services and promoting mental health policy, to include therapeutic methods based on psychodynamic approaches.

Working below the Surface has a distinctive intellectual and professional pedigree. It builds on the innovative body of work which developed at the Tavistock, both during and in the wake of the Second World War. This work centred on the nature of individual, group, and institutional processes: the ways in which internal states are inextricably linked with professional and group functioning, and the ways in which unconscious collective processes can affect, indeed at times determine, the implementation of tasks and goals— both organizationally and individually.

The present book, the first to focus specifically on current work within this tradition at the Tavistock, offers the fruit of the past decade's experience on the part of the staff and associates of the Tavistock Consultancy Service. It clearly and cogently sets out the new generation's extensive contribution to the human side of working with the problems endemic in organizations, and to the multi-faceted practice of organizational consultancy.

It draws on the original frame of reference, which sought to integrate a psychoanalytic perspective with systems theory and group relations. But it also develops new and suggestive theoretical models to address some of the rapid changes and challenges affecting the dynamics of the contemporary workplace: the increasingly competitive environment, the impact of globalization, IT, the culture of accountability, partnerships, and the ever-evolving structures of organizational leadership.

The editors and authors meticulously map this changing environment and both draw on and further develop the Tavistock Approach. In harvesting their extensive experience, they break significant new ground, whether in initiating new working methods, in offering innovative ideas and debates, or in furnishing challenging insights into the emotional worlds of a wide variety of organizations and their workplaces. The book offers a thoroughly contemporary understanding of the unconscious factors that affect all organizational functioning, as well as authoritatively contributing to the field itself and thus to the implementation of more effective managerial and social policies and services.

Margot Waddell
Series Editor

FOREWORD

It is a privilege to write the foreword of this book, the first on consultancy in the Tavistock Clinic Series. It describes the latest phase in the development of the Tavistock Consultancy Service (TCS) ten years after it was set up in 1994. Consultancy has been part of the Tavistock enterprise since the Second World War, when psychoanalytical ideas were first applied to groups and organizations. The ability to understand and consult to organizations has added a potent additional dimension to the Trust's activities of research, training, and clinical work. Working with the unconscious aspects of organizations has broadened and strengthened the Tavistock approach, enabling the Trust to engage with some of the endemic problems of organizations in the National Health Service (NHS) and in the wider society. It has also lent strength and authority to the Tavistock's engagement with social policy, where organizational change has a vital role in improving mental health services and social care.

The inspired application of Kleinian psychoanalytic concepts, developed by Bion and others, began the Tavistock's tradition of understanding the nature of unconscious processes and communication in groups and organizations. This has provided a rich and powerful model to apply to organizational difficulties and has allowed a capacity not only to work below the surface but to attend to resistance and negative processes in organizations. The application of the Kleinian concept of projective identification is fundamental to understanding the unconscious communication that takes place in organizations and groups. The addition of systemic approaches to this theoretical model has broadened the approach to understanding organizations, with the addition of further tools to the organizational consultant.

The theme of "working below the surface" is the distinctive approach used by TCS. Its working hypothesis is that bringing the emotional experience of organizations into view sheds light on the challenges and dilemmas facing the organization and provides a source of understanding and insight into the forces that determine its nature and ultimately its fate. This approach is part of the basic philosophy of the Tavistock and Portman NHS Trust, which is that an understanding of the unconscious contribution is essential to the delivery of its clinical work and training.

The work of the Tavistock Consultancy Service in the NHS, the public sector, and in private industry is taking place in a period of rapid and unpredictable social change, affecting the environment of all the organizations in our society. This has echoes of the period of social change which took place during the Second World War and its aftermath, when the Tavistock's organizational work first developed. At that time, collective social organizations, such as the NHS and the welfare state, were set up as a response to changes in society that followed the disaster of the First World War and the severe problems of the inter-war years leading into the Second World War. It could be argued that the social change at that time, involving mutually caring organizations, derived from reparative processes following the two wars, with their roots in the depressive position. Some have seen the present social change as going in the direction of more competitive, mistrustful, and paranoid forces within society and within organizations. As the editors point out in the introduction to the book, there are powerful factors operating; for example, globalization, intensified by the IT revolution, and increased mistrust of organizations with rigorous and imposed criteria of accountability. These changes in the environment of organizations affect the work of TCS because of the altered functioning of organizations and the need to develop new theoretical models and techniques.

The illustrative examples indicate the degree to which the boundaries of organizations are much more permeable. There is both the creation of partnerships across boundaries and the intrusion of external authority structures; for example, the many new agencies of inspection and performance management that represent greater government intrusion across the boundary of organizations.

The decline in the individual's trust in public organizations, including professional bodies, together with a competitive environment, leads to the fear that an organization will compete to seek its own ends rather than the benefit of its patients or customers. The demutualization of building societies is an example of this, where there has been a move from an organization providing mutual benefit to its members to a bank, which seeks to make profits from its customers.

The book offers explanatory hypotheses for these phenomena. The chapter by Cooper and Dartington considers the changed social environment. Horowitz investigates the problems that this change of environment brings to the leaders of organizations, looking carefully at some of the processes by which organizations and leaders have adapted. The rather idealized concept of leadership is examined, as are the ways in which leaders can continue to be effective and creative.

David Armstrong develops the important idea of institutional counter-transference. He advances the view that a great deal can be learned from the individual's emotional and irrational response to the organization. There is a conceptual shift from focusing on emotions as a source of disturbance in organizational functioning to regarding emotional experience as a rich source of information about the organization.

In considering leadership, the book reaches the conclusion that an organization in an unstable, intrusive environment may look to its leader as a crucial source of containment to enable it to continue functioning. There is a greater focus on the leader's need to mobilize personal qualities, including a capacity to create a psychological contract between the leader and followers. This is perhaps why executive coaching has become a much more common form of consultancy, focusing on the personal qualities and capacities of the leader.

This book lucidly sets out recent steps forward in the Tavistock approach to consultancy in its exploration of the social changes which are altering the nature of organizations and its exposition of new techniques and conceptual models in the psychodynamic framework. It marks the next stage in organizational work and in the history of the Tavistock Clinic.

Nick Temple
Chief Executive, The Tavistock and Portman NHS Trust
July 2004

Introduction

David Armstrong and Clare Huffington

The past decade has witnessed a series of cumulative transformations in the political, social, economic, and technological contexts in which organizations function. These changes have significantly affected the ways in which organizations have thought about themselves and the issues they are now having to address. In turn, they have challenged many of the conceptual frameworks and assumptions that underlie the practice of organizational consultancy.

The chapters contributed to this book have been written by the staff and associates of The Tavistock Consultancy Service (TCS), whose distinctive competence is in the human dimension of enterprise and the multi-faceted dynamics of the workplace. From their own perspectives, both distinct and shared, they tell a story of the experience of working as consultants with individuals, teams, and whole organizations over the past decade. The intention is to identify and explore some of the key themes that have emerged from this work and how they affect and influence the understanding of leadership and management in contemporary organizations. No attempt is made to reach a consensus, but rather to raise and map out a territory of continuing question and debate.

The Tavistock Consultancy Service

The Tavistock Clinic was founded in 1920. From the beginning, its consultancy work grew out of the experience of collaboration between psychiatrists, psychologists, and social scientists during the Second World War and its aftermath. It developed an approach to working with the organizational challenges of post-war reconstruction, drawing on methods of research and intervention first evolved within the context of military life (Trist & Murray, 1990).

In 1947, the Tavistock Institute of Human Relations was separately incorporated as an applied research body in its own right to pursue this consultancy mission as part of the Tavistock Clinic. The Tavistock Clinic itself joined the New National Health Service (NHS) in 1948. Both bodies shared the same premises until 1994, when the Tavistock and Portman NHS Trust was founded and the Tavistock Institute of Human Relations moved to its present location in the City of London and became the Tavistock Institute. Simultaneously, the Trust established The Tavistock Consultancy Service (TCS) as a specialized unit within the Trust to carry out consultancy work. The aim of TCS was and remains:

> To provide high quality psychologically informed consultancy on the human dimension of organizations to chief executives, senior managers and other professionals, which will enable them to work with both the conscious and unconscious aspects of their organizations in responding to the political, economic, social and technological challenges of today and in the future.

Over the decade since its foundation, the staff and associates of TCS have initiated programmes of work as consultants, researchers and trainers across a wide spectrum of private, public and voluntary organizations, both in the UK and overseas. These have included one-to-one assignments with senior executives in role consultation and executive coaching; work with top teams on organizational transformation and the management of change; whole organizational interventions in the field of cultural change; the implementation of strategy, mergers and partnerships; support to front-line teams in health and social services; stress, mediation and conflict resolution. They have also covered innovations in learning and development programmes, both generic and in-house, on consultative skills, group facilitation, managing continuous change and leadership (cf. Appendix I).

It is this range of work that both informs and is illustrated in the following chapters.

"Working below the surface"; an approach to organizational understanding and practice

"Working below the surface" is the phrase TCS has used from the outset to capture what is distinctive in the approach to consultancy that characterizes its work. It is an approach that focuses primarily on the human side of enterprise; both what is known and consciously attended to and also what is unknown, unattended, or unconscious in the individual and/or in the group. The working hypothesis that informs it is that bringing this undertow of experience and behaviour into view (to the surface) can shed new light on the challenges and dilemmas that an organization and its members are facing. This, in turn, can open up fresh and sometimes unexpected avenues for decision and action; in negotiating and managing change, handling conflict, rethinking work structures, or crafting vision and strategy.

This approach is distinctive in the field of organizational consultancy, a field that otherwise tends to view the study of non-rational processes in organizations as, at best, a side issue, or, at worst, irrelevant. In this respect, traditional approaches make little contribution, for example, to understanding and dealing with the complex responses to change, both positive and negative. The Tavistock Consultancy Service approach, in contrast, is significant in placing the exploration of non-rational, unconscious, and systemic processes at the centre of its work. This makes it possible to tackle conflict, stress and dysfunction head-on and thereby get more quickly to the roots, whether of organizational problems and dilemmas or of the challenges of creativity in individuals, groups, and organizations.

There are three principal frames of applied thinking and research on which this approach draws. First, there is psychoanalytic practice as a method of tracing the connections between conscious and unconscious mental processes and their significance in individual behaviour and development. Second, there is the extension of this practice to the study of group dynamics, sometimes called group relations. This practice is principally associated with the work of Wilfred Bion (1961) at the Tavistock following the Second World War, and has subsequently been developed by colleagues at both the Tavistock Institute and the Tavistock Clinic (Miller, 1993; Obholzer & Roberts, 1994; Rice, 1965). Third, there is systems thinking, which includes the Open Systems approach pioneered by social scientists at the Tavistock Institute (Miller & Rice, 1967; Trist & Murray, 1990, 1993) and the systems perspective developed by practitioners in family therapy and others (Bateson, 1973; Campbell, Draper, & Huffington, 1991). These variously overlapping frameworks constitute what is known as the "Tavistock approach" to organizational consultancy.

Our indebtedness to these three frames of thinking is apparent in many of the following chapters, without, we hope, being laboured. (Some of the key terms and concepts we draw upon are listed and briefly described in a concluding Glossary—Appendix II.) At the same time, part of the argument of this book is to question and/or to revisit aspects of this tradition of work, as applied to organizational life, which the changing contexts of the past ten years bring into view and may challenge. In this respect, just as organizations are increasingly having to question and reframe their conditions and tools of trade, so too are we.[1]

We have therefore been working directly from our experience of organizations to develop working hypotheses to explain some of the new themes in organizational life of which we have been becoming increasingly aware. We have compared and contrasted these ideas with existing frameworks, highlighting the gaps and, in some cases, coming up with new ideas of our own. The method is one of grounded theory (Hayes, 1997), starting with experience and deriving theory from this, rather than the more traditional scientific approach, which starts with a body of theory and hypotheses that are then applied to experience. It is in this spirit that we now outline some of the key changes in the context that have inspired our thinking and this book.

Changing contexts, emergent needs

That organizations are now inhabiting radically different and shifting external environments is the stock-in-trade of much contemporary political, social, and management discourse. Although the extent of change may sometimes be exaggerated, our experience is that few of our clients are unaffected by such change and the corresponding need to evolve new modes of adaptation, in the cause of survival and development, both individually and corporately.

The changes that have been most salient in the client organizations we are working with, which are often mutually reinforcing, include:

- the revolution in information technologies and the transmission of knowledge
- globalization of markets and hence competitive pressures
- increasing gradients of "manufactured risk"; i.e., "risk created by the very impact of our developing knowledge upon the world" (Giddens, 1999)
- changing social and cultural patterns; familial and generational, in attitudes towards gender and race, or work–life balance
- ecological awareness and sensitivity
- economic and political turbulence
- customerization and an increasing emphasis on consumer or client sovereignty
- the emergence of a contract culture, notably in the public sector, tied to rigorous and imposed criteria of accountability.

Associated with these changes are corresponding shifts in the structuring and patterning of organizations and the human requirements of the workplace. Organizational boundaries, both internal and external, are increasingly fluid; internal structures and roles less clearly defined and conventional hierarchies less evidently relevant. Mergers, strategic alliances, and partnerships have become commonplace. There has been a growing preoccupation with the language of vision, mission and corporate values, ownership, and "empowerment", alongside the harder edge of "outsourcing", "downsizing", and "target-setting". Within the business world and elsewhere, stable work groups are being replaced by project (some-times virtual) teams on short-term assignments, cutting across traditional professional and positional boundaries. An emphasis on innovation and creativity rubs up against the pressures on delivery and results.

The evolution of our thinking

The contextual changes listed above are significantly affecting the emotional world of organizations and their workforces; influencing and shaping what people feel and how they behave, both overtly and covertly, often in unfamiliar ways. Correspondingly, such changes both challenge some of the conceptual formulations we bring to our engagement with clients and their needs and also sug-gest new directions and emphases in understanding and working with the organizational experiences presented to us.

The chapters contributed to this book are not intended to offer a single unitary view of the new organizational order and its impli-cations for the theory and practice of our approach to consultancy. We set out to capture a "multi-verse" of perspectives rather than a "uni-verse" (Lawrence, 2003, p. 4); thinking in evolution, a journey rather than a destination.

It is possible, however, to discern a number of broad directions which this journey is taking.

First, there is a shift from focusing on emotions as a source of disturbance in organizational functioning to understanding the emotional undertow of people's experience in organizational life as a source of intelligence into the challenges and dilemmas they are facing. Our perspective on what can be called organiza-tional counter-transference significantly affects the way we think and behave in role as organizational consultants. This new con-sultancy mind-set is therefore presented at the beginning of the book, in Chapter One. Illustrations are given throughout of how this approach is applied to our work through the contex-tualization of what are often presented as individual issues. Chapter Nine on executive coaching, and Chapter Ten on media-tion and conflict resolution, are also detailed examples of this point.

Second, the loosening of organizational boundaries, both external and internal, is leading us to new constructs of contemporary organizations and their leadership. This feature of organizational life challenges traditional open-systems thinking about primary task and role, and therefore fundamentally changes how leaders might construe their exercise of power and authority. Some of the implications include, for example;

- The usefulness of making a new distinction between organization and enterprise in creating an engaging vision of the future of the organization; and of the need for a constant accommodation between the organization and its contextual embeddedness in order to keep its spirit and passion alive. This is addressed in Chapter One.
- The consequences for the dynamics of the organization of the need for the leader to focus on the psychological contract between leaders and followers. This is described in Chapters Two and Three.
- The challenge to individual leaders to act out of a personal sense of self rather than role and the ways in which changing role requirements and contexts mobilize different aspects of the self than were previously relevant; for example, the need to facilitate organizational creativity or to use political skills and know-how to influence decision and action. Linked to this is new thinking about the nature of organizational containment and the role of the leader in offering what we have referred to as "pro-tainment" or "the making present of an organizational idea embodied in a lively and enlivening sense of the enterprise which the organization frames". This is explored in Chapters Three and Four.

Third, and more widely, in an environment of constant change, the focus on the role of the leader in managing change and promoting creativity and innovation, covered in Section II, draws our attention to the idea of the existential primary task as a way of understanding people's responses to change. This is explored in Chapter Five.

Fourth, an underlying theme throughout the book concerns the struggle to promote creativity and innovation in the service of organizational health. This is most fully explored in Chapter Six, which both links and extends the conceptualization of creativity in psychoanalytic thinking to the dynamics of the workplace.

Fifth, the impact of the adaptations that organizations are making draws attention to new dynamic patterns in the relations between the individual, the group, and the team and, more generally, in the relatedness and identification of the person and the organization. This is addressed primarily in Section III, and developments in the practice of consultancy in addressing these emergent dynamics are described in Section IV. Chapter Seven discusses how, in the public sector, organizations are increasingly being subsumed within networks in ways that challenge many of the assumptions that have hitherto underpinned the practice of consultancy. These include the erosion of group attachments in the face of fears for individual and organizational survival (described in Chapters Seven and Eight), and the increasing focus on paired relationships, both positive and negative (described in Chapters Nine and Ten, respectively). The current organizational dynamic appears to emphasize basic assumption pairing (Bion, 1961) alongside the more recent conceptualization of basic assumption me-ness (Lawrence, Bain, & Gould, 1996). The greater exposure of the individual in organizations, the increase in personal vulnerability and the focus on pairs—those which function to contain creative work and those which do not—is reflected in the development of coaching and mediation work (Chapters Nine and Ten, respectively). The growing request for these services appears to represent a struggle and oscillation between basic assumption pairing and basic assumption me-ness, reflecting hope about future development and despair about individual or organizational survival. This struggle is vividly described in Chapter Eight.

It is not only our theoretical concepts and approaches that are being challenged; it is also the methods we use in consulting, and even the names we use for these methods. Thus "coaching", as we practise it, is not simply a renamed "organizational role consultation" but something distinctive in its own right. We have had to evolve new ways of working in group relations events. In the process, we have integrated techniques from family therapy into our consultancy and have explored ways of helping clients to lead creativity in their organizations. These and other methods are described in Chapters Nine and Ten and in Appendix I.

The structure of the book

The chapters contributed to the book are loosely clustered around five main themes.

Chapter 1 offers an overview of our particular "take" on the emotional world of the organization and its significance for understanding, decision, and action.

In Section I, Chapters Two to Four offer three different perspectives on the nature and exercise of leadership.

In Section II, Chapters Five and Six focus respectively on the dynamics of resistance to change, and creativity.

In Section III, Chapters Seven and Eight examine ways in which contextual change is reshaping the concept of the organization and the nature of our relatedness to it, both consciously and unconsciously.

Last, in Section IV, Chapters Nine and Ten consider different ways in which organizations are responding to issues of personal challenge or vulnerability and the significance of each.

While these themes may be general, the contexts in which we have encountered them are singular, arising out of the particular circumstances of particular assignments. We hope to have shared enough of this more singular experience to enable the reader to question our abstractions and make connections to their own experiences, as organizational players, consultants, or students.

In the interests of confidentiality, all references to clients are rendered anonymous and on occasion may represent a number of linked experiences that have been combined.

Who the book is for

This book is written for a wide range of readers.

- First, it is written for leaders, managers, and executives who are responsible for the smooth running of their organizational enterprise, offering new ways of understanding and managing the complexities of their environment.
- Second, it is written for organizational consultancy practitioners and students from a variety of backgrounds (including

people working in the Tavistock tradition, human resources specialists, and management consultants) who want to explore further their understanding of what is happening now in the underlying dynamics of organizations.

• Third, it is written for clinical professionals, counsellors, and psychotherapists interested in contemporary organizational dynamics and the impact that these may have on their work.

The tension of addressing such a wide audience is one that TCS has to hold on a daily basis and is represented in the content of this book, a tension that moves between TCS consultants' experiences, the client material (case studies), and the fusion of these with existing and emergent theory.

Note

1. An account of this perspective on organizational life, as represented at the start of the past decade, is given in a collection of papers, *The Unconscious at Work*, published immediately prior to the setting up of TCS by members of an ongoing workshop on Consulting to Institutions led by Dr Anton Obholzer at the Tavistock Clinic from the mid 1980s (Obholzer & Roberts, 1994). Their focus, however, is exclusively on addressing the dynamics of "human service" organizations.

CHAPTER ONE

Emotions in organizations: disturbance or intelligence?

David Armstrong

T his chapter offers a provisional account of the significance of emotions, the flow of feeling in thought and action, within organizational settings. This account seeks to build on but also in some respects to reframe earlier work within the "Tavistock tradition". It views emotions as a function of the organization-in-context, rather than simply of the individual and his or her relationships, or of the group. Correspondingly, it is suggested, alertness to the emotional undertow of organizational life can be a powerful source of information for managers and leaders in enlarging understanding, reviewing performance, foreseeing challenges and opportunities, and guiding decision and action.

Stating the obvious

Every organization is an emotional place. It is an emotional place because it is a human invention, serving human purposes and dependent on human beings to function. And human beings are emotional animals; subject to anger, fear, surprise, disgust, happiness, or joy, ease, and unease.

By the same token, organizations are interpersonal places and so necessarily arouse those more complex emotional constellations that shadow all interpersonal relations; love and hate, envy and gratitude, shame and guilt, contempt and pride.

Third, the interpersonal world of the organization is simultaneously a group world and subject to those tensions and conflicts that appear intrinsic to group life; between the wish to belong and the need to differentiate or between fear of the group and fear for the group.[1]

These are all, one might say, propositional truisms, in that they state something obvious that one hardly needs to be a psychologist or a psychoanalyst to recognize and acknowledge. Emotions are constitutive of organizational life because they are constitutive of all human experience. (Recently, neuro-scientists have suggested that they may indeed be constitutive of consciousness itself (Damasio, 2000).)

What these disciplines, and particularly psychoanalysis, add is a many-layered account of the *ways* in which emotions shape our experience, both consciously and unconsciously; their origin in early object relations, their expression in phantasy, and their pervasiveness and distribution within and across our private and public lives.

Questioning the obvious

It is one thing to acknowledge in this way that emotions are "constitutive of organizational life"; quite another to suggest that they may have something to tell us about a particular organization *per se*; for example, about the nature of its task or the way it is structured or the particular dilemmas and challenges it is facing. Emotions might be seen as independent variables affecting and influencing what happens in an organization but not otherwise intrinsic to it; an artefact, as it were, of the organization's dependence on human resources. It might, then, still be the case that an awareness of the emotional underpinning of behaviour, in oneself and in others, was a useful adjunct to management and leadership, enabling decision and action to be fine-tuned to the human realities of organizational life. This is the approach that informs the current vogue for "emotional intelligence"; "the capacity for recognizing our own feelings and those of others, for motivating ourselves, and for managing emotions well in ourselves and our relationships" (Goleman, 1998).

Similarly, much of the writing and practice of psychoanalytically orientated research and consultancy in the organizational field focuses primarily on disturbances to organizational functioning that arise out of individual or group dynamics, without further considering what, if anything, such "disturbance" may signify about the organizational field as a whole.

In what follows, by contrast, it is argued that emotional experience in organizations, at the level of both the individual and the group, should be viewed as a dependent rather than an independent variable. This could be put another way, that one cannot fully understand the place of emotions in organizations without reference to the boundary conditions that define any particular organization as a human construct. Making this shift of focus, it is proposed, significantly affects not so much how we understand the conscious and unconscious processes underlying emotional life in organizations, as their meaning; what they have to say about the organization as a system in context. One might express this as a move from emotional intelligence to the intelligence (as in "military intelligence") afforded by emotion. In turn, this move can open up new perspectives on the practice of organizations and their developmental needs.

An illustration

Before considering this position further the following material from a recent consultancy assignment offers a partial illustration.

> This involves consulting to a client who heads a team of IT staff working with a group of traders in a large multi-national investment bank. The consultation is part of a wider brief negotiated by a colleague with the boss of the IT division of which my client and his staff are a part. There is a close working relationship between the boss and my colleague and it is partly as a result of this that my client has sought out consultation. Both his boss and he himself believe that he will benefit from the opportunity to think through his role and how he works

within it. There is also an implication that he needs to hone his manage-ment and leadership skills as a prelude to possible promotion. He is aware of a number of apparent inhibitions in his approach to and exercise of those skills.

We start working together, ostensibly on a 2–3 week basis, meeting for two hours. I experience this work together as a tantalizing combination of hopeful feelings on my part—my client is young, bright, attractive, with a lot of technical flair—and frustration, amounting at times to exasperation. Sessions are cancelled or postponed at the last moment, sometimes without notice. Although my client will readily and appar-ently sincerely acknowledge much of what I try to put words to, it seems to make little or no difference to what he does and the tangles he gets into. I begin to feel we are going round in circles.

One recurring theme has to do with his relation to his boss, who is a powerful and dynamic figure with a highly successful track record. My client knew him from a previous company he had worked in and where he had built his reputation. The two of them had been quite close, socially as well as professionally, and it was through this prior relationship that my client had come into his present firm (just as it was through his relationship with his boss that he had come into this consultancy). In a series of four enigmatic pictures that, early in the consultancy, my client had drawn to represent how he experienced and felt about himself in his organization, his boss was the only represented figure he had been able to give a name to, placed on top of a kind of gantry, looking ahead.

The relationship between the two of them has remained close. They are often on the mobile phone to each other (including during consultancy sessions) and regularly meet when they happen to be in the same place at the same time (they are based in different countries).

Although their formal relation is that of subordinate and boss, the accounting relationship between them does not fit neatly into the conventional pattern of an organization chart. Indeed, one of the many apparently puzzling features of this organizational system as a whole, which my colleague and myself have been aware of from early on, is the difficulty of being able to gain any clear picture of the account-ability relationships in play. The IT Division serves traders in different parts of the world and trading in a variety of equities. My client is responsible for serving traders dealing in a particular type of equity in a particular country office, but with an additional and developmental global brief. At the time we began working together there was no appointed head of IT in this office, though this was on the cards and my client was potentially a candidate for it. Also, since traders can be fiercely attached to their own local view of their information needs, and since this attachment is likely to influence the ways in which local IT staff work with traders, any attempt to introduce a more global information system is likely to be an exercise in persuasion and certainly not dictat. In short, accountability relations within the division are fluid, and there is no formal, "special" relationship between my client and his boss that would distinguish him from a good many of his peers.

None the less, there is a "special relationship" between them. It gradually becomes clearer that this relationship has a peculiar quality. On the one hand it is expressed in a close, intimate, and probably collusive form, in which my client takes the role of confidante, backstop, gossip, bouncer-off of ideas or of judgments—about the business, about the people, about the politics. This relationship is shot through with positive feelings of affection, regard, loyalty, and admiration. Less consciously there is an undertow of envy, which tends to be projected in the guise of disparagement of other senior personnel in the bank, amounting at times to contempt.

On the other hand, the relationship can take a masochistic turn, in which my client is continually letting his boss, other senior staff, and himself down, through neglecting aspects of his immediate operational role or not taking up tasks he has been invited to do; for example, organizing "off sites." It is as if letting people down in this way is unconsciously and paradoxically a means of testing or proving their commitment or attachment to him.

This relationship is replicated in the (transferential) relations between client and consultant, in that I continually have the experience of being pulled into a kind of rescue mentality, i.e., being mobilized to do something that will save him from the consequences of his actions and in so doing demonstrate, as it were, that I genuinely consider him worth saving.

Things came to a head as a result of two events. I have mentioned that there was no appointed head of the IT office in which my client worked and that he was himself a potential candidate for this post—an expectation that he believed his boss had encouraged. Quite suddenly an appointment to this position was made from outside the firm. At first my client appeared curiously unaffected (without affect), neither particularly disappointed nor particularly angry. His relationship with his boss continued much as before, but with one significant twist—that he seemed now to transfer something of his "behind the scenes" role to his relationship with the new arrival: showing him the ropes, briefing him about the people and the politics, helping out with recruitment of new staff, etc., while simultaneously, if gently, complaining at the cost to other aspects of his work. (None the less, this relationship had a new emotional quality to it, in that the element of disparagement was much closer to the surface.)

The second event was the completion of a 360° feedback exercise for my client, which he had himself requested, once more perhaps following the example of his boss, who had recently done the same and had found it productive. The results from this exercise underlined the extent to which my client was at risk of compromising his good standing, personally and professionally, with his team, his clients (the traders), and senior management by what were seen as puzzling and frustrating inconsistencies in performance, especially in the more management and leadership components of his role.

Again, my client's initial response seemed emotionally flat. He was grateful for what people had said, pleased by the undertow of personal regard in which he was held and not apparently taken aback by the criticism. This, he felt confirmed his own view of his "weaknesses" and indeed it was in fact the case that his own self appraisals were often sharper than those of others.

I wondered if this would turn out to be just another circle we would go round. However, it did not prove to be so. I had decided, with the encouragement of my colleague, to propose a more active form of engagement in which we would meet more regularly, at my client's place of work, if possible weekly and at the end of the working day. Almost immediately I was struck by how much more focused he had become, both in how he presented himself and in the material he offered for work. For the first time he was able to acknowledge something of his anger and disappointment both at himself and towards his boss, but without sourness. At the same time he began to give up the "behind the scenes" role and rediscover and build on his real skills in offering technical leadership, both directly and indirectly. There continued to be setbacks, but it seemed easier now for him to pull back from both the internal and external pressures to "help out" or "make good", with their accompanying manic edge.

It occurred to me that what the 360° appraisal had done was not so much to tell him something that he didn't know about himself, but coming on the heels of his failure to be appointed as head of the office, as enabling him to *own* what he knew. To own what he knew in turn implied relinquishing something else, which had shadowed his self-knowledge in a way that robbed it of its emotional meaning—the illusion of the "special relationship".

It would be possible, I think, to read this whole episode from a clinical perspective, in terms of the enactment of oedipal phantasies, projected on to the relationship between my client and his boss (simultaneously my client and myself) and within a construction of the organization as a kind of extended family. And certainly there were occasions in working with my client when I wondered whether he might have benefited more from individual therapy, which at one point he was ready to consider. Although he rarely touched on personal areas of his life and history, I was aware of aspects of both that could have been seen to be part of a piece with his organizational experience.

However, and quite apart from considerations of my own competence and the boundaries of our role relationship (I was not working with him as a therapist), to have taken this route, either then or now, would have missed the opportunity afforded by a different and more organizational vertex.

In introducing the theme of my client's relation to his boss, I referred to the fluidity of accountability relations generally within the IT division and indeed within the bank as a whole. It was as if the whole organization and its various parts ran on the basis of informal relationships; networks of influence and persuasion that cut across and often seemed to subvert what an outsider would consider to be formal accountability lines. As my colleague put it, "there is often an apparent blurring of boundaries and difficulty in staying within the tasks and boundaries of the formal role".

From this perspective, one might consider the more pathological element in my client's relation with his boss as elicited by this structural "weakness" or "flaw", within which an internal patterning of object relations could take root and flourish. This would correspond with the position taken by Elliott Jaques, among others, in a well known critique of the relevance of psychoanalytic formulations to organizational functioning: that in so far as they are relevant at all, they are relevant only as a signal of the absence of "requisite organizational structure" (Jaques, 1995).

But this begs the question of what is "requisite structure" or, alternatively, of why an apparently "irrequisite structure" has evolved. In fact, both my colleague and myself found ourselves struggling for a considerable time with this issue. Were we at risk of seeking an explanation for what seemed to be evidence of individual pathology in normative assumptions about the appropriate structuring of accountability relationships?

The answer we gradually came to was affirmative—yes, we were. And in the process of arriving at this answer new light was thrown on my client's construction of the "special relationship". To summarize, and at the cost of some simplification, our hypothesis went as follows. The fluidity of accountability relations and the substitution of networks of influence and persuasion for formal lines of authority was an expression of at least two organizational realities. One corresponded to the developmental situation of the bank as a whole, which was expanding into new areas of business, buying up or buying in new bodies of expertise, often from diverse business and trading cultures. In this context there was some sense in keeping boundaries fluid and allowing a certain latitude in how things operated, even at the cost of a good deal of both organizational and psychological mess.

The second and more immediately relevant reality concerned the relation between the IT Division in question and its particular users—the business units and their traders. From a structural point of view the business units are dependent on IT to operate. Furthermore, and increasingly, IT applications can significantly add to the knowledge base of the business, both regionally and globally. In some respects IT could be seen as a leader in promoting and developing global operations, against the resistance of traders who, as mentioned earlier, can tend to focus rather on what they see as their more immediate local needs. On the other hand, it is the traders who have traditionally called the shots as the producers of revenue. For them IT is simply a service, and a very expensive one at that. In this structural and cultural context, there is a premium on building and cultivating special relations, through whatever means, as vehicles and levers of influence. At the same time, the pay-off from success in so doing can fall well short of felt considerations of equity. To use a very suggestive image offered by my client's boss in another context, the senior traders are seen as the "sun kings" who get all the glory, in a way which can "brew rebellion under-neath", feelings of being demeaned and undervalued.

One might say that this is a system that both puts a premium on special relations and simultaneously exacts a certain psychological cost; the inevitability of having to contend with feelings of envy and shame, which cannot be contained within a well-bounded organi-zational structure. But none of this is necessarily an indicator of unfunctionality. It may rather be an expression of something that is part and parcel of what might be termed the "psychic reality" of the organization.

From this perspective, my client's construct of the "special rela-tionship" could doubtless be seen as a defensive distortion of an organizational truth: to be understood not simply, or not only, as the enactment of an oedipal illusion, but as an idiosyncratic response to the in-actment of an organizational dynamic. Moreover, this is not just a theoretical point. It has consequences for both the client and the consultant, focusing attention on new questions: for example, about the nature of management and leadership in such a context, or about handling the tensions between personal and role relation-ships. It conveys intelligence, not just about oneself but about the nature of the "organizational animal" and its *modus vivendi*; a start-ing point for further exploration. To put this point apparently para-doxically, as he began to give up the phantasy of the special relationship, my client was able to get in touch with and explore the world of special relations he was indeed part of and how he could best cultivate and manage those relations, both individually and through the ways in which he supported his staff.

Transposing the argument: from the individual to the group

The example given above is intended to illustrate ways in which the emotional undertow of an individual manager's behaviour in the organization, which at first sight seems to have a purely personal significance, may simultaneously be a signal of (and a disguised response to) a present or emergent organizational reality, which has not yet been fully grasped.

The same may equally be true at the level of the group. It has been a feature of the Tavistock's work in the organizational field to draw attention to the importance of unconscious processes in groups.[2] These have generally been viewed as defensive responses to anxieties that have their origin in very early and primitive stages of development that are never fully outgrown.

In so far as such processes become evident within an organizational setting, however, a similar question arises regarding their significance. Are they to be understood as *en*actment of group pathology or *in*actment of an organizational dynamic; as an independent or a dependent organizational variable?

In a very influential and still widely cited paper by Elliot Jaques, first published in 1955, he proposes that, as he was later to put it, individuals unconsciously and collusively

> concoct organizations as a means of defence against psychotic anxieties thereby generating a fundamental cause of problems within those organizations. [Jaques, 1995]

This may be taken as an extreme statement of the enactment hypothesis. On this view it is as if organizations live two lives: one concerned with consciously addressing the requirements of particular tasks and one unconsciously aiming

> to externalize those impulses and internal objects that would otherwise give rise to psychotic anxiety and pooling them in the life of the social institutions in which (as individuals) we associate. [Jaques, 1995]

The emotional world of the organization then appears split off from its actual setting in the engagement of individuals with organizational work within particular structures and in social, economic, technological, and political contexts. Emotions in organizations function as extraneous "noise", something that needs containing or managing, but is not itself a signal of or response to the organization as an intentional object.

Over the next forty years, as he moved more into the fields of organizational research and consultancy, Jaques retracted this position. This retraction turned on his bringing into view and formulating a concept of the "organization per se", as

> an interconnected system of roles with explicit or implicit mutual accountabilities and authorities ... All human relationships take

place within such role relationships. Some form of organization must be explicitly established, or at least implicitly assumed, before it becomes possible for people to bring themselves or others into relationships with each other by means of taking up roles in the organization. In other words, organizations have to exist in their own right before people can collect in them. [Jaques, 1995]

This new position would not necessarily imply abandoning his previous stance. He could have argued, rather as Wilfred Bion and many of his followers have in relation to group life, that the organization can simultaneously be seen from two perspectives: as an intentional object and as an (unconscious) defensive construct.

But he does not do this. Instead, presumably bearing in mind the evidence of dysfunctional behaviour in organizations that his earlier work built on, he now argues that, in so far as we are prey to what he terms "psychological stresses" in the work situation, these arise primarily out of

the failure to clarify and specify the requirements of roles ... We get gross mismatches between the difficulty of roles and the capabilities of their incumbents. Or we fail to specify the accountabilities and authorities in role relationships, and leave it up to individuals to exercise personal power or otherwise manipulate each other in order somehow to get things done. It all becomes an unpleasant *paranoiagenic zoo*. [Jaques, 1995, italics added]

There is much to be said for this view. Moreover, the notion of the "paranoiagenic zoo" could itself be taken as an instance of how emotional turmoil in an organization may reflect and signal some unacknowledged feature of organizational functioning.

At the same time, there are two important qualifications to this position that can be made. First, it is not clear that Jaques's structural model is a rich enough specification of the organization as an entity "existing in its own right". (It is not only structures of roles that define the organization as an entity.) Second, as mentioned earlier, it can also be argued that Jaques's characterization of "requisite structure", at least in contemporary environments, may beg as many questions as it seems to resolve. More specifically, our prevailing concepts of role, authority, and accountability may be more problematic in the current contexts in which organizations trade than

Jaques appears to acknowledge. Correspondingly, our emotional experience in organizations, both positive and negative, may be a richer resource for probing organizational realities than he allows.

The organization as object

The argument advanced here may now be restated as follows. Instead of thinking of emotional life *in* organizations (the organization as one of the several arenas in which we live out our emotional inheritance, as individuals or as a species), we should think rather of the emotional life *of* organizations (the organization as an eliciting object of emotion).

With this view, every patterning of emotional experience within organizations, either in and between individuals or in and between groups, carries some reference to an organizational object. This "object" is an implicit third in all the emotional exchanges of organizational life, however intra- and interpersonal, or intra- and intergroup such exchanges may appear.

By "organizational object" we mean something that functions as a point of origin of psychic experience - "in its own right", to borrow Jaques's formulation—but which, like all mental objects, can elicit multiple responses, be subject to multiple readings, more or less conscious, and more or less in accordance with reality.

What then defines the organization as object? We suggest that it is defined by four boundary conditions. These are respectively:

- the organization as process (the task dimension)
- the organization as structure (the management dimension)
- the organization as enterprise (the identity dimension)
- the organization as contextually embedded (the ecological dimension).

It is these four dimensions of the organizational object that between them generate the emotional patterning within. Conversely, the emotional patterning within, whether located in individuals, in groups, or across the whole socio-psychic field, is a conduit of potential intelligence about the organizational object, seen under these four conditions.

The organization as process and as structure

The idea that emotional experience in organizations may reflect and be a function of an organization's process and structure is not new. It has been explicit in much of the work of the Tavistock Institute and the Tavistock Clinic and among colleagues influenced by this work, since the publication in 1959 of a seminal paper by Isobel Menzies Lyth, reporting on her study of the nursing service of a general hospital (Menzies, 1959).[3]

The title of this paper, "The functioning of social systems as a defence against anxiety", is borrowed from Elliott Jaques's earlier work, referred to above, and it has often been read as a vivid and detailed demonstration of his position at that time. In fact, however, it turns Jaques's thesis on its head. For Menzies Lyth the origin of the anxiety that mobilizes defences is not so much a matter of "concoction" as a response to characteristics of the nature of the organization's work, specifically the work of nursing. It is this "objective situation", as she calls it, that arouses feelings and associated phantasies linked to "situations that exist in every individual in the deepest and most primitive levels of the mind"; situations involving physical and emotional contact with illness, pain, suffering, and death.

Correspondingly, the intensity and complexity of the nurse's anxiety are to be attributed primarily to "the peculiar capacity of the objective features of the work situation to stimulate afresh those earlier situations and their accompanying emotion" (Menzies, 1959).

The originality of this paper turns on the ways in which Menzies Lyth goes on to show how much of the structural apparatus of the hospital, as this has evolved over time in the way roles are patterned, relationships regulated, and activities performed, can be seen as a sometimes conscious but often unconscious way of evading or defending against this undertow of anxiety intrinsic to the nursing task. The difficulty is, however, that these strategies of evasion, instead of serving to contain this anxiety may exacerbate it, through draining emotional energy and meaning from the nurse's relations with both patients and colleagues and through substituting rigid rules and procedures that inhibit the exercise of nurses' real and potential capabilities. The outcome can then be high and apparently intractable levels of sickness, often for minor illnesses, short-term absences, and a destabilizing pattern of staff turnover that further weakens the formation of strong and secure working relationships.

Much of the later work within the Tavistock tradition has drawn on and made use of insights stimulated by this paper (Obholzer & Roberts, 1994). Within this tradition the preoccupation has been with a reading of the emotional life of organizations, conscious and unconscious, in terms of the "goodness of fit" between organizational structures and the psychic demands associated with particular tasks and the processes involved in carrying them out. Simultaneously, charting the various ways in which organizations can get caught in evolving structures and ways of working that are designed to evade the burden of those demands as we register them internally is essential.[4]

Beyond structure and process

It is not only, though, structure and process that define the organization as object. No organization stands alone, insulated from its context, any more than each of us, as individuals, stand alone. While that context is relatively stable or predictable, it may be taken as a given, something to which an organization needs continually to adapt, but without having fundamentally to question either what it does or how it does it.

However, few organizations at present, either those we are members of or those we work with, inhabit such a context. Correspondingly our experience in and of organizations now is probably being shaped by challenges from without as much as, if not more than, anxieties from within. Since these challenges are registered emotionally, we suggest that they have to do not only with questions of viability, whether or not the organization will survive, but equally with the *cost* of viability, what will and what must be risked in the cause of survival.

Another and perhaps better way of putting this might be that as the relatedness of the organization to its context becomes more problematic and less predictable, the emotional experience within will both be shaped by and, in turn, signal questions of identity.

An illustration

Two years ago I was invited to facilitate an Away Day for the Board members and senior executives of a distinguished mental health trust. The focus of the day was to review and discuss clinical strategy, in the light of major challenges the organization was facing from outside. These challenges were being driven by a combination of political pressures relating to the provision of mental health services, that were in turn related to new arrangements and requirements on the part of commissioners and funders. In response to these challenges, the organization needed to consider a range of issues concerning the scope and substance of its clinical services and how these could best be presented or marketed to a new configuration of stakeholders, especially purchasers.

Towards the end of the day I became aware in myself of two pervasive feelings. One was a feeling of an absence; more exactly, the absence of "passion". The other was an accompanying sense of loss, associated with what I knew of the past history of the organization and its founding vision. These feelings were linked in my mind to a difficulty the meeting appeared to have in formulating a view of what was unique about the organization and its work that could, without embarrassment, inform how it presented itself to the outside world.

I wondered aloud whether these feelings, registered in myself, were being carried by me on behalf of others. I suggested that these missing elements might have tended to restrict the creativity or boldness of people's responses to the various challenges addressed in the review documents. This was not to say that important and constructive work had not been done. But there was something of a flavour of"none of this is of our choosing and we wouldn't be embarking on it if we didn't have to".

The response to this observation was muted and hard to read. Was the consultant importing something from outside, linked to his own image of the organization's history and identity or was he speaking to what was present in the room. I remain unsure. Someone commented that one would not expect passion here. Its locus was rather in the day-to-day engagement with patients. But then, unless one can access such experience in addressing strategic decisions, what guarantees can there be that such decisions may not put the quality and distinctiveness of that engagement at risk?

My sense is that the absence of "passion", understood as the spirit of the work, was serving as a defence against the acknowledgment of risk. Or rather the acknowledgment of a felt tension between two types of risk; the risk to survival, the viability of the organization in its market; and the risk to identity, the preservation and integrity of a particular enterprise.

Enterprise and context

By "enterprise" we mean a distinctive practice or set of practices that embody an organization's implicit or explicit concept of the work it does; that define what the social philosopher, Alasdair MacIntyre, has termed its "form of activity"; its conception of the ends and goods involved; its standards of excellence and sources of knowledge (MacIntyre, 1981).

The enterprise and the organization are not one and the same. One might think of the relation between them in terms of Wilfred Bion's model of container and contained (Bion, 1970). (One need not necessarily assume that the term "enterprise" has a realization in every organization, though I am inclined to think that where this is not the case, it seems likely that the "organization-as-object" will no longer carry meaning, will be experienced as psychologically empty.)

Rather than using this model, however, enterprise is considered here as a factor in the "organization-as-object". This factor, it is suggested, is always potentially held in tension with the outward-facing function of the organization—its contextual embeddedness. Similarly, structure is always held in tension with process. This tension surfaces whenever the context in which the organization operates challenges the terms on which and the means through which the organization has, as it were, been trading.

Most, if not all, organizations, are now having to face such challenges, be they public or private. Correspondingly they experience, consciously or unconsciously, the dilemmas of balancing the claims of survival and growth against the cost to identity, to embodied practice. It is such dilemmas, arising from a dissonance between these two boundary conditions of the "organization-as-object", that underlie much of the emotional experience presented by the clients we are currently working with—whether they are from banks, consultancy firms, pharmaceutical companies, or schools, colleges, hospitals, or prisons. The forms this experience can take are many and may present themselves as "suitable cases for treatment", either of the individual or of the group; stress, burnout, resistance to change, intergroup or intra-group conflict, loss of competence, intractable splitting between managerial and professional functions, etc.

We are only now just beginning to understand the underlying dynamics that relate specifically to this dimension of organizational life and what it may evoke from our inner worlds or our group inheritance. But we remain convinced that we will go seriously astray if we collude with the pull into pathologizing.

No emotional experience in organizational life is a suitable case for treatment. It is rather a resource for thinking, releasing intelligence.

Notes

1. The classic account of these tensions and conflicts, on which much of the later work of the Tavistock has drawn is to be found in Wilfred Bion's, *Experiences in Groups* (1961), and the distinction he draws between two modes of functioning in groups; work group activity and basic assumption mentality (dependence, fight–flight and pairing). See Appendix II: Glossary for further explanation.
2. A useful, if partial review is provided in Miller, 1990, and in the series of theoretical and applied papers collected in Obholzer and Roberts, 1994.
3. Recently, the term "systems psychodynamics" has been introduced to describe this tradition of work (Gould, Stapley, & Stein, 2001).
4. Elsewhere I have suggested introducing the term "primary process" to describe the emotional undertow intrinsic to an organisation's work, and its management (Armstrong, 1995).

SECTION I
PERSPECTIVES ON LEADERSHIP

Introduction

Clare Huffington

Organizations in all sectors have had to cope with massive change, both externally and internally. One effect of this turbulence has been to alter irrevocably the psychological contract between organizations and their employees. For the first time, in some cases, organizations have had to think about what they can do for their staff as well as what their staff can do for them. In this context, leadership as well as management effectiveness has become crucial. Leadership is needed to pull the whole organization together in a common purpose, to articulate a shared vision, set direction, inspire and command commitment, loyalty, and ownership of change efforts.

In the first chapter in this Section, "Leadership, followership and facilitating the creative workplace", Anton Obholzer with Sarah Miller, using core ideas from the Tavistock approach outlined in the Introduction to the book, draws our attention to the changing psychological contract between leaders and their followers.

Obholzer takes us through his view of the core functions of leadership considered in relation to both leadership and followership and how they can be thought through and negotiated in order to develop a creative workplace. In his focus on the pairing, or collaboration, between leaders and followers, he is reflecting the new preoccupation in organizations with the changing psychological contract between organizations and their members. He is, however, exploring this relationship in the context of a notion of stable organizational boundaries in which the primary task of the organization and organizational roles can be negotiated without too much difficulty.

Chapter Three, "What women leaders can tell us", is concerned with women's experience of leadership, taking as its starting point a research study of women in top leadership roles. In common with the theme of Chapter Two, women leaders are also focused on the relationship between leaders and their followers, but within a context of uncertain and loosening organizational boundaries both at home and at work. Their account of leadership is rooted in the person element of the person–role–system model, as if the leader is more than ever needed to embody the enterprise in the absence of traditional organizational boundaries. Simultaneously, this approach to leadership creates a need to question the concepts of primary task and role used in their original sense and brings to the foreground the concept of "pro-tainment" as a different kind of containment needed in the leadership role.

Chapter Four, "What is the emotional cost of distributed leadership?", looks at the role of the leader in embodying the enterprise, no matter what has been shared with or distributed to others in order to deliver the current agenda of devolved and delegated decision-making patterns. It focuses on the importance of horizontal as well as vertical leadership, how these interact and their effect on the emotional life of the organization. While there can be a devolution of responsibility downwards, there is also, perhaps, an unrecognized and simultaneous evolution of accountability upwards. The chapter concludes with a reassertion of the importance of the leader offering a singular, inspiring vision to integrate and contain the elements of leadership distributed to others.

All three chapters provide ample evidence of the constant questioning of identity—of the individual leader, the work group or team, and the whole organization—that is shaped by, and in turn shapes, the turbulent context around it.

CHAPTER TWO

Leadership, followership, and facilitating the creative workplace*

Anton Obholzer with Sarah Miller

Introduction

L
eadership would be easy to achieve and manage if it weren't for the uncomfortable reality that without followership there could be no leadership except, perhaps, of a delusional sort. What is more, for the organization to be creative it requires followership to be an active process of participation in the life of the common venture, and this, in itself, may carry with it some discomfort.

By definition there is thus an inherent tension between leadership and followership. This chapter is an attempt to address the complexity of this interface, to place the relationship in the context of the overall containing organization, and to investigate some of the factors that make for, and facilitate, a creative versus a stuck workforce and workplace. It is worth noting that in many other

---

*This chapter is a re-worked version of "The leader, the unconscious and the management of the organisation", which first appeared in L. Gould, L. Stapley, and M. Stein (Eds.) (2001), *The Systems Psychodynamics of Organisations*, New York: Karnac.

models of leadership and of management, working at understanding one's experience and the experience of others in connection with management do not necessarily go together. Further, that the sort of personal work and institutional introspection that goes with the approach to be described here is seen as unnecessary, gratuitous navel-gazing. The chapter postulates this latter view to be profoundly shortsighted.

The core functions of leadership

The primary task and the visionary function of leadership

Above all, leadership is about vision and strategy for the future. Differentiation is made between vision and strategy because there is, and has to be, a degree of passion and, indeed, of fervour in vision. Strategy, by contrast, is a "colder" element of leadership, but nevertheless an absolutely essential one in providing a focus about where the organization needs to be in future years. So strategy acts to temper vision and ensure that reality is the cornerstone on which achievable goals are set. It is strategy that enables vision to be achieved. But leadership vision, unchecked by strategy and out of touch with an active and responsible followership, risks creating a delusional system and, at worst, leads to *folie-en-masse* (group madness). This can be seen, for example, in cult disasters, such as the mass suicide in which all the members of the Jim Jones cult in Guyana, without questioning, emulated the suicide of their leader. On a more work-based plane, some of the recent accountancy scandals have made it clear how very strong the conscious and unconscious group pressures can be and how it can be almost impossible to become a "whistle blower" and thus stand up against institutional pressure.

The main institutional "ballast" that keeps the organization, both membership and leadership, steady must be the awareness of the *primary task* of the organization. The primary task of a commercial organization, for example, is to increase its shareholder value. Miller and Rice (1967), Rice (1958), Obholzer and Roberts (1994), and others have written about the danger of the primary task being infiltrated and corrupted by defensive processes arising from the work of the organization. A core leadership task, therefore, is to ensure that the concept of the primary task is not only uppermost in the minds of the membership of the organization, but that it is constantly reviewed in the light of the changing external environment and that the organization adapts in accordance with this (cf. the rather different perspective on primary task, as explored in Chapter Three).

Rice (1958) originally developed the idea of the primary task, which he defined as follows:

> Each system or sub-system has, however, at any given time, one task which may be defined as its primary task—the task which it is created to perform. . . . In making judgements about any organization two questions have priority over all other. What is the primary task? How well is it performed? [pp. 32–33]

Later, Rice, working with Miller, refined the concept, making the point:

> The primary task is essentially a heuristic concept, which allows us to explore the ordering of multiple activities (and of constituent systems of activity where these exist). It makes it possible to construct and compare different organizational models of an enterprise based on different definitions of its primary task; and to compare the organizations of different enterprises with the same or different primary task. [Miller & Rice, 1967, p. 25]

However the concept of the primary task is defined, its importance to institutional functioning is that an ongoing debate must be held about what the institution is about and where it is heading. Where the primary task is clear, debate is likely to be minimal. For example, the primary task of a school could be defined as educating pupils; likewise, the primary task of a hospital could be defined as treating patients. Where it becomes more complicated and where there is therefore likely to be more debate, is when an organization has multiple tasks. For example, the primary task of a prison could be defined as punishing and/or rehabilitating offenders. Similarly, the primary task of a pre-school nursery could be defined as educating and/or caring for those children attending it. This concept is thus a key element in member–member and leadership–followership interaction.

Leadership and the management of change

From the above, it is clear that leadership is essentially about the management of change, both internal and external to the organization, and the establishment and maintenance of mechanisms that enable the two components to link and cooperate with each other at a pace of change that is emotionally possible and realistic to both external and internal needs. The key question here is whether change is ever "internally" driven, or whether it is determined by external events. With the possible exception of succession issues, most change seems to be driven by changes in the environment. An example of this would be the imperative for organizations to embrace diversity training and policies as a result of a growing concern about the endemic nature of institutional racism.

Change that has its origin in the environment cannot, as it were, be "wished" away and has to be taken account of, though obviously for a time the existence of the external pressure can be denied by the process of "turning a blind eye" to it (Steiner, 1985). Change that is internally generated, by contrast, can be hived off or "encapsulated" (the institutional equivalent of the body walling off an infection, or the psyche encapsulating a traumatic experience). So, for example, changes in staff practice, staff rights and options are often "hived off" into the personnel or human resources department. Here they linger—policies on paper that can be produced at critical moments but that have little effect on the overall function of the rest of the institution.

Unless external factors affect the institution and augment the pressures contained in the encapsulated part, it is likely that the process of institutional resistance to change will reach an equilibrium, with the result being no change. Resistance to change, therefore, inevitably resides in the institution (cf. Chapter Five).

In other instances, new ideas do arise in institutions, but what often happens is that the ideas, and those that embrace them, form a discrete "enclave" within the organization. If they do find favour, this often happens through being taken up by others outside the organization or by the creation of a new external structure to pursue the idea or produce the product. Leadership is, therefore, about managing a quite sensitive "titration" process—too much external reality overwhelms in-house values and the strengths of the past are lost; too little titration of reality leaves the organization at risk of being bogged down, irrelevant and, at worst, conceptually and financially bankrupt.

Leadership and the "osmotic" boundary-keeping function

For the work of the institution to be reality based, what needs to be aimed for is an institutional "chemistry" where there is sufficient awareness of the pressures impinging from, and opportunities afforded by, the external world. For example, a review of the British National Health Service (*c*. 1990) caused a great deal of organizational turmoil as the system changed to a "market" orientation. The risk was that members of staff would either ignore the changes, thus putting the enterprise at risk, or alternatively be so taken over by the "ins and outs" of the market process that they neglected or ignored the organization's primary task, history, traditions, and their core skills and contributions—in short, both their institutional competence and wisdom.

What was required for sufficient awareness of change to enter the system was for key office bearers, through a process of titration of external reality, to make clear that the core marketing responsibility would be undertaken by a small, designated network of workers who performed this function on behalf of all, thus leaving the rest of the staff to continue working at what they were good at, but in a changed context.

This "osmotic" boundary-keeping is, of course, a two-way function, with the values, ideals, worth, and products of the organization also needing to be communicated to the outside world. Further, in setting up and maintaining the necessary structure for the institution to run effectively, there also needs to be an awareness of everyday practical issues that are integral to the well-being of an organization. These include matters such as group size for effective working, clarity of task and role, and of boundaries differentiating various work-related functions (Obholzer & Roberts, 1994). In order for this to be effectively managed and overseen, the leadership needs authority and power. Authority is a product of organization and structure, be it external, as in the organization's sanction, or internal, as in the inner world of the leader or leaders' experience. The leader needs to have a personal identity with a sense of confidence, based on past experience, that the task about to be tackled is manageable and that the anxieties aroused by embarking on the task can be dealt with.

Leadership, power, and authority

Authority, although necessary, is not sufficient. Power, which is having the resources to be able to enact and implement decisions, is also required. For example, a leader authorized by the organization and personally in touch with his/her inner world issues to a resolved degree will, nevertheless, be quite ineffective if the means to effect decisions—money, staff, equipment, and so forth—are not available. In this regard, it is also important for attention to be paid to the terminology of authority. Appointing someone as chief executive gives quite a different message from appointing the same person as co-coordinator, even though they might have access to exactly the same resources to implement decisions arising from their authority base. All authority must be exercised in the context of the sanction of the followership as noted, but any such sanction or lack thereof must be measured against the benchmark of the primary task of the organization.

This means that the giving or withholding of sanction for change must be measured against the benchmark of what the change is intended to achieve. If the change is in the service of developing and furthering the primary task of the organization and the followership withholds approval, then the withholding of approval should be taken to mean resistance to change. This would then require work on the part of the management to address the underlying anxieties that are presumably at the root of the process, while also encouraging work to be done as part of the membership to produce alternative models of achieving the necessary movement towards change.

In connection with the above, an awareness of the presence and workings of unconscious personal, interpersonal, group, intergroup, and intra-institutional processes among both leaders and followers is essential. As a basic minimum, such awareness can help to prevent, in whatever role, collusion with, or being caught up in, anti-task institutional processes; for example, endless meetings that never come to a decision. Such awareness enables pro-activity in expecting these processes to make their appearance at certain strategic stages of institutional development, and to ensure that they cause a minimum of disruption.

Many of the unconscious dynamics of personal and family life are at risk of flaring up again and being enacted in institutional functioning, particularly if the institution is led and managed in such a way as to turn a blind eye to such issues. This in itself can, for example, be a recreation of a leader's personal past dilemma, say where a parent ignored the noxious effects of sibling rivalry, or worse, played upon these issues. Many an organization is beset by a re-enactment of such dynamics in their staff group—for example, where two peers find themselves competing for a promotion—and whilst a "family type" or therapeutic intervention is never justified, an awareness of the presence of such issues and a refusal to play into them can go a long way in creating a task-orientated team.

Leadership and institutional dynamics

In many organizations, thinking about institutional dynamics and their management is delegated to the human resources function. In my view, this is the equivalent of a splitting process with perceived "soft" elements effectively being disowned (and more worryingly, not addressed) by part of the organization. In therapeutic and human service organizations the process often takes a related form—here personnel does not deal with it, but instead a member of staff with a suitable "valency" for this sort of work takes on the role, often as part of an unconscious institutional process (Bion, 1961). The end result, however, is the same—the dynamic is not owned as part of the overall functioning of the system, but instead it is lodged with the individual.

A "therapeutic" style of management, of the kind often found in mental health sector organizations, runs the risk of missing the primary task of the organization, namely, the welfare of patients, and instead, of replacing the task with a focus on the well-being of staff and, perhaps, particularly those staff whose valencies result in their picking up some of the more challenging roles on behalf of the organization. Leadership and the management matrix should, of course, have a therapeutic and staff development side to it, but only in the context of the overall primary task and institutional processes.

In all organizations, the health of the entire workforce must fall within the remit of management, who also have a particular responsibility for minimizing the effect of "toxic" processes arising from the nature of the work in which the organization is engaged. This applies equally whether the toxins are physical products inherent in the manufacturing process or whether they are toxins "in the mind", with an effect on the personality of the kind one finds in people changing organizations, be they educational settings or mental health organizations. Jaques (1955) and Isabel Menzies Lyth's (1990) work on social systems as a defence against anxiety were particularly innovative in this area. Menzies Lyth suggested that the anxiety arising from the nature of the underlying work and the breaching of societal taboos that are often an essential part of carrying out one's duties can have a significant effect on the state of mind of the worker. For example, the daily work of nurses brings them into contact with dying and seriously ill patients. The distress this causes requires them to find ways of overcoming it simply to continue with their task. As a result, work patterns are organized in the service of psychic defence mechanisms rather than in the pursuit of the primary task. It is axiomatic that in instances where one's work provokes anxiety, an organization's membership will be particularly caught up in enacting defensive processes, through personal valency (Bion, 1961) and vulnerability.

Bion borrowed the concept of "valency" from physics, where it denotes the proclivity of an atom to combine with others. In his applied sense in the field of human unconscious group/institutional processes, he used it to mean "capacity for instantaneous, involuntary combinations of one individual with another for sharing and acting on a basic assumption." The connection between the individual and the institutional process is thus via the valency factor of the individual's personality. Additionally, a multi-disciplinary or multi-grouped organization also allows for splitting processes to happen, so that the defences can take the form of intergroup and interdisciplinary issues and rivalries, thus masking the defensive processes and flight from work. All of us will be able to think of examples of where we have heard of experienced managers blaming the workforce and the workforce blaming management for a stalemate.

Other dimensions of leadership

Leadership and management

If leadership is about the elements described earlier; vision and strategy, boundary and change management, and containment, what then of management? How is it different? Management, if practised unimaginatively, is leadership without the vision, and therefore, to a degree, the management and administration of the status quo. While this, in itself, is an important function, it is not enough to produce satisfaction in either the managers or the managed. The response is often that the managers fall into states of increased bureaucracy, both "in the mind" and "in the system", and the managed fall into states of denigrating management. This can either take the form of casting managers as parasites who live off the work or creativity of the workers, or else for management not to be seen as real work. "When can we get this over with so that I can get back to my real work?" was the parting comment of a senior colleague whose role straddles leadership and management. Not seeing management, and to a lesser extent leadership, as "real work" perpetuates the problem cycle and confirms the self-fulfilling prophecy about management. Preferring to do "the real work", whether as an engineer, lawyer, accountant, or psychotherapist is, of course, a "face-enhancing" or at least face-saving way out of attending to the difficulties of having to perform a managerial or leadership role.

Leadership styles and the group process

At an unconscious level the leader is perceived as giving the group a message: "I think I'm better than you are". While leaders and followers would deny any such intent in their conscious perception and dealing with each other, the facts often speak otherwise. Leaders and managers are experienced as siblings who have reached "above their station" and, in the cauldron of unconscious institutional processes, are thus perceived as "fair game" for a process of bringing them down to earth, that is, unconsciously, to the same "level" as oneself. This attack on a "sibling" is often dressed up as helping the individual(s) concerned to be more "in touch with reality"; helping them therapeutically not to fall victim to "omnipotent projections"; or generally helping them along. It would be wrong to see such activity only in terms of an envious attack on a sibling rival; it would be equally inappropriate to sweep these processes under the carpet to pretend that they don't exist.

Bion (1961) has described different states of group, and, by implication, of organizational functioning and thus of leadership. Dividing the most primitive mode of functioning, which he named "basic assumption functioning", he described basic assumption fight–flight, pairing, and dependency. (See Glossary for definitions.) Each has an accompanying "in-house", "across-the-boundary", and leadership implication. The leader of an institution that is in fight–flight mode thus needs a fight–flight dynamic in order to function effectively, and, if that is no longer forthcoming on account of changed institutional or environmental conditions, is at risk of gratuitously stoking up more fight, of being ousted, or else of needing to change his or her style. There is, of course, no immutable basic assumption state, and there is always a contribution from other basic assumption modes to the overall functioning of the institution. Bion also elaborated the dynamics of a more mature style of institutional functioning, which he described as the "work group". Here, the direction of the institution is essentially aware of the primary task and the basic assumptions are harnessed in the service of carrying it out. Bion termed this process "the sophisticated use of basic assumptions".

Although Bion, in his writings, never made a direct link between his thoughts on institutional functioning and Melanie Klein's (1959) concepts of the paranoid–schizoid and depressive positions (cf. Glossary), there is nevertheless a clear and helpful parallel between the two sets of concepts. There is a clear connection between the competent functioning of an individual, essentially in a depressive position state of mind, and an institution in work group mode. Similarly, paranoid–schizoid position functioning in the individual has much in common with a basic-assumption institutional state of functioning.

These concepts describe and determine the behaviour of individuals in groups and institutions, and the resulting leadership requirements, both unconscious and conscious. It is the individual with the most suitable valency that will take up the leadership role to enact the requirements, both good and bad, of the institution. Both Freud and Jaques have taken the story of Judith and Holofernes from the Apocrypha (Book of Judith, Chapter 10: 1–13: 20) and shown with great clarity the interaction between unconscious group process, leadership style, and the consequences of such a dynamic.

In essence, Holofernes, the leader of the vastly superior besieging army, ran the army on the basis of charismatic leadership with the followership in a basic assumption dependency state of mind. When Judith cut his head off and displayed it to his troops it was as if they in turn had "lost their head" , given their dependency state, and all fled the battlefield, a sobering example of the price of charismatic leadership and dependency if ever there was one (Freud, 1921c, p. 97, Jaques, 1955, p. 481).

The core functions of followership

Followership is and must be an actively participative process. It needs to be differentiated from a passive, dependent state of mind of the individual or the group, and also from an uninvolved or not responsible state of mind, which leads to a "boarding house" mentality. By this I mean a state of minor participation only in as much as it affects one's personal comfort or work, or the state of one's immediate grouping, but in which there is no responsibility acknowledged, or taken, for the overall venture. Nor is there any passion about it. It is of course, legitimate at times to represent the needs and point of view of one's sectional interests; it is harder to draw the line between a sectional partisan approach and one's responsibility for the overall organization. The risk inherent in this process is that the overall perspective is delegated at both a conscious and unconscious level to senior management, leadership, or the leader, resulting in a splitting process and the disowning of personal responsibility for the overall good of the organization. We all know of examples of how individuals, teams, or departments who have doggedly fought their corners have held their organization and its development hostage.

So, how does the process of active followership function? It must clearly be based on a process of consultation, participation, and involvement. It cannot, however, operate on the basis of consensus management, for that, in effect, means the unspoken but nevertheless true exercise of a power of veto, often on behalf of sectional interests, sometimes in the service of resistance to change. Consensus management can only come into play when decisions are either inevitable or of no consequence. As decision-making, in essence, is about the weighing-up of risks and the probable consequence of such decisions, it is not surprising that it is at these crucial stages that decision-making by consensus falls down and therefore does not justify a place in the management process. On the very rare occasions where a decision is reached by consensus, the outcome is often misleading because the "consensus" rapidly falls apart and then the process has to be embarked on all over again in order to achieve a better reasoned and worked through decision which transparently acknowledges the issues and concerns of all parties.

The creation of an arena for debate, both in the mind and in reality, is obviously a key requirement for exercising one's followership role. In question, however, is how long the process of debate and consultation should take. Sometimes the latter decision is taken out of one's hands by events beyond one's control. For example, deadlines might be imposed by financial factors, legislative acts, and so forth. But, even then, it is not unusual to have disputes about time available, with management curtailing time for discussion, presumably fearing the worst, while the followership wants to extend the time, presumably also fearing the worst. A senior colleague once said to me, "You speak a lot about authority and leadership, but you seem not to believe in 'working through' "; an interesting comment reaching to the heart of the leadership–membership interface and the question of how much time is needed for "working through" and how much is too much time. "Working through", as a basic psychoanalytic concept, implies the state of coming to terms with and accepting a psychic situation; for example, the loss of a loved one. It is therefore a process of coming to terms with a loss and an acceptance that a new state of affairs prevails. A certain amount of time is required for the process—in the case of mourning, traditionally about eighteen months. There is, of course, no guarantee that after that amount of time the issue will have been worked through—it may be that the loss is as unacceptable as ever and that a near delusional state of harking back for what once was prevails.

Any change requires the giving up of something, be it a way of working or a state of self-perception, and the fact that what is being given up might have only been ambivalently valued, as it could be with an ambivalently loved or even hated person, makes no difference to the process of working through and mourning. The same of course also applies to working practices that one had mixed feelings about and that one fights to retain once they become a part of the process of managing change, or part of management proposals for change. The core question, thus, is whether giving up something is an appropriate activity in the service of moving forward on the path of organizational change, or whether it is an inappropriate, often fashion-determined request for the giving up of something that is best retained as part of the overall institutional culture. Is resistance to giving something up then resistance to change, or is it on-task valuing of tradition? There is no easy answer to this question. No doubt, however, the question needs to be debated (see also Chapter Five)—robustly at times—but such a debate has to be held against the backcloth of the primary task, for it is only against that parameter that a true measure of continuity for the organization, its members, and its products can be reached.

It is a striking fact that whereas outsiders and leaders regularly see, speak about, and attempt to understand and to manage resistance to change, it is remarkable how the very possibility of being caught up in resistance to change is something that is never debated or acknowledged in discussions with membership. Being "too busy" to have time for discussion or consultation, or not having time to reach that item on the agenda is about as near to a semi-acknowledgement as one can get. Perhaps one should not be surprised by this; after all, one would not expect a patient in psychotherapy or psychoanalysis to "own up" to being in the grip of resistance to an interpretation. And yet, viewed more positively, the very same process described above is also the process that stops omnipotent flights of fancy in leaders and helps to bring them down to the depressive position reality of what can, or cannot, be achieved and in what timescale.

Facilitating a creative interaction
between leaders and followers

Leadership and working at differences

It must follow from what has been said so far that difference of opinion, and particularly between leadership and followership, is a healthy and necessary part of institutional debate and functioning. The very same debate, however, also carries within it the seeds of destructiveness to the institution and its various component parts. How is the process of debate to be managed?

I believe that clearly bounded structures with clearly designated tasks and a spelt-out system of authority and constitution are essential for the debating process to work. The risk is that, if there are too many forums and too much reporting back, individual and structural responsibility is fudged or disowned, and decisions that have been taken, and legitimately so, are gone over again—part of a time-wasting exercise often condoned by management in the belief that "if we have everyone's fingerprints on the decision, then we'll have general acceptance". Sadly, this does not follow at all, and certainly does not make up for foot-dragging, time-wasting, and the haemorrhage of creativity. The question about how important structure is in the area of institutional "working through" of issues is often raised. A lack of structure makes for a process that easily succumbs to the basic assumption activity described so lucidly by Bion. The situation is even worse if it takes place in a large group (Turquet, 1975). If the debate is structured and competently chaired, it has the highest chance of complying with work-group criteria (Bion, 1961). But the design of the meeting and the interconnectedness of meetings (if that is necessary given the size of the organization) must be planned and co-ordinated, or else the result is a combination of misunderstandings and a free-for-all. For example, in a business management meeting, relevant issues might have been competently addressed but, unless the meeting and its decisions are seen in the context of, and relayed to, the whole organization, the value of its work may be lost. Bion's concept of containment (cf. Glossary) gives a good indication of how a work-group orientated discussion of issues might be had.

On the other side there are many situations where the organization is managed or directed with the minimum of discussion or consultation. The end result of this style is often either a "boarding house" mentality, noted previously, where there is no sense of a common venture, or alternatively a factional or tribal sort of break-up of the membership, with some being drawn into the roles of "favourites of the director" while others feel very undervalued. So the result of this process is that there is a spectrum of favouritism and, instead of the business focusing on its primary task, there is a tendency for staff to be tipped into various states of sycophancy in order to catch the eye of the directors and to maintain or enhance their position in the pecking order of the organization.

In attempting to find structures to further dialogue and debate concerning the organization's future, certain pitfalls appear with regularity. One is a reopening of the debate as to the primary task of the organization. This is tricky, for whilst at some level going to one's sponsors, paymasters, or patients, and saying, "What do you want us to do?" is obviously good practice, it is not something that can be done as an ongoing process, nor is it realistic always to expect coherent or reasonable answers in response to the question. There has to be continuity of task, as there has to be a vision and strategy for the future.

The leader's membership and the members' leadership

In any leader–member structural dichotomy, there is always the risk of splitting and projective identification, with unwanted, unac-knowledged, and disowned aspects of staff being seen often with crystal pseudo-clarity in the other, leaving one free, virtuous, misunderstood, and self-righteous. Thus, there needs to be the opportunity for the leader and the leadership to engage in ordinary and everyday membership activities, and for the leader not to spend his/her time in their private dining room being protected by a "loyal" personal assistant. Such activities would seriously impair their capacity to encompass and conceptualize the reality of mem-bership of the organization. So, for example, it would be very help-ful if, as part of the leadership function, the leader varied their route through the building in going to the office, shared drinks in a vari-ety of settings, used a variety of toilets, and generally acted in a normal citizen role as part of the organization. Equally, members must take on leadership roles open and available to them to allow their creativity and managerial skills to develop and for them to have an opportunity to identify with the hardships and vicissitudes of management and leadership, and perhaps particularly with the loneliness inherent in the decision-making requirements of the role. Reluctance to do so would alienate them further from management and create a widening of the psychic split between management and membership.

Concluding thoughts: leadership, followership and facilitating the creative workplace

By now it is clear that the individual member of the institution, in whatever role, has to tread a careful path between a variety of loci of power and influence, and in the process must maintain his or her individuality while yet remaining in touch with the requisite group process. Pierre Turquet (1974), in "Leadership: the individual and the group", addresses this issue in its full complexity, but it is not only the members of the institution who must tread this careful pathway; it is also the leaders. However, being preoccupied with this process can itself become a perverse form of leadership, with such preoccupations taking up a great deal of time and thought, and providing a distraction from serious attention being paid to future directions (Obholzer, 1995).

The idea of the leader keeping an eye on the future direction of the organization draws our attention back to the need for the leader to balance vision with strategy, see the whole picture, have a sense of the history and future of the enterprise along a time continuum, as well as to provide a sense of containment in order to ensure creativity within the workplace.

CHAPTER THREE

What women leaders can tell us

Clare Huffington

This chapter focuses on the implications of findings from a research study into women's leadership (Coffey, Huffington, & Thomson, 1999). The study revealed a vivid picture of changing cultures in organizations, the new demands on and for leadership and how women are meeting them. The women leaders tended to speak from what they felt to be a marginal position, partly because they are so few in number and partly because of their particular sensitivity to organizational change and the evolving psychological contract between leaders and followers. In this respect, they can be seen as offering a vision of the future for leaders, whether these are men or women. This chapter focuses on what the women leaders told us and the implications of their stories for our conceptual framework around leadership and organizations, particularly the concepts of role and primary task and the containing function of leadership.

The changing world of life and work

The world has changed and is going to go on changing at a dizzying rate. It is now impossible to predict future developments accurately, even a few years away. At the same time, a social revolution is going on, hand-in-hand with business changes. Family life is no longer static over the period of children growing up and children themselves are viewed as consumers whose views are sought. Both men and women work and their expectations of how they wish to work, how they view careers, and what they want out of life as a whole is changing just as rapidly and just as unpredictably (Doyle, 2000). All this puts a premium on businesses identifying what is happening in the environment around them and being able to deploy resources rapidly to follow these changes and transform themselves so as to be ready to meet them (Taffinder, 1998).

In turn, the need for agility and a sharper focus has created powerful drivers for change in organizational structure and leadership. There is a shift away from the traditional "command and control" hierarchies towards greater flexibility. Decision-making is more likely to take place closer to the point of contact with the client or consumer in order that it is better tailored to his or her needs. This has been called distributed leadership and is explored in Chapter Four. Lateral relationships—between people, groups, organizations, and systems—now have more primacy than the vertical relationships of the traditional hierarchy, calling upon different skills in management and leadership. Employees involved in decision-making need to be able to understand the business as a whole and to continue learning about it over time. All employees need to become more involved in the business, in terms of both input (creative thinking and ideas, and handling feedback from clients and consumers) and output (the effective delivery of targeted products and services) (Hirschhorn, 1997). For example, staff in call centres need to be able to channel feedback from customers to a strategic planning group in the organization so that products and services can be tailored to emerging needs.

This kind of move has huge implications for organizational cultures, many of which are not yet able to meet these demands. It is becoming more apparent that what separates the best performing organizations from the others is not just about the mechanics of the business but about how good an organization's people are. It is also about how well they are led and motivated and how well they are integrated into their teams and into the organization as a whole. Organizations also need to be more concerned about how their employees live their lives outside work as it is those organizations that invest in helping people with quality of life issues who manage to hold on to their best people (Burns, 2000; Guest, 2000). Most business thinking these days emphasizes the importance of so called "soft skills" to world-class performance.

This focus on people in successful businesses is both about those inside the organization—its employees—and those outside—the customers, clients, or consumers, suppliers, partners, and competitors. Any organization that fails to listen to its customers will not survive for long. The interesting shift here is towards the increasing diversity of the customer or client base, in particular the growth of women as key consumers, and not just in traditionally female markets. Tom Peters, in *The Circle of Innovation* (1997), reports that 57% of motor tyres sold in the US are bought by women. Women's economic power has increased hugely in the past twenty-five years, both because they earn money in their own right and also through their influence on major family buying decisions, including the purchase of houses, cars, furnishing, holidays, clothing, and computers. As traditional family units continue to give way to other arrangements and more homes become single adult occupied, women's economic power will grow further. Organizations increasingly need a mix of people at the top of their management structures that can reflect the reality of the marketplaces they serve—people who think the way their customers think. So they need more women, more ethnic minorities, more people with disabilities, more older people, and so on. Those organizations that continue to under-utilize the pool of potential talent in this way are likely to suffer because they will not be attuned to the needs of their customers or clients, nor will they attract the best people to work for them. Thus, they will lose out to competitor organizations that have managed to be more internally and externally responsive in this way. Although this seems an obvious point to make, it is still the case that women hold fewer than one in ten of the most senior positions in public life in the UK (Equal Opportunities Commission, 2004). Julie Mellor, of the Commission, says

Almost 30 years since the Sex Discrimination Act was passed, women are still massively under-represented in positions of influence in Britain. No one can argue any more that it's just a matter of

time until more women make it to the top. . . . If we select our leaders from only half the population, how can we expect to get the best
person every time. . . . Leaders have less legitimacy if they reflect
only part of the population.

The research study

The purpose of the research study was to try to find out why so few
women reach senior positions in organizations in the UK, despite
many organizations wishing to increase the numbers of women
leaders. We wanted to explore the nature of the individual, group,
and systemic blockages from both above and below the surface;
we wanted to see if there was any additional support that could be
provided to help women progress into leadership roles. Fifty-two
senior women leaders from organizations of all sizes and types were
interviewed in depth about their organizations and organizational
cultures, their experience of leadership within them, factors enabling and blocking career progression, family background, schooling
and education, home circumstances, and how they saw the future of
leadership and organizations. The results are fully reported in the
(Coffey, Huffington, & Thomson, 1999) book about the study, but
here we are focusing on what the women said about leadership and
organizations and their own experiences in leadership roles.

Changing organizational cultures

When the women were asked about their organizational cultures,
they made some important points:

> Our industry is changing and growing fast. Our competitors are
> changing every day. Technology and the markets are changing. We
> are globalising. Unless we can let go and let people make their own
> judgements, we will lose out. None of us at Board level has enough
> wisdom to identify trends and to take action quickly enough for
> today's world. The corporate culture and leadership has to be
> enabling. You have to have a clear strategy and support framework
> to enable people to get there, for them to put flesh around the bones
> of the strategic frame you have set out. [Board Director, FTSE 100
> company]

There was a sense in interviewing these women of a real shift in organizational life. It resembled the "completely different emotional–psychological landscape" described by Shere Hite in *Sex and Business* (2000, p. xii). Many women were part of the new because they were not part of the old. They were part of organizational cultures they had no hand in shaping and thus had less invested in the way things used to be. So many of them had become unwitting pioneers of organizational change. Thus, they described organizational cultures in transition; they were still characterized by one particular set of values and norms while at the same time espousing another set. For example, an organization could promote a woman to the board and genuinely welcome that appointment, and at the same time manifest organizational behaviours that made it very difficult for her to succeed. Many women described very inhospitable organizational cultures with a competitive, macho leadership style that they associated with bullying and that no longer inspired others to follow. This "masculine" culture seemed particularly ingrained in manufacturing and technological organizations, but the culture of many of the organizations the women described was predominantly male. The culture can thus be seen as ungendered or undifferentiated as to gender (Wajcman, 1998). The women vividly described some of the struggles they had to make a difference. However, some women had been able to create organizational change or had set up their own organizations, which had a very different culture, such as the one described below.

> The culture is very values-driven. We concentrate on treating people as individuals, both staff and clients. We are always trying to do things better. I've had a "good ideas hotline" telephone installed on my desk to try to promote good ideas and give people direct access to me. It's often used at weekends, I've found, when people have had a chance to reflect. The ideas are of excellent calibre. Most people identify themselves and I always go back to them and thank them. I want to promote a real culture of flexibility and thanking. [Chief Executive, Voluntary Organization]

There are signs that both men and women want organizations of this new kind. Young people want very different things out of work than their parents, and in particular they want a life too (Brooks, 2000). The Industrial Society reports from large scale employee surveys that a "friendly working atmosphere" and "good working relationships with colleagues" are the most important elements to job satisfaction (Doyle, 2000, p. 21). Those who fail to find this are leaving large corporations to set up their own companies where they can create the culture for themselves. A Barclays survey in 1999 (Oldfield, 2000) showed that women founded 31% of new businesses in 1999. These may be the same women in their thirties and forties who are dropping out of corporate life. It is not just women who want something different: Those over fifty , "third age entrepreneurs", are also starting new businesses, 15% of the total (Gribben, 2001). So there is a real challenge for organizations to face in attracting and retaining good staff of either sex; the pressure for change in organizational life coming as much from inside, in order to have good people to do the work, as from the outside, in terms of a competitive external environment.

Women's experience of leadership

If this description of organizations of the future is accurate, then leadership and management need to be quite differently focused. The women in the research described it as being more people-centred and personal, less about control and more about influence, less about management and more about leadership. This means inspiring and influencing people to follow and it seems likely that they will follow more willingly where they have had a hand in helping to create or re-create their own organization. This implies a rather different blend of skills and intelligence for successful leadership in the future, which is more about developing collaborative relationships with followers or other stakeholders (Drucker, 1999; Fukayama, 1995; Litwin, Bray, & Lusk Brooke, 1996). This is the same theme of basic assumption pairing (Bion, 1962) set out by Anton Obholzer in Chapter Two, and might imply that women leaders are more likely to have a valency for this style or approach to leadership. Here is an example of what it might be like.

> I am strong underneath but I have learned to be delicate. There is a North American Indian saying which goes "He who is tough inside and soft outside is a healer. He who is hard on the outside and soft

inside is useless!" A tough, hard, macho style is no good. If you have no tenderness in you, you can't do it. And if you are soft or weak inside, you can't do it either. True strength is delicate. [Principal, College of Further Education]

Intuition, in the sense of using one's own and others' emotions as data in decision-making, alongside rigorous analysis, has its place here; an investment banker quoted in Stein and Book's *The EQ Edge* (2000) says " Most deals are 50% emotion and 50% economics" (p. 28). Negotiated authority, which is acceptable to and acknowledged by the leader and led, is also critical (Mant, 1997). This means that collaboration becomes an important skill as does having the courage to present oneself as a human being to one's colleagues, warts and all. The "glue" that integrates the organization is of a different kind, not based on deference but on shared values (Covey, 1992). The women talked about making themselves more vulnerable, by being more transparent and accessible, the prize being the building of a more enduring mutual trust and support. Their experience was that this tended to hold and contain people more effectively than traditional organizational structures. Here is an example of this kind of thinking.

We are getting out of kilter with our client base. A lot of management requirements these days play to feminine management skills. Consulting is about building empathy with your client, reaching consensus, being consultative. It is also about caring for people, not dealing with people as if they were armies to be moved around, like players in a game of *Risk*! [Partner, Global Professional Services Firm]

Women talked about their skills in facilitation, collaboration, and the development of people in organizations, combined with their commitment to learning, confirming other, earlier research (Baker-Miller, 1986; Helgesen, 1995; Martin, 1993). For example:

Relationships in my firm are friendly. It is a flat organization and completely female. In the leadership, we value motivation, innovative ideas, energy, intuition and initiative. Everybody has a second job within the company to develop her abilities. I deal these out according to their strengths. [Managing Director, Retail Company]

The women in the current research had clearly articulated sets of principles and values that guide them at work, confirming previous research studies (Kabacoff & Peters, 1999; Loden, 1985). Women tend to talk about their leadership as strongly connected with who they are as people. Here are two examples of strong women leaders in action.

> There was a major disturbance on the wing with fifty men out of their cells, up in arms about what they thought was poor quality food. I knew we had to do something or we would have a riot. I checked the kitchen—there was nothing else. All the staff and prisoners were looking to me. What I decided to do was to order 100 or so Macdonald's Happy Meals. I took delivery of them myself and took every single one personally to each prisoner. Life in prisons can be wrecked over food. It was crucial that I carried the prison officers with me and the prisoners were happy as they felt they had been heard. [Assistant Director, Civil Service]

> It is my job to create the strategy, to set the framework, the values, the behaviours for this division. Then I am the facilitator. I need to give them the things they need to get on with it. I have always found that people exceed my expectations, but you need to religiously enforce the values. . . . Sometimes I find pockets of behaviour that hit my hot buttons. I am clear about what I expect from people and this seems to go down really well because there is nothing worse than lack of clarity about what is expected of you. [Board Director, FTSE 100 Company]

While what is described above might equally be said by men in leadership roles, there was some evidence that women leaders' experience in organizations was gendered in some respects. For example, their perception of enablers and blockers to career progression, work–life balance issues, and sexuality in the workplace.

In terms of women's perceptions of external forces that had facilitated career progress, nearly all the women referred to the crucial role of support from family members; formal mentoring and coaching; informal support from within their organizations, where it was available; and high visibility because of being a woman in a senior role. This could be enabling if it led to more scope and recognition, but also might lead to anxiety due to a feeling of pressure on achievement, which is reminiscent of what Kram and McCollum (1995) call a "visibility–vulnerability spiral". In terms of blockers, the women were reluctant to see any, but then spoke of lack of self-confidence, a lack of people to identify with, male or female, and a lack of natural networks at senior level. All the women talked a great deal about life–work balance and their struggles to maintain it, given the high priority they place on their roles as parents. They felt they had to deny the pressure they were under in order to be seen as committed and equal to male colleagues. This quote illustrates the problem.

> People in the workforce are waiting for you to collapse at work, almost taking bets on when that will be when you are juggling these bits of life. How can you do a presentation when you haven't slept through the night? You need the support to get through. [Managing Director, Executive Search Firm]

The women in the research talked about how sexuality, as a component of gender, was relevant to the exercise of power in organizations. While they spoke of oneness between who they are as people and how they exercised leadership, it was clear that they left quite a lot of themselves at home, and this was mainly connected to their sexuality. They described the lengths to which they had to go to show they could do the job like their male colleagues; some of them had to hide the pressures connected with being a working mother, like the woman in the quote above. Many of them, especially in large corporates, had to dress a certain way, in business dress with high necklines, sober suits, or in a dress code acceptable for women in the organization (for example, in the legal profession until quite recently, no trousers). This was so as to fit into rules set by men and so as not to attract attention that would lead to them being treated as sex objects and thus inferior to men. This was partly defined by men and partly defined by themselves for their protection. They did not tend to see their sexuality as a source of strength or power over men in an organizational context. Some of them talked of the stress and constriction they felt in donning this gender-neutral armour for work. Others spoke of attacks on their leadership framed in terms of their sexuality. For example, one interviewee was unjustly accused of having affairs with several of her staff. These attacks were not only from men but also other women. Hite (2000) points out that it is difficult for women to take each other seriously at work because they see men as the real power centres as this is still the reality in most organizations today.

The envy that people feel towards those in leadership positions may play a part. Those most idealized or most elevated are most likely to be deposed; football managers and high profile chief executives spring to mind as examples. Stokes (1994) points out that envious attacks on male leaders will generally be around such traits as money-making, decision-making, defining strategies, all of which represent supposed areas of masculine potency. Attacks on women leaders tend to centre around their feminine potency such as their appearance, creativity, or reproductive or parenting ability. Media portrayals of women leaders with children as "superwomen" or "having it all" reinforce envy rather than create role models; especially when women who lose out in the boardroom are often depicted by the same media as being forced to leave the office to get back to their "neglected" children. The attacks on men may be felt to be more distant or external to them, focusing on professional skills and competence, whereas attacks on women are more personal, focusing, for example, on mothering roles, and so may be experienced as more fundamentally destructive. The fear of such attacks from others may discourage women from taking up leadership roles or may lead them to "bale out" as soon as they have children. Clearly it is important for organizations who do not want to lose talented women to provide explicit support for them in their leadership roles, especially those who have children, whether this is in the form of flexible working hours, support for childcare or personal coaching.

Whereas any expression of sexuality has been excluded from the workplace on the grounds that it threatens both production and control, Wajcman (1998) and Hite (2000) both talk about the ways in which men in organizations use their sexuality to maintain their dominant position. Men tend to work, network, and play (on the golf course, for example) in exclusively male groupings that women find almost impossible to penetrate. There can be in this sense a feeling of "psychological institutional homosexuality" at the top of organizations, even today. For women, on the other hand, the use of their sexuality in the workplace would have the opposite effect, to "degrade" them into passive roles, so they can be forced into a position of denial of their sexuality to succeed. It is only recently that management and leadership styles dubbed "female" have been seen as the way of the future. This may be another reason why some women have set up their own companies in order to create a culture in which they can bring more of themselves to work, including their sexuality. It has been pointed out that the growth of e-commerce may favour women's development because you can be gender-neutral in cyberspace and thus escape the prejudices about women in leadership roles, as well as wear what you like (Civin, 2000).

While it seems that the women in the research may be describing successful leadership in very similar terms to men, in that this is what leadership needs to look like today (Hirschhorn, 1997), their marginal position at the top of organizations, just in terms of sheer numbers, gives their account particular poignancy. What is important is what the women alert us to about the new demands of leadership and how this helps us to reframe what leadership, organization, and change might now be about.

A reframing of leadership, organization, and change

As we have seen, the rate of change in organizations today requires more people to be involved in decision-making on the vision and strategy of the organization as it evolves day to day. Thus, people have more power in and over organizations, both as decision-makers and as consumers. This may explain the sense of synchronicity between women's approach to leadership, based firmly on people, and the demands arising from the context. These are for a closer engagement by the organization with the diverse needs of both external clients, partners, and suppliers and also with the needs of people working within the organization so as to attract and retain the best people as employees.

Women's leadership is rooted in the person element in the person–role–system model of looking at the way an individual negotiates his/her position in the organization (Miller & Rice, 1967). Leadership is about personal qualities and values and a sense of oneness and integrity between the person as an individual and himself or herself as a leader. It is important to be visible and to be seen to connect to the people and activities of the organization. It is as if the leader has to embody the organization in the absence of traditional boundaries and to compensate for the sense of depersonalization that would otherwise dominate in the large group experience of organizations now (Turquet, 1975). The "boundaryless" organization (Hirschhorn & Gilmore, 1992) can stimulate large group phenomena such as feelings of loss of identity, lack of coherence and connectedness. This version of leadership with a strong personal definition appears to be a way of avoiding or compensating for the consequent discomfort and confusion. In Chapter Seven, Andrew Cooper and Tim Dartington quote Castells (2000) on the theme of identity in organizations:

> Identity is becoming the main . . . source of meaning. . . . People increasingly organize their meaning not around what they do but on the basis of what they are are, or believe they are.

The women's stories reflect this view. They tended to experience and also be tuned in to the full blast of the organizational culture and, although they often referred to leadership teams as a source of support and strength, they present a picture of holding the organization together in a unitary and solitary fashion. Self-doubt, as opposed to certainty, seems to be an important quality, connected to the readiness to experience the vulnerability and potential impermanence of the organization. It signals the leader's need for constant reflection on oneself in role so as to make change possible when it is needed. Stress on the personal element in leadership success may also offer an explanation of why the one-to-one executive coaching market has grown so rapidly in the past ten years or so. This is further explored in Chapter Nine.

The emphasis on the importance of the person in organizations and the dismantling of rules, roles, and management structures seems to explain the importance of the exercise of power through politics in organizations today, rather than through bureaucracy or management structures. Politics in this sense means the use of personal power to get things done, via influencing others, rather than by the use of authority deriving from one's role. Caulkin, in an article in *The Observer* newspaper entitled "Politics, be proud of it!" (2000), suggests that the idea of a company as a politics-free zone is getting harder and harder to sustain. He maintains that organizations are inherently political places, essentially about "resolving the clash of competing causes". From experience of coaching both male and female leaders, it is clear that they are struggling with how to get things done when there are no longer these hierarchies and bureaucracies to help. The emphasis is on lateral relationships between equals rather than top-down control, thus influencing skills become important. Collaborating with others, persuading others of your point of view, building mergers and coalitions and dealing with differences and conflict are all part of the new skill set. It centres around how to use the person element effectively in the system. Some leaders get it wrong by using personal power in a coercive fashion, and this may account for the number of cases of bullying and harassment in organizations (cf. Chapters Five and Ten). There seems to be widespread distaste in both men and women for this approach to leadership.

The need is for something much more subtle. The women in the research talked about their dislike of organizational politics as "game playing" and unethical behaviour. They preferred to reframe politics as "influencing skills" in which they felt they needed more development. There is clearly something being avoided here, the "nasty" bits of leadership, including conflict resolution, and hard decision-making. Women in top roles must, however, have used these skills effectively to have succeeded at all. In fact, this is the territory that is the focus of much of the coaching with clients in leadership roles; to own and use political power in the best interests of the organization, occasionally being prepared to be hated for it. It is possible that male and female leaders need to develop a new "relationship technology", as one client described it, to manage and lead in organizations without fixed rules and roles.

Leadership can be viewed as a flexible set of behaviours, playing up and down the scale of "soft" to "hard", and there is little sense of the "person" element being mediated through a notion of "role". It is as if the idea of a leadership role is deconstructed as too constraining of the creativity, individuality, and autonomy leaders need to try to exercise themselves and to promote in the people they lead. What the women leaders instead stressed was a "hard" set of values or principles around a shared purpose or enterprise that binds people together in pursuit of a common goal. However, the way the organization needed to achieve this goal was "soft" or flexible, based on collaboration and care for the individual and the ability to mutate according to the needs of the time. The supermarket which now sells financial services or acts as the community post office would be a good example.

Thus, the leader connects people with the enterprise rather than with the organization. I am using here David Armstrong's definition in which he describes enterprise as "endeavour" or "carrier of organizational identity that defines its 'what-ness' or 'it-ness'". (Armstrong, 2002). An example would be that one way of describing the enterprise of a school is that it is to create a learning environment, but the organization built to deliver this learning environment could take many forms; from a traditional school building to teaching students in their homes, offering counselling to parents, developing leadership skills in teachers, and so on. Armstrong uses this idea of "practice", "primary spirit" or "animating principle" to flesh out Bion's concept of the work group. This can otherwise appear a kind of notional or threadbare counterpart to richly delineated basic assumption functioning. His idea is that it is the "practice" that breathes life into the organization, not the primary task, which seems rather a limiting condition within which "practice" is required to be framed.

Traditional ideas of role and primary task and the leadership, authority and power derived from these seem less useful when "organization" appears to be such a provisional concept. Many organizations, especially public sector organizations, seem to be in a state of deconstruction and incoherence, in which traditional organizational boundaries have broken down. Patients on trolleys in the corridors of hospital accident and emergency departments are a stark illustration of this. Organizations are required to do so much more, or such different tasks, or to such different ends, and to change so rapidly that the "primary task" has shifted. People have lost a sense both of the primary task and of the purpose and enterprise underpinning it. There seems to have been a de-coupling of enterprise and organization that is experienced as deprivation, persecution, and loss, rather than a developmental opportunity (cf. Section III). Attempts at role clarification or reinstatement of the primary task of the organization can appear to be a retreat from working at some of the differences and divergences about the enterprise itself and, consequently, how it could or should be framed organizationally. The interpersonal conflict and bullying that is prevalent in organizations today can alert us to the need to work at some of these differences. Sadly, these problems are often seen as connected to individuals and to be resolved through processes of mediation and conflict resolution, frequently cut off from an opportunity to expand or reframe the notion of enterprise so as to bind people together. (See Chapter Ten for a fuller exploration of this theme.)

Case study

An example of a woman leader who has managed to work at some of the tensions between organization and enterprise and come up with a creative solution is the Principal of an inner-city comprehensive school—and she is creating a "Communiversity" Her school is in a very deprived part of London. Six out of seven families have no adult in full-time employment. Fewer than 50% are registered with a GP. Twenty per cent of students are on the Refugee or Looked After Children Register and 72% have free school dinners. Individual work with the head teacher, as she was then, and with her leadership team began four years ago in the wake of a failed OfSTED inspection. The school was classified as "failing" and was put on "Special Measures". This meant they had to improve their performance to specified standards within two years or face closure. The consultancy role was to work with the head teacher and her leadership team to help them out of this crisis and beyond. Although they had an action plan, they were feeling traumatized and low in confidence, yet determined to "get off Special Measures". What is interesting about this example is both the "before" and "after" and the shift between in terms of the leadership stance adopted. The "before", the period of "getting off Special Measures", required a survivalist stance; a tough, uncompromising attitude in the head teacher to reach the standards required, for example taking immediate action on issues like "the blind eye syndrome" of staff towards bad student behaviour. Creative ideas were put on the back burner as "too risky for now" (cf. Chapter Six) The head was determined that the school would prove to itself, however unfair the inspectors had been, that it could achieve this task. It required her to be somewhat persecutory, or "zero tolerant" in her treatment of her staff, though not of the students, to achieve this end and, while she found this very difficult at times, she was prepared to do it in service of the enterprise as a whole. This kind of stance was recently described by Anton Obholzer, former Chief Executive of the Tavistock and Portman NHS Trust, psychoanalyst and organizational consultant, as "depressive position zero tolerance" (Obholzer, 2003). I think she was already formulating the next step in her mind.

The school was very successful in achieving most targets and, more than this, raised achievement to unprecedented levels, from 13% to 27% A to C Grades at GCSE level in 2001, above the 25% benchmark set by the Secretary of State for Education. They were widely congratulated both locally and nationally and received visits from the Chief Inspector of Schools and other important people. Several of them suggested that the school buildings needed upgrading. At this point, the school itself had three problems. The first was the ongoing one of constantly keeping the staff motivated; after such a long period of crisis management and fighting to restore their reputation, what was the new organizational purpose? It was essential to have one or the fear was that performance might slip back and the school might find itself on Special Measures again. The second problem was getting the school fit for the purpose of twenty-first century learning. The third was that, as the school had improved, so had problems from the outside community grown. Ex-students, some who had left and others who had been excluded some years before (not as part of the recent drive on school improvement), and young people from other local schools gathered at the school gates and attacked students leaving the school; gangs hung around alleyways at night and there were break-ins. Should they build higher fences, get extra gate keepers and strengthen the organizational boundaries? Work with the school at this point was very important. There were several meetings held with the head teacher and leadership team in which they worked at the meaning of the attacks from the community. The most important question addressed seemed to be about what the ex-pupils outside the gate might be thinking and feeling that made them attack the students. This led to the idea that they were expressing envy and rage at the school moving on and growing when they were no longer part of it; also that the school owed them something—and then that perhaps the school should not be thought of as ending at the gates, with a closed boundary between it and the community. It was possible also that the community round the school might set limits to what the school itself could achieve.

And this is where the idea for the "Communiversity" was born; the idea of using the rebuilding of the school as an opportunity to develop on the school site an integrated multi-faceted learning community, or "Communiversity". This would not just be for eleven- to eighteen-year-olds, but for all the community as a resource for learning and employment, including business units, skills training, a leisure centre, crèche, GP surgery and counselling centre.

The head teacher managed to inspire her governing body and various other organizations to sponsor her to carry out a six-month feasibility study for the project. This has now been extended. She has widely consulted school staff and students, including some who have become "Ambassadors" for the "Communiversity". These students have joined with her in making presentations to government ministers and others to raise money. It was at this point that her job title changed from head teacher to Principal, to reflect the more executive nature of the role in relation to the enterprise as a whole. Thus, the head teacher has shifted her survivalist leadership stance to a developmental one and her "hard" to a softer, more facilitative approach. She has unleashed the creativity that had to be suppressed in order to survive as an organization. She has thus expanded and reframed the practice of education to include the community as a whole. The enterprise is not only contained in the organization of the school but in the wider organization of the "Communiversity". This example also incidentally challenges Lewin's (1947) idea of what organizational change consists of. "Freeze, movement, refreeze" becomes "Freeze, movement, *reframe*", highlighting the need to reformulate the organization in an open-ended way rather than to restore it to some pre-existing state.

This example also alerts us to another aspect of leadership described by women in the research; that of the centrality they give to encouraging creativity in others. They describe their leadership as being focused on providing the facilitation and containment others need to collaborate with one another and develop the new ideas the organization needs to move forward. The leader formulates an idea of the enterprise that people can work at from divergent points of view, mobilizing hope as against feelings of despair. This points to a neglected aspect of leadership and of consultancy. From a psycho-analytic point of view, it can sometimes seem as if the role of the leader is merely about working at the destructive or pathological aspects of organizational functioning so as to minimize these, allowing growth and development to take place. The containment offered is about helping others to work through frustration or act as a shield from overwhelming anxiety. It can seem as if the leader has nothing to contribute to non-pathological or healthy organizational functioning. However, recent work in child psychotherapy by Anne Alvarez, brought to my attention by my colleague, David Armstrong (2002), has described a different kind of containment that is relevant to our understanding of the leadership of organizations. This is containment that can communicate the pleasures of self-discovery and discovery of the world and encouragement for exploration and curiosity. This is a kind of *joie de vivre* and links to what Lacan (1977) has called "*jouissance*" and Hirschhorn (2003) has called "flow". This containment can be about making an object alive and present and promoting lively interaction with it.

The leaders in this research, in their stress on encouraging others' autonomy and creativity, support the idea that leadership today is more about this newer meaning of containment than the traditional view. This may be because of the co-evolutionary potential in the interaction between people and organizations. People *can* actually have a lively interaction with their organizations and change them as a result.

In the example described above, the risk of destruction of the enterprise of the school through a demotivated staff and an envious community was transformed into a lively interaction between staff, students, community, and other organizations with the co-created and reframed enterprise of the "Communiversity".

Conclusion

The example described above brings alive what the women leaders in the research were saying about leadership and organizations today. In particular, what is highlighted is the shift from authority derived from role and task to that derived from embodying or representing the enterprise and, in so doing, binding people together to work at it. It expands the emphasis given to the person in organizations to include the idea of the leader making the link between the organization and the enterprise in promoting a lively engagement with both the external environment of clients, consumers, partners, and competitors and with those working within the organization, its most precious resource.

CHAPTER FOUR

What is the emotional cost of distributed leadership?

Clare Huffington, Kim James, and David Armstrong

"I am paid for being able to think more clearly than anyone else but I don't know any training that can help me do this in relation to my industry"

CEO, Pharmaceutical Company

"These leadership development programmes have nothing to do with what I have to do every day—which is basically to fight my corner with other directors"

Director, NHS Trust

"People here are used to leadership meaning being top of a hierarchy and your authority coming from your experience and expertise. It is quite a new thought to them that leadership means inspiring loyalty and influencing people externally. They thought they got that automatically with the role and did not realize you have to earn it"

CEO, Local Authority

What is distributed leadership?

While there may be various styles of leadership (facilitative, charismatic, authoritarian, etc.), there are also different leadership concepts held by organizations; for example, hierarchical, distributed,
matrix. The leadership concept encompasses more than a set of
competences or an idea of a style of leadership that is considered
desirable. It touches upon the assumptions in the organization that
are held about the role of leader, the way leaders should use their
authority, the way followers should relate to leaders and the way
the leaders relate to each other and the outside world. The leadership concept that is widely subscribed to in the organization,
whether consciously or unconsciously, will impact on the emotional
relations in the organization. Thus, the patterning of emotional relations may change when a new leadership concept is espoused or
when leadership development activity enables people to reflect on
the leadership concept informing their behaviour. New organizational dynamics will then emerge.

One of the strands in the debate about the importance of leadership in organizations today concerns distributed leadership or
"leadership at all levels". This is seen as a requirement in new, flatter hierarchies with horizontal networks, inter-functional and cross-
functional teams, and strategic alliances with suppliers, customers,
and even competitors. Decisions need to be taken away from the
centre of the organization, at the point of contact between the organization and its environment. Even the most traditionally hierarchical of organizations such as the army, the police, and education
are developing a leadership concept that involves devolution of
decision-making. Gregory (1996) analyses the concept of leadership
for the management of educational change, for example. He argues
for a model of shared or distributed leadership for transformational
change. Distributed leadership also implies collaboration in leadership activity. If leadership is distributed among many, it must
also be integrated across the organization. The notion of collaborative leadership brings together the characteristics of the learning
organization with leadership (Dentico, 1999). The term collective
leadership is also used to describe this concept. Denis, Lamothe,
and Langley (2001) argue that creating collective leadership in
which members play complementary roles appears critical in

achieving strategic change. However, they note that collective leadership is fragile in a context of diffuse power and multiple objectives.

These writers argue the advantages of distributed, shared, collective, and collaborative leadership. However, it is clear that achieving this different approach to leadership is hard in an environment in which individual leaders are the focus of attention; any management magazine or newspaper will dissect the virtues and vices of political leaders, football managers, and entrepreneurs in terms of their individual characteristics. Locke (2003) explores different models that underpin these terms and also raises the questions of what role the top leader plays when new models of leadership emerge. He argues that top leaders are engaged in eight key tasks (vision, core values, structuring the organization, motivating employees, selection and training, communicating, team building, and promoting change). We argue that a shift to distributed leadership requires not only a mindset change in the concept of leadership, an understanding of the tasks of leaders at various levels, but also a different understanding of the emotional challenges facing leaders in these settings. Locke's analysis does not include key emotional aspects of top leadership and distributed leadership.

In this chapter we draw on a number of recent experiences of consulting to organizations seeking to implement or experiment with distributed leadership, to explore the dynamics associated with these challenges, and what they may indicate about the limits and conditions of the concept.

Taking up and giving up: the challenge of transition

The difficulty in implementing distributed leadership emerges in client work not only as an issue for organizations that are explicitly adopting this model, but equally for more traditional organizations trying to move away from the notion of one leader to a more corporate team approach at senior levels.

An example is of a large technologically driven organization that had recently brought in a new CEO who had an international reputation as a charismatic leader. After two years, during which he had brought about major change in culture and customer focus, he decided he needed a strategic group that exercised more leadership across the organization and did not depend upon his ideas and initiative alone. He brought together his top team in a series of workshops, the purpose of which was to encourage the team to operate as a cohesive leadership group and take a whole organizational business perspective rather than focusing on their particular individual remits within a strategy he had or would set. Given such senior team members had extensive leadership roles themselves, often managing large businesses within the overall organization, he was frustrated that in the wider business setting they seemed over-dependent on his leadership and disempowered themselves as leaders of the organization as a whole. During the workshops, some of their dilemmas emerged. The first was that the leader's charisma had meant that there was an element of "hero worship" for him in the organization that interfered with others' self-perception of being leaders in their own right. The second was a related and implicit perception that it was the CEO who needed to change *his* style in order to let others share in the leadership. The possibility of challenging him on this was considered a difficult issue—it seemed like a big risk to engage in such a conversation. The irony of this perception—that he needed to lead the change in style so that they, the team members, could change their own behaviour—was lost until the workshop leaders played this back to them. It was as if the only way they could make the required changes was by using the old paradigm of following the leader rather than by addressing the risks of making changes themselves. They acted as though they could only change once the leader changed, rather than understanding that a change in relationship would be dynamic and required all of them to initiate adjustments in behaviour.

In the event, and following the workshops, the senior team redefined their task as responding to the leader's invitation to engage in a wider leadership role in the company rather than the narrower task of running their own businesses. Having some of their assumptions and behaviours played back to them during the workshops enabled them to see that "it is about . . . evolving the role from one that accepts decisions handed down by the leader to engaging and influencing together with the leader the shape, the performance of the company". Subsequently, the CEO and other directors were very receptive to ideas that these executives began to develop around some key issues that the leader had wanted them to engage with.

The importance of this example is that it demonstrates how, even at the highest levels in the organization, senior executives can be disabled by feelings and perceptions, explicit or implicit, from taking up distributed leadership roles. These may include feelings of dependency, fear of challenging and being challenged by others—seniors or peers—and the struggle to contain anxiety about exercising one's own authority as a leader on a wider organizational front.

To take up such roles can require facing up to and dismantling ("giving up") established assumptions and relations—in this case assumptions and relations around the construct of the CEO as charismatic leader—which may also have served both to contain anxiety and to displace reservations and doubts about both one's own and the organization's capability. Giving up the idea that the charismatic leader is the only leader needed, engaging their own leadership capabilities, meant being more in touch with the risks and potential failure, as well as success, associated with exercising shared leadership. The CEO would need to give up the easy acquiescence of his directors to his ideas and face more challenge from them as they engaged in collective leadership of the business.

To put this another way; distributed leadership, at any level, will tend to heighten and, as it were, to equalize feelings of vulnerability—personal, professional and organizational; simultaneously removing the apparent, if illusory, protection afforded by more hierarchical structures. Hirschhorn (1997) talks about the shifts in leadership required in such organizational settings. In contrast to organizations that used primarily to emphasize external authority—the chain of command—these new organizations require people across the organization to exercise personal authority themselves. Accessing personal authority without recourse to bureaucracy, position, or formal power, is essential if the individual is to be capable of exercising choice, making independent decisions, bringing their imaginations and ideas to create new options, and persuading others to follow their direction.

This shift from external, hierarchically embedded authority to a more personal and laterally distributed exercise of leadership is psychologically demanding. On the one hand it presents challenges to one's individual competence, professional, technical, and managerial; to one's readiness to make and act on judgements and handle the risks consequent on uncertainty, while accepting accountability for decision and action. On the other hand, it may involve the dismantling of projections on to, and expectations of, others—the external authority figures to whom one has previously looked for containment or direction: idealized, envied, or denigrated.

At the same time, the example also shows how bringing such assumptions and relations to the surface can enable a more realistic engagement with the challenge of distributed leadership, in which these can be, if not fully relinquished, at least open to the test of practice.

Distributed leadership and upwards accountability: a necessary tension

It is not, however, only past assumptions surrounding the leadership concept of the organization that present challenges of transition. Equally, there are apparent paradoxes in relation to accountability as this can be experienced and felt by role holders.

> This was a central feature in consulting to a new marketing division of a multi-national pharmaceutical company. The President of the division was seeking to transform how the enterprise and his senior group of regional Vice Presidents were operating and managing across very diverse markets. He saw that the volatility, unpredictability, and diversity of these markets required knowledge, strategy, and decision-making to be located as close as possible to each theatre of operation. His Vice Presidents correspondingly needed to be freed to experiment with and exploit new ways of penetrating and exploiting market opportunities without over-reliance on, and control from, central headquarters. They, in turn, would need similarly to transform something of their working relation with their immediate subordinates—the line managers responsible for particular country markets—some of which might be equally diverse.

> This transformational intent, accepted and welcomed in theory, nevertheless gave rise to unintended tensions and dilemmas around the experience and practice of leadership. For example, Vice Presidents would seek to use the President to ask advice on strategic options or challenges they were experiencing. The President would not offer such

advice; it was up to them to make their own judgement on the ground. On other occasions, however, the President would challenge decisions a Vice President had made or complain of something he had not been informed about. Leadership became seen as ambiguous in its practice; the President, as it were, simultaneously distributing leadership downwards and then taking it back. It was difficult to acknowledge that this ambiguity might itself be intrinsic to what the President was attempting. Or, to put it another way, that in distributing leadership among the Vice Presidents, the President was not simply abdicating or withdrawing his responsibility for keeping informed, monitoring or challenging from his position on the boundary of the enterprise as a whole. The Vice Presidents were experiencing the ambiguity around leadership as a tension that needed to be resolved. But it could also be seen as a tension that needed to be continually maintained: that there *might be no single answer to the question* "Where does the authority for decision lie?" Rather, that this question had to be continually negotiated and explored in the light of the team's evolving experience.

This example draws attention to what might be understood as a double-edged aspect of the vulnerability of distributed leadership; that it heightens the sense of individual responsibility but without necessarily removing the burden and need for an accountability to others. On the contrary, the devolution of authority may require more accountability rather than less—a greater responsibility to report back, be open to monitoring and receive feedback.

Distributed leadership and the negotiation of roles

The example just given suggests that one of the central challenges of distributed leadership turns on the ability to acknowledge and manage the necessary uncertainties and ambiguities surrounding one's own role in relation to those of others, both vertical and lateral. Where such acknowledgement and management are lacking, the consequence can be an explosion of more personal dynamics surrounding relations with colleagues and/or superiors, in which the tensions around the location of leadership get played out in accusation, hostility, and recrimination.

This may, in part, account for the recent sharp increase in complaints of bullying within organizations, including, at senior levels, grievance procedures and the corresponding rise in requests to consultants to help with conflict resolution and mediation (cf. Chapter Ten). It is as if distributed leadership both exacerbates and in turn fails to contain anxieties arising from the exercise of one's roles.

An example of this was a senior director of pan-European services in a large company. He had been disciplined for bullying some of his staff, managers heading services in each European country. While this was historically a strong hierarchical organization in which each country manager was directly responsible to the senior director, the creation of a pan-European organization meant that certain aspects of leadership had been delegated to local level. There were tensions about which aspects had been delegated and which had not; whether central directives could be customized to the local situation or not; and how much autonomy the country managers actually had. In psychoanalytic terms, the dynamics of projective identification were very differently patterned.

Complaints about bullying occurred during the implementation of a very large project in which it was essential that all European countries adopted exactly the same policies and practices. It was a very stressful time as country managers found that the policies and practices did not fit their local situation. Some staff in different countries took longer than others to implement the changes. Country managers did not always keep the senior director informed about what they were doing, or in the same ways, and seemed to resent the need to do so. There was one week in which the senior director telephoned the manager in Germany eight times with no call back. When he did finally reach him, after hearing that he was in regular communication with his counterpart in Spain, he exploded, reprimanding him about the quality of his work and his failure to communicate. This led to the country manager and two of his peers complaining of bullying to the European Managing Director, the senior director's boss. They complained of distress, inability to sleep due to anxieties about their work, and fear of losing their jobs. The senior director, who was then disciplined about his behaviour, was deeply shocked about being called to account, as it had never happened before. He felt he had a right to expect regular contact from his country managers. He felt personally accountable and responsible for the outcome of the project as a whole and did not trust country managers to deliver. He had been very stressed at the time, attempting to hold the project together across a huge geography and then feeling that he had failed and "lost it"(his temper and his power and authority). As a result of the disciplinary procedure, he too was stressed, unable to sleep, and in fear of losing his job. Both "sides" thus felt out of control and caught in a powerful mutual projective system.

In this example, we can see that the tensions associated with distributed leadership led to intense personal vulnerability. It is as if those to whom authority had been delegated saw themselves as wholly accountable and supporting or authorizing each other laterally (Germany and Spain) and not vertically through the senior director as they once would have done. So, the telephone call from the peer was returned immediately, but the call from the boss was not, as if he was not now relevant to the authorization process. When he came down hard, this was experienced as persecutory and as a personal attack rather than the legitimate exercise of authority in the role of line manager to direct report. While he may have exercised his authority in an over-forceful way due to anxiety, stress, and so on, it also appears that he was seen as making the "mistake" of seeing the accountability as all his. The fact that the European Managing Director disciplined him rather than offering support in working through what had taken place between his colleague and himself could be taken as emphasizing the difficulties the organization was experiencing in facing the structural rather the personal tensions in play; a failure in containment. Anton Obholzer in Chapter Two spells out the role of managing boundaries in leadership and the importance of the individual leader needing to create a "containing structure conducive to creativity and thought . . .". It is clear that these aspects of leadership are particularly challenging in the situation of distributed leadership

Distributed leadership in partnership

So far we have been focusing on some of the dynamics surrounding the introduction and practice of distributed leadership within the single organization. The concept may also be considered, however, in the context of the recent emphasis, especially within public sector organizations, on the development of partnership working. In this context, distributed leadership may be taken to refer to leadership being delegated to managers who negotiate in the best interests of their own organization with managers from partner organizations.

The tendency here is for two opposing difficulties to arise. One is that partners get so preoccupied with their own reading (explicit or, more likely, implicit) of the nature and/or requirements of the work that "partnership" cannot get off the ground. The other is that the energy or commitment released in partnership leads to a watering-down or abandonment of real differences related to the nature of the work. One way of expressing the appropriate dynamic of partnership is that it turns on the ability to contest with the other, without this either deteriorating into conflict or being evaded as a way of dealing with fear of conflict. The danger is of stimulating a pairing valency designed partly to keep fight–flight or dependency at bay.

> For example, in local government, services now need to be delivered by partnership organizations across the boundaries of existing statutory and voluntary organizations. In dealing with homelessness, this could require involvement from housing, health, education, and voluntary organizations. How could assistant directors of services in a local authority in the south of England exercise leadership horizontally in a partnership of peer organizations, all of whom might be looking for a leadership role and might have varying degrees of responsibility or accountability for the final outcome? In a workshop exploring these issues, assistant directors identified that their traditional way of working was to work solo in expert roles in which they could demonstrate individual competence. In working across organizational boundaries they discovered that expertise must be exchanged and colleagues would need to work together seamlessly to deliver a satisfactory outcome. This meant that individual competence did not have to be demonstrated in the same way. It would need to be combined with the skills of creating personal relationships with strategic partners, and expertise needed to be seen as the material that could be shared, bartered, and consulted. This meant that the leadership development of these assistant directors had to focus on personal development, group working, and influencing skills in which they would learn to lead from an awareness of personal values and principles and learn skills in collaborative working. Simultaneously, they would need to be able to balance and resolve any issues deriving from the constant need for systems of accountability and responsibility. It was as if they had to blend hierarchical and horizontal leadership together so as to weave

the weft and warp of a new organizational fabric. One outcome of help-ing these directors to work across the organizational boundaries was that they began to form a strong support group within the organiza-tion. This led to some of the difficulties in directorate management teams working together being tackled and, paradoxically, the organi-zation as a whole began to work in a more robust and efficient way.

This example draws attention to the way in which, in different contexts, distributed leadership may require one to re-frame one's own personal construct of leadership and the skills and capabilities that underpin it.

A related example comes from a looser idea of "partnership", where leaders from different organizations, but within the same broad domain, work together as a collaborative leadership group to implement best practice learning by sharing and reflecting on current practice across their institutions.

The initiative in question was a "collaborative leadership learning" project for leaders of educational institutions. Collaborative leadership learning deliberately has a variety of connotations—learning together about what leadership means, personal learning for leadership from and with others in the group, and learning about the leadership of learning in schools or other educational institutions. In a group acting as a "*collaborative* leadership learning" group, the concept of leadership, both in their everyday organization and in their group, was an impor-tant area for inquiry; what does collaborative leadership mean? Does the idea of equity and collaboration make the role of leader redundant or different from the common view of leadership? Could it be mean-ingful in their organizations? There were difficulties in discussing these issues even though group members expressed a wish on the first day that their conversations would "have depth", "go beyond the business as usual agenda".

Coming from a highly competitive environment, from institutions that have hired them for their personal leadership and visionary character-istics and a high degree of personal responsibility and sense of voca-tion, these are leaders accustomed to "going it alone". In the groups, they found it hard to share examples of competence, while they were ready to talk about their failings or concerns. They experienced collab-orative learning as anxiety-provoking because it challenged the projec-tion of omniscience that they had unconsciously accepted in their day-to-day work. Staff and students in their institutions expect them to "know everything". In collaborative leadership learning, it was as if they had to deny their leadership capability in order to create a mind-set whereby they could learn from each other. This stance, while being a defence against envious attack, created an impoverished learning environment, despite the fact that they consciously set out to avoid this. The sign that they had been able to move from group dynamics characteristic of dependency was conflict in the group that had previously been characterized by politeness (see, for example, Bion, 1961). The emergence of difference in the group enabled some genuine personal engagement between members of the group. That was the beginnings of real collaboration.

These examples illustrate how leaders in partnership or collaborative projects need to be able to debate and contest their differences if they are to develop real, as opposed to a false or neutered, engagement with one another. They also illustrate how difficult it can be for all parties to address themselves to the task of partnership in this way, expecting that *they* will need to change too and dismantle existing ways of working in service of a greater potential shared good.

Anxiety, containment, and leadership

The experiences illustrated above indicate something of both the challenges and the risks, psychological and organizational, associated with the concept of distributed leadership as this emerges in practice.

In summary, we would argue that distributed leadership and the devolution of authority in response to sensed changes in the organization's relatedness to its environment raise the level of work-related anxiety on the part of role holders. Simultaneously, the containment offered by protective processes such as clarity of structures, lines of accountability, assured role boundaries, are reduced or dismantled. The importance of containment of anxiety in order that an organization can focus on the organization task has been long documented (see, for example, Jaques, 1955; Menzies, 1959). Lack of containment, in turn, may reinforce anxiety in ways that can significantly reduce the mental space, within the individual and/or the group, available for generativity in decision and action, which the transition to a distributed model is designed to promote. Hence, the kind of comment sometimes expressed, albeit without acknowledgement of complicity, by senior managers, "we empowered them [sic] but they did not want it really" (James & Clark, 2002).

Where this is the case, work anxiety may spill over into a more diffuse sense of personal vulnerability, loss of confidence or self esteem, the questioning of one's own competence and professional identity; or, alternatively, into persecutory feelings and responses directed outward at superiors, colleagues, or subordinates. Heifetz and Laurie (1997) affirm the importance of providing what Winnicott (1965) described as a "holding environment" in leadership roles. They argue that the "regulation of distress" and providing a space for processing experiences is a key aspect of the leadership role. This requires the leader to possess personal presence, poise, and resilience, and the emotional capacity to tolerate uncertainty, frustration, and pain without getting too anxious themselves. They argue that this is the most difficult aspect of leadership and we suggest here that this poise is under threat in situations of distributed leadership in which the exercise of personal authority without recourse to bureaucratic power leaves people feeling vulnerable.

Correspondingly, a central challenge facing organizations seeking to implement distributed leadership is how to mobilize or create new processes and structures that enable anxiety to be held and worked through outside conventional hierarchical channels. It would be possible to interpret the recent vogue for executive coaching, in both private and public sector organizations, as one response to this challenge (cf. Chapter Nine). In this respect, executive coaching might be viewed as the out-sourcing of the containing function of leadership. However, quite apart from questions around the merits and demerits of such an approach, a focus on the single role holder (or series of single role holders) cannot in itself carry the containing function now needed. To put this another way, such a focus risks construing distributed leadership as an issue for the individual rather than for the group or the team. The challenges and risks of distributed leadership represented in each of the examples we have offered are all concerned rather with the relations and relatedness *between* individuals, who are having to negotiate roles and accountabilities within continually changing contexts. It is at this level—that of the group or team—that containment may need to be carried; through sharing and processing experiences, suspending judgements, engaging with conflicts, challenging and exploring differences of perspective, both overt and covert.

One might describe this process as one of cultivating a culture of corporate reflection and one of the dilemmas here may be the extent to which such a culture can appear counter-intuitive in increasingly competitive, results-driven environments. To put this point more paradoxically, the same external forces that are stimulating this transition in the organization's leadership concept can get in the way of the transformations, in culture, process, or structure that it may demand.

Distributed leadership and the idea of the organization

We noted earlier that distributed leadership cuts two ways. On the one hand it implies *devolution of authority downwards*; on the other hand what might be referred to as an *evolution of accountability upwards*. Expressed in the language of boundaries, distributed leadership, if it is to mean more than just delegation, implies a measure of acceptance of accountability for the overall functioning of the organization and its direction. In other words, to accept distributed leadership involves a bringing into view of the outer boundary of the organization as a whole in relation to one's own or one's group's sphere of decision and action; this means keeping in mind the overall system of organizations and influences of which this organization is just a part. This is what one might term its ecology.

Without a clear and shared idea of the organization and how it is defining itself in relation to its context, what it is seeking to achieve, how it frames its practice, and the values that inform this, its standards of excellence, and the competencies that underlie these, distributed leadership will be prone to fragmentation and/or the dynamics of conflict and evasion referred to above in relation to partnership working.

We propose coining the term *"pro-tainment"* to capture this aspect or function of leadership; the making present of an organizational idea embodied in a lively and enlivening sense of the enterprise ("an organization of persons and materials around some human endeavour"), which the organization frames (Armstrong, 2002). We would suggest that the importance of the leader offering a containing leadership idea or vision is ever greater in circumstances of ambiguity and consequent anxiety where so many traditional structures and processes are in flux.

In a paper on the "psychology of vision", Hirschhorn (1998) uses the notion of the "basic idea" that the leader (by implication singular) is able to offer the organization. The basic idea he suggests is not mystical, but deeply grounded in the organization's history, culture, and current context. It may connect with the leader's personal history and have some creative element, but it must articulate the organization's experience in such a way that followers can buy into the vision and allow the leader to take risks on their behalf (Hirschhorn, 1998). Our experience of working with organizations seeking to deploy the concept of distributed leadership suggests that exercising this articulating function is a pre-condition, both psychologically and organizationally.

A highly imaginative leader of an inner-city college with whom we have been working uses Richard Dawkins' idea of *memes* (the cultural equivalent of genes) as a metaphor of the transformational process she is engaging with. Much of her leadership comes from her ability continually to offer a language of imagery, reference, and naming that "gives suitable expression to something already in the air" and at the same time opens up new ways of understanding and developing the organization's practice in an evolving context of opportunities and challenges. Over time, this evolving language has become embodied in an unwritten "lexicon" that serves to give meaning to and to monitor both practice and culture across the college; that informs but without controlling what might be termed the mental habits or mind sets of staff at every level.

In contrast to Hirschhorn's position, we would interpret this process of articulation here as one that allows *others*, not just the leader, to take risks on behalf of the whole. Simultaneously, it provides a third term, without which the processes of containment referred to in the previous section can become organizationally ungrounded.

In this respect, distributed leadership does not so much remove the need for singular leadership or "leadership from the top", as qualify it—drawing attention to functions that may have been neglected, taken for granted, or subsumed in the language of strategy, mission, and goals.

In summary, we have drawn attention to some of the tensions arising from the new organizational dynamics around distributed leadership. It is clear that, while there are considerable potential benefits to be gained from sharing, collaboration, and devolution downwards of decision-making in and between organizations, simultaneously there are anxieties and conflicts to be contained in new ways. Far from diluting the influence of the leader in the central role, it appears even more important for the person in this role to offer a singular inspiring vision or idea to integrate and contain the elements of leadership distributed to others.

SECTION II
CHANGE AND CREATIVITY

Introduction

William Halton and Linda Hoyle

E ven in periods of rapid change, new structures crystallize, emotional bonding takes place, loyalties develop, patterns emerge. The tension between present stability and future possibilities always exists and change gives rise to an experience of fragmentation as structures and patterns dissolve. Opposite and complex currents of feeling, mourning over loss, hope for the future, and anxieties about personal survival, are stirred up and need to be acknowledged and contained until a new configuration is achieved. Traditionally, this process has been conceptualized as the container and the contained, with the leader offering containment of anxiety during a period of uncertainty and change. For example, the tension between present and future puts a strain on relationships within the organization. The present is known but the future is unknown. It can only be seen obscurely as through clouded glass. Change is a gamble that has to be taken in order to survive. In this section there are two chapters that explore emotional responses to the hopes and fears involved in change and examine ways in which leaders can promote creativity and innovation as well as contain anxiety.

Chapter Five, by Linda Hoyle, "From sycophant to saboteur— responses to organizational change", provides an exploration of a continuum of responses to change. At opposite ends of the spectrum are those who cannot engage with change; believing their personal survival is at stake, they either blindly oppose it or they blindly embrace it. In the middle of the spectrum are those who recognize the need for change in principle and are able to think about it from the point of view of what is best for the organization. They have worked through organizational reasons for a negative or positive attitude towards the change. This chapter also draws attention to the idea of the existential primary task as a way of understanding people's responses to change, and demonstrates that the way managers handle the change process can influence the position staff take up on the continuum.

Chapter Six, by William Halton, "By what authority? Psychoanalytical reflections on creativity and change in relation to organizational life", explores links between organizational change and psychoanalytic thinking about creativity and change. It looks at how the leader's personal style of creativity affects organizational development. Tensions in the change process can be flexible and creative, or inflexible and stultifying, depending on the leader's capacity to allow the expression of conflict between loss and gain without identifying with one side or the other. It is also suggested that, in evolutionary creativity, the process of disintegration and reintegration in relation to assimilating a new object may involve an oscillation between manic-depressive splitting and integration within the framework of the depressive position.

Both chapters illustrate how consultants need to be aware of complex emotional dynamics and make a consultancy intervention adapted to the current emotional state of the organization. In this way, the intervention provides a temporary organizational framework for containing the fragmentation and tensions of the change process and for promoting creativity and innovation.

CHAPTER FIVE

From sycophant to saboteur—responses to organizational change

Linda Hoyle

Introduction

During any period of organizational change, there is the potential for heightened creativity. When the purpose of the change is to develop new ideas about improving services or to create innovative products, this opens up the opportunity to review the current organizational structures and put in place more appropriate working practices. However, as people connect with their creativity to bring about change, they will also be taking risks, generating uncertainty, and facing the possibility of failure, which can evoke anxiety in themselves and others around them. There may be other potentially negative consequences of organizational change that evoke understandable anxiety, such as threat of job loss, and the loss of known ways of working.

The anxiety evoked by the process of change can be a major barrier to implementing successful change and it is, indeed, the central tenet of the psychoanalytic theory of the sources of resistance to change. The aim of this chapter is to explore how people respond during a period of organizational change and to examine the contribution of psychoanalytic theory to understanding such responses. It begins with an outline of the seminal work conducted in the 1950s by Jaques and Menzies on the unconscious sources of resistance to change. Findings from two case studies are presented to explore two new working hypotheses to understanding responses to organizational change.

Psychoanalytic theory of resistance to change

The most influential work on sources of resistance to change has been that of Elliot Jaques and Isabel Menzies. Jaques's main finding (1955) was that a source of resistance to change was that the social system in the organization, designed for work purposes, was also being used by people as a defence against "psychotic" anxiety. It follows that any attempt to change the social system would result in resistance to change, with individuals and groups trying to maintain the current system because it served to defend them against anxiety. In using the term "psychotic", he refers to the individual mechanisms of defence against the recurrence of the early paranoid and depressive anxieties, which were first described by Melanie Klein (1946).

Jaques says that the institutions did not become "psychotic" but that

> individuals may be thought of as externalizing those impulses and internal objects that would otherwise give rise to psychotic anxiety and pooling them in the life of the social institutions in which they associate. [Jaques, 1955, p. 278]

Jaques applied this theory to an analysis of the Glacier Metal Company, which was in the process of negotiating a change to methods of wage payments. Although the management and workers both desired the change, they had not been able to reach a decision. Jaques proposes that the workers had split the management into being good when they worked together but that the same managers were bad when negotiating wage changes. The workers projected their destructive impulses into the union representative, who deflected this into the negotiations with the bad management. This social system served to maintain good working relationships between management and workers on the task of the organization, and also provided a defence against persecutory and depressive anxiety for management, workers, and the union representative in the negotiating situation.

Another interesting aspect of this social system was the management's idealization of the workforce. Jaques proposed that this was a defence mechanism to diminish the guilt stimulated by the fear that exercising their managerial authority would in some way damage or destroy the workers and also their fear of retaliation by the workers. Jaques describes how this was the basis for a reinforcing, circular process. A partial resolution occurred when Jaques was able to focus attention on working through and restructuring the social relationships rather than focusing on the wages problems.

Following from Jaques' work, Menzies (1959) undertook a study of the nursing service of a general hospital so as to understand why change to nursing methods and training could not be implemented. She had found high levels of tension, distress, anxiety, turnover, and sickness in the nurses. Menzies analyses the nature of this anxiety, which can be summarized as follows. The primary task for the hospital was to accept and care for ill people who cannot be cared for in their own homes. The work of the nurses, therefore, arouses strong and mixed feelings of pity, compassion, and love; guilt and anxiety; hatred and resentment because of the aroused feelings; envy of the care given to the patient. The nurse also has to deal with the psychological stress of others, for example, the patient's relatives, due to their own anxieties about illness. As Menzies puts it "by the nature of her profession the nurse is at considerable risk of being flooded by intense and unmanageable anxiety" (*ibid.*, p. 110). However, she states that this alone cannot account for the high level of anxiety in the nurses and continues by outlining the defensive techniques used by the nursing service to contain and modify anxiety; for example, by splitting up the nurse–patient relationship; detachment and denial of feelings, and the attempt to eliminate decisions by ritual task performance.

Menzies agreed with Jaques that the social system is used by people to defend them against anxiety. However, she also points out that the social organization aroused anxiety within the nurses and that the social defence system *itself* aroused anxiety. For example, there was anxiety due to the threat of crisis and operational breakdown, and anxiety from the nurses' excessive movement, underemployment, and deprivation of personal satisfaction. In conclusion, Menzies comments that stress and anxiety in the nursing service could not be accounted for by the task alone and that the social defence system is inadequate in alleviating anxiety because it also evokes anxiety.

The findings of these studies provided important insights to understand the unconscious source of a resistant response to organizational change. In the following sections, two more recent case studies are presented to examine different responses to change and to explore the source of that behaviour.

Health service case study

Background

This case study is based on a consultancy project in a health service organization (Health Trust) with staff who provided residential care for adults with learning disabilities (the residential service). The residential service was undergoing major changes based on government policy. First, the service was soon to take part in a competitive tendering process. They had to submit a proposal giving details of the cost and quality of the service, which would be judged against other service providers, including private sector organizations. Second, the service was moving from being in the health service sector to being in the social services sector. This meant that the model of care used by the staff in the residential homes had to change from a "health model" of care, which focused on the physical care of the client, to a "social model" of care, which focused on the social needs of the client.

> The consultancy process was designed to involve staff in the changes and enable them to identify, understand, and work with resistance to change. The consultant worked with five groups of staff from the Trust, who worked in residential homes for adults with learning disabilities. The groups included care assistants, domestic cleaners, administrative staff, and residential home managers. Interviews were conducted with senior managers of the Health Trust who were responsible for implementing the changes to the homes.

The project design involved three phases; diagnosing, exploring working hypotheses, and action planning. During each phase, group discussions were facilitated with staff groups from the residential homes. The phases can be summarized as follows:

Phase 1:   Diagnosing: The aim was to enable the staff groups to explore the current dynamics in the homes, examine their present role and relationships, and what the future state and future role might be.

Phase 2:   Exploring working hypotheses: Each group was given a summary of the themes and working hypotheses relating to their group in order to explore the working hypotheses with the group members. There was also further discussion of the possible future state of the service.

Phase 3:   Action planning: The combined data for each residential home were presented to each group of staff from that home to develop the working hypotheses. The presentation included a review of two possible scenarios for the future of the service that had been put forward by staff. A Force Field Analysis technique (Lewin, 1946) was used as a framework to help the staff to think about what they would like the future of the service to be, to put forward what actions would enable change to be implemented, and to discuss what would be barriers to that change.

The outcome of the consultancy project was a final report that was presented to senior management, which contained the views of staff about the current service, how they would like the service to develop and what actions they could personally take, and what actions they wanted senior management to take.

The data from the consultancy project were also analysed to examine the contribution of psychoanalytic theory to understanding the responses to change and unconscious sources of resistance.

Summary of main findings

Social system as a defence against anxiety

There was evidence that the staff in the residential homes perceived their senior managers to be critical, unsupportive, and unavailable. In return, the senior management identified with these projections from staff and behaved in a critical, unsupportive, and unavailable way towards them, thus reinforcing the projective system. It could be argued that this process of projective identification served to defend against the anxiety evoked in the authority relationships that existed in the organization.

In a similar way to Jaques's findings in the Glacier Metal study, the care assistants in the home tended to split the role of the Home Manager into being good when they worked alongside them as a carer, but bad when they took up a management role in the residential home. However, the Home Manager seemed unable to contain or understand the hostility and either displaced it on to senior management or on to the consultant. It seemed that this enabled them to take a scapegoat or victim position, which could serve as a defence against anxiety. The proposed changes to the residential homes threatened to change the authority relationships, in that staff were expected to take up more responsibility in their role and the Home Managers were expected to take on more of a management role than a carer role. This meant that the changes threatened to remove this part of the social defence system, which can therefore be seen as a source of resistance.

Similarities with Menzies' case study were also apparent; the care staff seemed to use socially structured defence mechanisms as a defence against the anxiety evoked by close contact with clients and the defence mechanisms themselves evoked anxiety in the care staff. However, in Menzies' study, the work-load was broken into different tasks for each care staff as a defence against close contact with the clients. This was not the same here. In contrast, the majority of care staff had close contact with clients and each staff member had responsibility for the care of particular clients. It seemed that the major social defence mechanism in the residential homes was the intense conflict between groups of staff. There were also different responses to change; while it is apparent from the case study that theories developed in the 1950s are still relevant to current organizational dynamics, the main focus in this chapter is to outline two new working hypotheses that were developed from the case studies. These are that there is a continuum of responses to change, and that the existential primary task can be a source of resistance to change.

Continuum of responses to change

The main finding from the case study was that groups of staff and the senior management team demonstrated different responses to change. The different ways that people were responding seemed to be a source of conflict between groups of people within the homes and between staff and senior management. The responses were more apparent because the staff members had self-organized into groups for the meetings they had with the consultant, despite the attempts of the Home Managers to divide staff into other specific groupings.

The different responses to change are represented on a continuum ranging from "sycophant" response, "positive and challenging" response, "negative and challenging" response, to "saboteur" response (see Figure 1).

A description of each of these responses is outlined below.

Sycophant response

The term "sycophant" response is used here to describe a response to change that can be seen as an unthinking and unchallenging state of followership. This particular word has been used to capture perceptions expressed by participants during the case study and to illustrate the attributes assigned by other people to those who demonstrate this type of response, i.e. other people perceived this

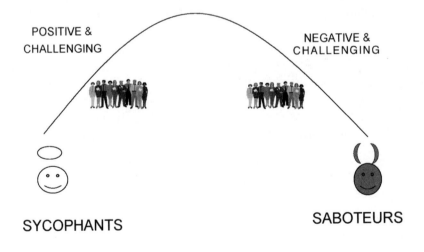

Figure 1.   Continuum of responses to change.

response as grovelling to higher management and that these people were only looking out for themselves. The behaviour of the senior management can be categorized as a sycophant response to change. The proposed changes were directives from government policy and the directors of the Health Trust. The senior management were responsible for managing the implementation of the changes and were in full agreement with the proposed changes. However, they seemed to be unthinking in their followership and appeared to be unwilling to listen to any challenges or criticism that staff may have had of the changes. In this way, the senior management were resistant to changing their views about what the change should be and how it should be implemented. The senior management seemed determined to push through the changes regardless of what impact the changes would have on staff. It may have been that their behaviour served as a defence against anxiety and a source of the anxiety was the fear that the change programme would not be successfully implemented, which could jeopardize their career progression.

Positive and challenging response

Group members who had this response represented positive support for the changes and offered constructive challenge during the consultation process. Staff in these groups participated fully in the consultation process and thought creatively about how they could influence the content of the changes and help with the implementation. These groups consisted mostly of young care assistants who had joined the service because they believed in a social model of care. These staff members were enthusiastic about the changes to a social model of care, which meant that staff would facilitate the development of the clients to become as independent as possible, rather than doing everything for them and encouraging dependency.

Negative and challenging response

Group members who represented the negative and challenging response to change were against the changes in principle and offered reasons why they disagreed fundamentally with the proposals. These tended to be older women, mostly night staff, who had been working in the home for many years using the health model of care with clients. They believed that clients were dependent on care staff and that clients did not have the capability for development. At the beginning of the consultation, they were extremely angry and resistant to the proposed changes and displaced their anger on to senior management and the consultant, i.e. people in positions of authority.

Saboteur response

The term "saboteur" response is used here to describe a response to change where individuals or groups unconsciously attempt to sabotage a change. This particular phrase has been used to capture perceptions expressed by participants during the case study and to illustrate the attributes assigned by other people to those who demonstrate this type of response, i.e. other people perceived this response as an attempt to sabotage the change. For example, there was evidence in the case study that some people behaved in a way that threatened to sabotage the consultation process and ultimately the proposed changes to the organization. The behaviour of these people ranged from outward displays of sabotage, such as disruption of the discussion groups, to passive forms such as non-participation in the consultation process.

The most extreme saboteur response came from one of the Home Managers, who behaved in a way that encouraged conflict between groups of staff in the home; she was extremely anxious about potentially losing her job. She was also against the social model of care and seemed threatened by the younger care assistants who supported it as she seemed to fear that they would take over her role as manager.

It can be seen that the sycophant response represented extreme support of the changes and the saboteur response represented extreme resistance to the changes. However, these extreme responses are similar in that the source of resistance seemed to be that these people expressed anxiety based on fear for their personal survival in the organization.

The less extreme responses in the middle of the continuum represented a range of responses depending on differing levels of support for the change and, in particular, whether people supported the social model of care or the health model of care. There is a parallel here with the work of Miller & Gwynne (1972). Their study was of residential institutions for people with incurable conditions and they identified two models of care; the "warehousing model", which is similar to the health model, and the "horticultural model", which is similar to the social model. Miller & Gwynne proposed that both care models were working practices that served to defend staff from the anxiety evoked by the kind of work they did and the contact they had with clients. In a similar way to Menzies' (1959) study, the anxieties inherent in the tasks performed by staff gave rise to a social system of work practices that served as a defence against anxiety.

In this case study, there was conflict between groups of staff within the homes. The conflict was between those people who supported the social model of care, i.e. a "positive and challenging" response, and those who supported the health model of care, i.e. a "negative and challenging response". However, there was also evidence here that the responses of these groups of staff were based on their own beliefs and values. In both cases, these staff became enthusiastic when they talked about the way they worked with clients and held very strong values to justify the different model of care they favoured.

Based on this finding, a working hypothesis was developed that the values held by people can also be a source of resistance to change.

The existential primary task as a source of resistance to change

Staff expressed frustration that the beliefs and values in the health service had changed and that the service was being run as a commercial business. It could also be argued that the beliefs and values of individuals were at the core of their attitude to different models of care and were connected to the meaning that the work had for them. For example, it seemed that for some staff the work had meaning when they were caring for clients as if they were unable to make decisions for themselves, i.e. a health model of care. In other cases, staff seemed to derive meaning from nurturing and developing clients, i.e. a social model of care. In addition, there seemed to be a connection between the different meaning that work had for staff and the different responses to change. For example, groups of staff who had a positive and challenging response to change were in favour of the changes because the social model provided a source of meaning in their work. In a similar way, groups of staff who had a negative and challenging response to change were against the change to a social model because the health model of care provided a source of meaning in their work.

It could be argued that there is a connection between the meaning that work has for people in the organization and the existential primary task, which is an idea put forward by Lawrence & Robinson (1975). They develop the concept of primary task by making a distinction between;

> the *normative* primary task as the task that people in an organization *ought* to pursue (usually according to the definition of a superordinate authority),
>
> the *existential* primary task as that which they believe they are carrying out, and
>
> the *phenomenal* primary task which it is hypothesized that they are engaged in and of which they may not be consciously aware."
> (Miller, 1993, p. 17, original italics).

The optimum position in an organization would be when the normative primary task and the existential primary task are in alignment. In other words, the task that staff are being told to pursue by people in authority is in alignment with the task that staff believe they should carry out. In contrast, when the normative and existential primary tasks are out of alignment, then the resultant behaviour is the phenomenal primary task, which could be resistant behaviour. In this way the existential primary task can be seen as a source of resistance to change.

At the time the health service case study was developed, the internal market of the health service was a good illustration of the normative and existential primary tasks being out of alignment and with the resultant phenomenal primary task behaviour. For example, there was evidence in the case study that people experienced the internal market as follows:

- The normative primary task declared by the government, and in turn by directors of the Health Trust and the senior managers, was that staff ought to provide a cost-effective service to patients, within a restricted budget. In the health service case study this was seen as the basis for the compulsory competitive tendering process;
- The existential primary task of staff was that they should provide the highest standard of care to patients regardless of cost, although they had different models of care that they believed would result in the best care for clients;
- The phenomenal primary task seemed to be the different responses to change outlined above. These ranged from sycophant behaviour from senior management who were protecting their promotion prospects by imposing the normative primary task, positive and challenging behaviour from those who believed in a social model of care, negative and challenging behaviour from those who believed in a health model of care, and saboteur behaviour from those who believed they could protect their jobs and retain their role by preventing the changes from coming into being.

The working hypothesis that the existential primary task can be a source of resistance to change was explored further in a private sector banking organization case study

Bank case study

Background

Two human resource (HR) professionals were interviewed at the head office of a high street bank ("the bank"). The organization provided banking services to customers through branches located in the majority of towns and cities in the UK. It had undergone several major changes over the previous ten years in that it was originally a building society, it had merged with another building society, and it had become a bank. The directors of the bank had also recently proposed a major change to the HR function within the organization, which had a direct impact on the two participants in the case study. Both HR professionals, Susan and Joan had been working together for a year as internal change management consultants. However, Joan recently had a change in role, which was in line with the overall changes to the role of HR professionals in the organization. It had been decided that there would be a move away from having a centralized HR function that worked on the traditional lines of implementing and monitoring the use of personnel policy throughout the organization. The HR director was responsible for implementing the changes. He was new in post and was an accountant by training, which was described by the interviewees as an illustration that the basis of the change was really a cost-cutting exercise.

The change would mean that the responsibility for implementing and monitoring personnel policy would be decentralized to branch managers with a small team of HR professionals based at head office in an advisory capacity. It was planned that Joan would take up the role of Team Leader for the small team of people who would advise branch managers about personnel policy. They were to be based in a call centre, similar to front-line staff, which would be set up in one office and staff would be equipped with computer terminals and telephones to receive and log the calls from branch managers. The HR director said he wanted the team of advisory HR professionals to take up a "consultancy" role rather than the traditional "policing" role of the personnel function. The change to the HR function would mean fewer staff would be required, which meant some would be made redundant.

Susan remained in the role of internal change management consultant working with the HR director to implement the changes to the HR function. This meant that the relationship between Susan and Joan had changed. Previously they had worked together as internal consultants, but now Susan was in a consultancy role and Joan was a member of the client group. The interviews were conducted in the week after Susan had facilitated an "away day" workshop about the planned changes for the HR director and all the HR professionals, including Joan.

Summary of main findings

Continuum of responses to change

There was evidence that the main response to change was a sycophant response from the HR director and a saboteur response from the HR staff. The director demonstrated a sycophant response in that he formulated and attempted to implement the changes without any consultation or communication with staff. He avoided hearing any negative feedback by avoiding consultation with staff and instructing those who were undertaking consultation with staff that he did not want to hear any feedback. This could be seen as a lack of reparative creativity that managers require when managing a process of change in organizations (described in Chapter Six).

There was evidence that staff initially had a negative and challenging response to change when they voiced their concerns informally. However, the response became more intense when the director did not provide an opportunity for staff to voice either positive or negative and challenging responses to change. In addition, staff did not feel able to express any thoughts or feelings and believed this would be seen as a challenge to the authority of their managers, which reinforced the sycophant response of the director.

This resulted in a saboteur response, which was most intense at the workshop that Susan facilitated for the HR staff. Up to that point, people had not been given any other forum to express their views and it seemed that their concerns about the changes had intensified. At this point, their feelings seemed to be acted out as sabotage towards the consultation process and the hostility about the changes seemed to be displaced on to Susan in the role of internal consultant.

The existential primary task as a source of resistance to change

Susan and Joan felt that the organization had changed in such a way that it had an impact on the meaning their work had for them. The normative primary task of the organization, advocated by the directors and senior management, was for proposed changes to bring about cost cutting. The participants reported that the first stage of this had been completed, in that the management development department had been "wiped out". The second stage of the proposed changes was to decentralize the HR function, make many HR professionals redundant, and set up an HR call centre at head office. This was done without consultation with HR staff. In contrast, the existential primary task of the participants was to facilitate change, consult, involve and engage staff in change projects, and to provide personal development for staff. They had both informally voiced a negative and challenging response but had not been listened to. Whereas Susan was the target of sabotage when she facilitated the HR workshop, Joan admitted that she had also attempted to sabotage the proposed changes by non-participation during the same workshop. However, the end result was that they both decided to leave the organization and they did so a few months later.

This finding builds on the working hypothesis that the existential primary task can be a source of resistance to change, i.e. when a proposed organizational change has the potential to change an individual's role so that it no longer provides them with a source of meaning, they will be resistant to the change. As the outcome of this misalignment was that both participants left the organization, it could be argued that an understanding of the existential primary task is important for the consideration of retention, as well as recruitment, of employees.

Conclusions

The findings of the bank case study supported the model of the "continuum of responses to change" and builds on the working hypothesis that the existential primary task can be a source of resistance to change. However, there was further evidence to indicate that people had the potential to move between the different responses to change on the continuum. For example, it was reported that, in the early stages of the bank change project, some people had a negative and challenging response to change, but, when the director blocked them from voicing their concerns, they developed a more extreme saboteur response to change. In other words, these people moved along the continuum from a negative and challenging response to change to a saboteur response to change because they were not able to voice their concerns. In contrast, the people in the health service case study who had a negative and challenging response to change maintained that response, rather than becoming saboteurs, because they were given the opportunity to voice their concerns and opposition to the proposed changes.

In a similar way, people with a positive and challenging response have the potential to move to an extreme sycophant response. The senior management in the health service case study were positive about the changes and said that they began the change project by being facilitative and consultative with staff. However, when they were met with extreme opposition to the changes from staff they admitted that they became more autocratic and tried to push the changes through. It seemed that they moved from a positive and challenging response to a sycophant response when they were faced with opposition from staff. In a similar way, the HR director in the bank case study seemed to move to a sycophant response of imposing the change as a way of avoiding consultation and contact with HR staff whom he sensed would be angry.

In both cases, it seemed that the sycophant response to change was used as a defence against the anxiety evoked by this aspect of their work, i.e. bringing about change through the authority structures. Unfortunately, in both cases, this sycophant response of management was reinforced in a circular pattern of behaviour in the relationship between staff and management in the organization. It seemed that staff perceived the managers to have a sycophant response; for example, they were seen as imposing change in order to achieve career progression, which seemed to intensify the anger and hostility of staff towards management. When staff expressed hostility towards management, the result seemed to be that management avoided contact and consultation with staff. This not only seemed to reinforce the staff's perception that management had a sycophant response to change, but also seemed to result in staff moving from a negative and challenging response to a saboteur response.

This movement to an extreme sycophant position is in contrast to those groups of staff in the health service case study who had a positive and challenging response to change. Although they had the potential of moving to a sycophant response because they were extremely angry with the people who were resistant to the social model of care, they maintained their initial response. It could be argued that this was because they had an opportunity to express their views during the consultation process and make a valuable contribution to the consultation.

The evidence outlined above demonstrates the impact of the interpersonal relationships and interactions between different people in the organization and how this can reinforce certain behaviours in response to change. These examples also seem to illustrate how the unconscious process of projective identification could move people from the positive and negative challenging responses to the extreme behaviours of sycophant and saboteur response to change. It seems that when people hold opposing views of the change process there is a potential that their behaviour could reinforce the negative perceptions they hold of each other until their behaviour becomes more extreme and results in a polarization between groups in the organization. In addition, the extreme behaviour of the sycophant and saboteur responses could be seen as evidence of people reverting to Klein's paranoid–schizoid position. In contrast, the behaviour of the positive or negative and challenging responses could be seen as evidence of people being in Klein's depressive position. When people had a positive or negative and challenging response they seemed able to think creatively and make a valuable contribution about what the changes should be and how they should be implemented, which indicates that they seemed to be in the mature depressive position.

There was evidence in both case studies that using a process consultancy model (Schein, 1990) to provide an opportunity for people to voice their concerns increased the potential for people to move to a more creative depressive position in relation to the change. In this way the process consultancy model also enables people to reach an internalized level of learning and a more evolutionary view of change in comparison to the catastrophic view they may have had at first (cf. Chapter Six). In view of these findings, it could be argued that senior managers and directors would benefit from consulting, involving, and engaging staff in the change project so that staff have a mechanism to express positive or negative and challenging responses to change, rather than moving to a sycophant or saboteur response.

It is important to remember that all adults have the potential to revert temporarily to the paranoid–schizoid position when faced with a situation that evokes anxiety, such as change in an organization. It is, therefore, possible for any adult to revert to extreme sycophant or saboteur response to change if the particular change evokes anxiety. To give an example, the proposed changes for Joan in the bank case study had the potential to take away the aspects of the work that gave her meaning and she resorted to extreme behaviour in her non-participation. This example illustrates a strong link between the existential primary task as a source of resistance to change; if the change in the organization has the impact of taking away the meaning that work has for someone then there may be more potential for that person to move to an extreme saboteur response to change. It follows that if the change in the organization increases the meaning that work has for someone then there may be more potential for that person to move to a positive and challenging response to change.

There was evidence in both case studies that some people remained in extreme positions even when they were given the opportunity to express their concerns. These people seemed to be preoccupied with their personal survival in the organization, which was also the basis of their existential primary task. In both cases, these individuals seemed to have a limited capacity for personal change and did not take up the opportunity to engage in the consultation or move from their extreme responses. It could be said that the extent to which an individual has capacity for personal change also links with the level of learning of which they are capable. The process consultancy model may have limited impact with these individuals, but could be used help other people in the organization to identify, understand, and deal with such extreme behaviour.

Based on the findings from both cases studies, there seems to be a connection between the extent to which people have the capacity for personal change, the extent to which they are in favour of organizational change, and the resultant response to change. This led to the development of an additional model, which represents the dimensions of responses to change (see Figure 2).

It seems that the basis of a sycophant response could be that those people have a lower capacity for personal change and are more in favour of organizational change; for example, the HR director in the bank. In a similar way, the basis of the saboteur response to change could be that those people have a lower capacity for personal change and are less in favour of the organizational change; for example, the home manager in the health service case study. In contrast, the basis of the positive and challenging response could be that those people have a higher capacity for personal change and are more in favour of organizational change. Likewise, the basis of the negative and challenging response could be that those people have a higher capacity for personal change and are less in favour of organizational change. A process consultancy model is particularly useful with people who seem to have a higher capacity for personal change. In particular, it would be important during a change project to provide an opportunity for those people to express their concerns

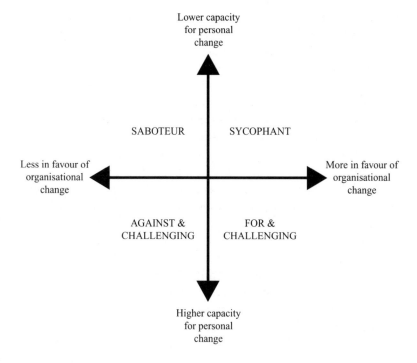

Figure 2. Dimensions of responses to change

about change. It would also be important for management to take these concerns seriously and give feedback indicating that they have been listened to, which could reduce the potential for the behaviour of different groups becoming a more extreme saboteur or sycophant response.

In conclusion, the findings of the case studies can be applied to developing the process consultancy model by:

• Using the continuum of responses to change as a model when thinking about how people respond to change and how the behaviour at the extreme positions could be reinforced by projective identification.
• Providing an opportunity for people with a negative and challenging response to voice their concerns and potentially move to a more thoughtful and constructive response, which could reduce the tendency for a saboteur response to change.

- Enabling those with a positive and challenging response to make a valuable contribution to the content and implementation of change, which could reduce the tendency for a sycophant response to change from senior managers and directors.
- Helping people to move along the continuum from the extreme positions of saboteur or sycophant to the middle of the continuum so as to be more involved, thoughtful, and potentially constructive in the change process.
- Using the dimensions of responses to change when thinking about the connection between the capacity for personal change and the extent to which someone is in favour of organizational change. Applying this model to the process consultancy approach could help consultants to accept that some people have a limited capacity to change and will not move from the extreme positions of saboteur or sycophant. This can help the consultant to decide what interventions are most useful to address different responses to change.
- Identifying and understanding an individual's existential primary task as a source of resistance to change. Also, using a process of bringing the existential task into conscious awareness to enable the individual to understand the source of their anxiety and see their resistance as a misalignment with the organizational normative primary task. In particular, this could be helpful in addressing organizational issues of retention and recruitment, as well as individual career counselling and personal development.

CHAPTER SIX

By what authority? Psychoanalytical reflections on creativity and change in relation to organizational life

William Halton

Aglance along the bookshelves of organizational literature reveals a strong orientation towards the new and a preoccupation with creativity as a means of bringing the new into existence. Psychoanalysis also has its preoccupations with creativity, but usually more in relation to the arts. This chapter takes a theoretical look at some possible points of contact between organizational life and psychoanalytic ideas about creativity.

Drawing on psychoanalytic authors from a variety of sources, three different strands of thinking about creativity can be identified that are related to three different stages of childhood development. These three strands could be gathered together under the headings initiatory, reparative, and evolutionary creativity. Although developmentally and conceptually distinct, in any concrete situation they may all be present to different degrees, if only because earlier stages of development are always residually present in later ones.

Initiatory creativity

The initiatory strand relates particularly to the mental power of the individual. In psychoanalytic theory, omnipotent creativity is an element of early infancy (Milner, 1934; Winnicott, 1951). The infant plays with the phantasy that it has created its own world, including the mother herself. To see the mother is to have created her. There is a fusion between the baby's self and the mother in such a way that they live and die together. This is a normal stage of development during which the mother provides a supportive environment, protecting the infant's omnipotent creative impulse in a bubble of safety until it is ready to face more frustrating reality. As long as the mother provides support, the illusion of omnipotent creativity can be sustained. This is only half the story. The other half is that her absence arouses the baby's fear of helplessness and disintegration. The baby moves between these two separate emotional states; one in which the "good" mother, when present, is loved as a protector and provider; and the other in which the "bad" mother, when absent, is hated as an abandoning and anxiety-generating monster. This emotional division between two different mothers is known in Kleinian terms as the paranoid–schizoid position, "schizoid" because of the split and "paranoid" because of the fear of being destroyed (Klein, 1946). These two states of mind are kept separate in such a way that when the baby is in one state there is no awareness of the other state and it becomes a "blind spot". A version of this paranoid–schizoid split may be reactivated in response to organizational change.

How does initiatory creativity relate to organizations? One point of contact might be with those charismatic leaders who have a sustaining self-belief in the achievability of their own vision. In a simplified form, charisma functions like childhood omnipotence; to persuade others to follow a better way to a new world. The constraints of existing realities that hinder other organizations can be brushed aside as counting for nothing, and frustrating considerations of risk and dependency on other people can be split off and left behind in the old world, as it were. Followers feel that by participating in the enterprise their ordinary lives are elevated to a higher plane. Charismatic leaders demonstrate a capacity for implementing their vision, often in an idiosyncratic manner, breaking known boundaries and devising new methods of working. As long as the environment continues to be supportive of this initiative, success may follow. If the environment changes, say through government legislation or social mores, or other factors, then the leader may be in trouble (cf. case example in Chapter Eight). Contemporary examples may be found among small businesses, private schools, hospitals, and children's homes; enterprises that face change in their way of operating, contrary to the vision and values of their founders. Organizations founded by charismatic leaders eventually arrive at the question of leadership succession. Because of the emotional fusion between founder and organization, separation poses the fear of disintegration for both sides. A common anxiety is that when the founder leaves, the creative impulse that sustains the organization will disappear and it will collapse into the nothingness from which it came. Another connection is that, when the founder leaves, the new leader may be experienced as the second "bad" mother, the anxiety-generating monster, coming to destroy the organization.

Initiatory creativity can also be detected in the heady excitement of those new ideas that will change the world; the great leap forward (political); at a stroke (financial); too cheap to meter (nuclear power); the paperless office (information technology); the dotcom revolution (internet). It can be found in the inventor who believes that the genius-properties of the invention will by themselves overcome the constraints of production, marketing, and distribution. It is present in the service that believes that the high quality of its product alone will protect it from environmental change. The initiatory style blocks off constraining and limiting aspects of reality that in the end have to be confronted. Sometimes consultants are employed in the initiatory stage as an "insurance policy" against anticipated challenges, but more often they are called in when the other half of the story has to be reckoned with.

Reparative creativity

In psychoanalytic thinking, the reparative strand of creativity relates particularly to the capacity for care. Reparative creativity focuses on repairing damage done by aggression (Klein, 1940; Segal, 1991). This strand is based on a different stage of development, known in Kleinian terms as the depressive position. This is formed when the infant brings together the two halves of the story into a single narrative; coming to recognize that the supportive mother that is loved and the anxiety-generating mother that frustrates are one and the same person. This integration of opposite perceptions and emotions represents first steps in psychological integration and formation of a worldview—a realization that the self contains conflicting emotions, that other people are separate from the self, and that they have other relationships in a family system. The anxiety of the depressive position is that, since there is only one mother, aggression against the frustrating mother may also damage the loved mother. This anxiety triggers reparative creativity that aims to repair damage done. In the depressive position, there is a different kind of division in the internal picture of the mother; there is only one mother who is either in a damaged and disintegrated state or in a repaired and lively state. Reparative creativity transforms the first picture into the second. But if guilt for aggression cannot be borne because the damage is too overwhelming, then there may be denial that aggression exists or, if aggression does exist, then denial that its impact is serious. The emotional extremes here are manic–depressive; on the one hand, the depression that the damage is too great to repair and the loved mother is lost, and, on the other hand, the manic feeling that the damage doesn't matter and nothing can harm her. This manic denial renders reparation unnecessary.

How does reparative creativity relate to organizations? The reparative style of creativity in organizations is based on a concern to repair damage arising at work. It recognizes the human dimension of organizations; that organizational structure is not an abstract system of roles and functions but is an interpersonal reality in which every role-holder, whether employer, employee, or customer, is a person. It keeps in mind the needs and feelings of the individual performing the role and recognizes that everyone has other people to deal with apart from the immediate transaction with oneself. The reparative style accepts that this standard of interpersonal concern is not always attainable and that organizations may treat people as objects of some kind, resources or personnel, and that organizational change produces losers or casualties. It acknowledges that destructiveness and aggression are an inevitable part of organizational life, as, for example, competition between colleagues, hatred and fear of authority, in-group and out-group dynamics. Managers try to direct aggression and competition into the service of the primary task by identifying the organization's internal and external challenges. But, when aggression gets turned inwards it undermines relationships between departments, between managers and their teams, and between colleagues. Suspicion, mistrust, and hidden rivalries interfere with the healthy exchange of differences. Reparative intervention by the leader becomes necessary, while recognizing that they themselves may be part of the problem. Organizational consultants may be engaged to help with situations in which destructive dynamics have got out of control; such as personality conflicts, prejudice, bullying, scape-goating, sabotage, lack of cooperation, stress, burn-out, and so forth (cf. Chapter Ten). On the other hand, a culture of denial in which aggression and its consequences are denied allows the problems to fester below the surface. This denial often takes the form of so-called positive thinking. The messenger declaring that something is wrong is labelled unhelpful, or paranoid, or disloyal, or displaying negative attitudes, or talking down the organization. Reparative creativity depends on a willingness to recognize the existence of destructive dynamics in the interest of creating more constructive relationships.

Organizations frequently have mechanisms for responding to potential damage at work and examples of these are occupational health and human resource departments, equal opportunities, codes of good practice, grievance procedures, customer services, recall of faulty products, environmental clean-up. Again, the creation of such reparative procedures depends on the mobilization of a sense of guilt and recognition that something has gone wrong. Some organizations are engaged in reparation as the primary task; health care, social care, environmental care, pressure groups, and charities, for example. Those who work in them are exposed to burn-out through hyperactive reparation and exhaustion.

Evolutionary creativity

A third strand of creativity in psychoanalytic thinking, evolutionary creativity, is connected particularly with a capacity for openness to uncertainty. It is based on the need for further development within the depressive position (Bion, 1970; Meltzer, 1983) As the child grows, its picture of the world and its place within it also grows. One worldview gives way to another by a process of evolution, with notable milestones such as weaning, starting school, work, marriage, parenthood, career change, religious/political conversion, midlife crisis, retirement, etc. Whereas reparative creativity is a response to aggression, evolutionary creativity is triggered by the need to develop. Evolution of worldview and sense of identity are stimulated by the need for personal growth, the search for knowledge, the desire to emulate potency and creativity in others, and the mobilization of undeveloped parts of the self. The creative drive that pushes towards challenge and risk has its roots in an unconscious part of the personality—an unknowable mystery-source, a hidden interaction of masculine and feminine parts, *mysterium conjunctionis*. It is represented by the image of an internal parental couple that generates new connections, new insights, new ideas, new possibilities, new objectives, that suddenly pop into the imagination as if from nowhere (Meltzer & Harris Williams, 1988, p. 83). As a psychological process, shifting the balance from conscious to unconscious activity involves giving up control and directedness of conscious thinking. In evolutionary creativity there is an element of surrender to non-purposive thinking that opens the boundary between conscious and unconscious parts and allows a free flow of ideas, images, dreams, feelings, memories, perceptions, and new imaginings to enter consciousness. The current integration is dissolved into a fluid state of disconnected elements that allows a new idea to emerge, possibly with an explosive or revolutionary force. The evolutionary strand of creativity requires a mental attitude of patience. It cannot be hurried or controlled. Bion describes this attitude as one of reverie over disparate elements until a new pattern evolves or a "selected fact" presents itself as the basis for a new synthesis (Bion, 1962. p. 72). The transition from an old synthesis to a new one involves a period of flux during which there are feelings of both loss and gain. The existing integration represents a hard-won sense of self, a coherent picture of the world, a sense of reality and sanity, a pattern of relationships and commitments, and a record of achievements. During the flux these well-functioning structures are felt to be at risk of being lost because the existing integration is weakened but the new one is not yet secured, may not be achieved, and is of uncertain value.

This view of evolutionary creativity as developing from unconscious promptings by internalized parents harmonizes with Klein's statement that creativity arises from gratitude for what has been received. For Klein, one of the motives for creativity is a "wish to return goodness received" and she believes that a "feeling of generosity underlies creativeness and this applies to the infant's most primitive constructive activities as well as to creativeness of the adult" (Klein, 1963, p. 310). This seems to suggest that the disconnection of elements involved in evolutionary creativity does not imply a destructive attack on what exists now, however radical the change, and that, unlike reparative creativity, its motive is one of appreciation rather than guilt. Evolutionary development, therefore, takes place within a depressive position framework. Perhaps it is unfortunate that the creative flux was described by Bion as a state of mind analogous to the paranoid–schizoid position (Bion, 1970, p. 124). On the positive side, this analogue may capture the element of disconnection associated with the dissolution of cognitive structures to produce a state of unknowing. But on the negative side, a paranoid–schizoid split tends towards rigid black-and-white certainty rather than fluidity leading to new connections, and it is only fragmentary and chaotic in its most pathological form as a defence against overwhelming anxiety. Moreover, when the qualifying term "analogous" is dropped, as often happens, it might also give credence to the notion that creativity involves the splitting of love and hate, with the consequence that the good object is put at risk of further destructive attacks, characteristic of paranoid–schizoid functioning (cf. Britton, 1998). Such attacks might give rise to further reparative creativity but they would be incompatible with the gratitude on which evolutionary creativity is based.

An evolutionary proposal gives rise to disruption and loss of a current well-functioning state but the motivation for the proposal is the need for further development. From the motivational point of view, therefore, the unavoidable disruption is not a destructive attack on something good, any more than the birth of a new baby is an attack by parents on existing family relationships. The loss that arises from evolutionary creativity may give rise to a process of mourning but it is a loss without an attack. Evolutionary disruption and loss has to be distinguished from disruption and loss caused by destructiveness, which is motivated by hatred that aims at causing damage rather than development.

If the splitting involved in evolutionary creativity is not paranoid–schizoid, how can it be conceptualized in the Kleinian framework. The new and the old have to be brought together through a second type of flux that has a manic–depressive quality and during which the containing function of the parental couple is shaken but not lost. This manic–depressive flux is a type of splitting that remains within the depressive position. Klein discusses manic–depressive flux in relation to a different situation, namely bereavement. She describes how in grief there is a feeling that everything of value has been lost, and that the forces of destruction have triumphed, and the internal world is in danger of collapse. The mourner goes through manic–depressive states, oscillating between: "Nothing is lost" and "Everything is lost". This manic–depressive split eventually resolves itself into a new integration.

> Just as the young child passing through the depressive position is struggling, in his unconscious mind, with the task of establishing and integrating his inner world, so the mourner goes through the pain of re-establishing and re-integrating it [Klein, 1940, p. 354]

The emotional flux required for evolutionary growth through the assimilation of something new could be seen as comparable to the process of bereavement. Disruption and rebuilding take place in both cases. In evolution, feelings towards the new object oscillate between a depressive fear "There is everything to lose by it and nothing to gain from it" and a manic hope "There is everything to gain from it and nothing to lose".

In organizational terms, an example of a manic–depressive response to evolutionary creativity occurred in the following way. At a team meeting a senior manager presented a proposal for a major organizational change that had been developed by a small working party. The first team member responded by commenting enthusiastically on the creativity of the proposal. A second team member questioned the proposal, saying that it seemed to imply the reorganization of the existing team. The first team member replied that it was wrong to think about future consequences, as that would put a brake on things; the momentum had to be kept going. In this exchange both team members had a depressive position concern for the welfare of the organization but from opposite points of view—one was concerned with gaining a new future; the other was concerned about the future loss of something that was working well in the present. As the remaining team members aligned themselves to one or other of these two perspectives, a manic–depressive loss–gain dynamic became established. Personality factors, life experiences, and team dynamics may influence how individuals position themselves along an emotional continuum from depressive loss-resistance at one end to indiscriminate change-mania at the other. In any organization there will be different perceptions about the need for change, perhaps related to the different time-spans of different roles or to different kinds of contact with the external environment. There will also be different judgements about the merits of new proposals.

Sometimes the resolution of the manic–depressive process does not succeed and development is blocked by a paranoid–schizoid response. The integration of the depressive position is not just shaken; it is dissolved. The containment breaks and a paranoid–schizoid disconnection occurs. This implies that either the existing state is idealized and the new idea is seen as purely destructive, to be resisted at all costs or, on the other hand, the new is idealized and what exists now is denigrated. In a paranoid–schizoid response there is not just tension between opposite points of view but a breakdown into hostility and fear. Each side sees the other side as a dangerous threat to the welfare and values of the organization. In an interpersonal or intergroup situation, communication breaks down and antagonism, impasse, and fragmentation are likely to occur. For example, a voluntary sector community service unit found itself in an impasse over making changes in order to win new funding. The division within the staff took the form of a paranoid–schizoid polarization to such a degree that opposing factions could no longer be in the same room together. If the unit remained the same, it would go bankrupt and cease to exist; if it changed to get new funding, its identity and values would be destroyed. Each side saw the other side as bent on the destruction of the agency.

Returning to individual development, evolutionary creativity struggles to retain what can be preserved while including what can be added. It involves disruption and loss of a secure and stable integration. In a manic–depressive response, the disruption, however conflicted and painful, is felt to come from the need to grow and develop, that is from a part of the self that needs to give fuller birth to the self, from an unconscious internal parental part, from a life force. Internal parental figures provide psychic containment while the evolutionary tensions of loss and gain are resolved. In a paranoid–schizoid response, on the other hand, the proposal for change is seen as a hostile and damaging attack on a sufficient level of integration that needs no further development. In this view, the new idea is felt to arise from a destructive part of the self such as excessive greed or envious competition, and the requirement to change is seen as a pressure to self-destruct that comes from a monster-parent, from an annihilating death force.

How does evolutionary creativity relate to organizations? In a constantly changing environment, the creative evolution of the organization, its mission, its tasks, its boundaries, and identity is a continuous process. An essential attribute of evolutionary leadership is openness to the new rather than closure around existing success. Evolutionary creativity disrupts the existing configuration, its loyalties, values, and achievements. It requires the presence of a trusted leader, who, like the internal good parent, contains the tensions that are part of the change process. The leader recognizes that the emotional components of evolution are depression, elation, and anxiety; depression because something is lost, elation because something new is coming, and anxiety because the future is unbounded and uncontained. The paradox for the leader is having to contain a change process that contains the future as an uncontainable term. Individuals involved in the change will identify with different emotional aspects and group tensions will arise. In a manic–depressive response, each side recognizes the concern of the other side for the welfare of the organization. Advocates of the new emphasize the hopeful aspects of new possibilities and point out that failure to evolve puts the organization at risk. The depressive side emphasizes that proven current ways of doing things will be lost and that untried developments may also put the organization at risk. Leaders need to be in touch with the validity of both sides and allow adequate time for the debate to be worked through (cf. Chapter Two for a discussion of the difficulties of this process). In evolutionary creativity, the leader holds the boundary between present and future with one foot on either side in order to hold the balance between different viewpoints. The positives and negatives have to be expressed, old loyalties have to be aired and relinquished, implications such as mergers, redundancies, demotions, promotions, etc. have to be acknowledged and anxieties about the unknown consequences of the new have to be honestly faced. In evolutionary creativity, the balance of loss, gain and risk has to be resolved. A. K. Rice believed that the

> leader has the onerous task of evaluating change and resistance to change: . . . change can be destructive as well as constructive . . . One of the important tasks of leadership is to make this decision. [Rice, 1963, p. 263]

One danger in evolutionary development is that the manic–depressive division between loss and gain may degrade into a paranoid–schizoid polarization in which each side sees the other as an enemy trying to destroy the organization out of personal self-interest. The leader may unwittingly add to this downward spiral. If the leader is over-identified with the future, the present situation may be denigrated—slash-and-burn—and the depressive side may be treated as the enemy of change and given no voice. The manic leader, for example, extolling the merits of a new system to an increasingly depressed staff is not an unfamiliar sight. On the other hand, if the leader is over-identified with the present, then the proposers of change may be blocked as disruptive troublemakers. An organizational consultant entering this situation tries to distinguish between these two configurations, manic–depressive and paranoid–schizoid, as they call for different kinds of intervention. A paranoid–schizoid breakdown between non-communicating factions may require a mediation process or a divorce before the evolution itself can be addressed. It sometimes happens that a consultancy project goes through two different stages, beginning with reparation of a paranoid–schizoid impasse before moving on to support evolutionary creativity through a manic–depressive phase.

Since evolutionary creativity always involves tension between old and new, the present and the future, some organizations adopt the strategy of splitting off the creative function to special teams or units with a research and development brief. Rice recommended that the design stage of change programmes needed "complete protection" from "interference" (Rice, 1963, p. 256). But eventually assimilation is necessary and the tension has to be addressed. A study of corporate creativity centres in America showed that many were closed down despite generating successful ideas because of resistance from ongoing businesses. The report concluded that, for evolutionary creativity to succeed, every level of the system should be involved in innovation. It was a sign of organizational health if managers were continuously facing difficult choices between new strategies (Hipple, Hardy, Wilson, & Michaelski, 2001). The organizational dilemma is that evolutionary creativity needs to be public in order to involve everyone and reduce the likelihood of a paranoid–schizoid impasse, but openness about new ideas in their embryonic stage may stimulate attack before the new development can be properly formulated.

Envy of creativity

This leads to a final point of connection with psychoanalysis; ambivalence and envy. Creativity is a nuisance. It upsets the status quo. We need it for survival but it exposes us to loss, risk, and uncertainty. However, there is more to this ambivalence than just fear of change. Creativity itself, as an internal parental birth-giving function, stirs up envy both towards our own creative capacity and towards that of others (Klein, 1957, p. 202). The evolutionary idea gives rise not only to hope but also to envy. This envy is based on the feeling that the new idea was conceived by someone else, internal or external, and not by oneself. Envy of creativity intensifies resistance to change, over-attachment to existing arrangements, exaggeration of risks involved, ridicule of the new absurd notion, obtuse misunderstanding and obfuscation by proliferation of alternative proposals.

An example illustrating organizational envy of a disruptive idea comes from a working conference on creativity and authority. The example occurred in the opening few minutes of a large group discussion that took place during the conference, recorded immediately after the event. The purpose of the meeting was to explore issues of creativity in organizations. The seating had been arranged in a concentric format with a small circle of chairs in the centre of the room and other chairs in circles behind them, also facing towards the centre.

All the chairs are occupied. The meeting begins with a short silence.

First speaker, sitting near the middle: *I don't feel comfortable with the way the chairs are arranged. I can't see everyone's face. I would like to move my chair.*

Second speaker: *I agree. I feel uncomfortable where I'm sitting.*

Third speaker: *I don't like it either but I think we should give it a try.*

Fourth speaker: *I can see quite a lot of faces. There are only a few faces I can't see.*

Fifth speaker: *It's been arranged on purpose like this. If we move the chairs it would spoil the pattern.*

Sixth speaker: *If we moved the chairs, maybe we wouldn't find out what we are supposed to be learning.*

First speaker: *Well I still feel uncomfortable. I want to move my chair.*

Seventh speaker: *If you are the only one who moves and the rest of us don't move, you still won't see all our faces.*

Eighth speaker: *I want us all to move and sit in a large circle. So we can all see each other.*

Ninth speaker: *In one large circle we would be too far apart across the room.*

Tenth speaker: *I like sitting where I am. I have space around me. If we sit in a large circle I would have someone close to me on either side. I don't want any of us to move.*

Eleventh speaker: *I like sitting in the middle. It is nice in the centre. I feel I have more power in the group. If we sit in a circle I'll lose my position of power.*

Twelfth speaker (at the back): *I can see everyone from here. I have no one behind me. I am happy on the back row. I don't want anyone to move behind me.*

Thirteenth speaker: *The arrangement of chairs is designed to manipulate us.*

Fourteenth speaker: *I don't feel manipulated but if we move the chairs into one large circle, it would be like any other group. We would lose what is special about this arrangement.*

Fifteenth speaker: *I agree. It's not for us to move the chairs. I think it would be destructive towards the people running the conference. They would be angry if we alter anything.*

Sixteenth speaker: *Yes, I think moving the chairs would be aggressive and like trying to take over the group.*

First speaker: *I wasn't trying to take over the group or the conference. I just feel uncomfortable sitting here.*

Seventeenth speaker: *Can't we talk about something else? We're just going round in circles.*

The arrangement of chairs set out by the conference managers could be seen as an existing configuration of an organization. The proposal to move a chair doesn't seem in itself to be a substantial creative idea but in the context of the theme of the conference it could be regarded as symbolizing any creative or divergent move in an organization. Taken in this light, the proposal reveals the emotions that can be stirred up when a new idea opens a gap between the status quo and a future possibility.

Within the space of a few minutes, a wide range of arguments has been deployed to imply that disrupting an existing organizational configuration is self-seeking and morally wrong. It would result in loss of output (learning); it would upset the equilibrium of the system, vested interests in the centre would lose power, and those on the periphery would lose security. It will be defeated by non-co-operation of the peer group and punished by management as an aggressive usurpation of their role; it is a covert bid for power and a desire to take over the group. Behind these arguments lie sibling rivalries, competition for power, inability to face loss, hatred of change, and fear of authority. Cumulatively it amounts to a spoiling attack that suggests an underlying envy of anyone who is not controlled by subservience to the powers that be, whether sibling or parental; in short, envy of creativity itself. Such group obstruction would be likely to deter anyone from making or carrying out any proposal and it is true that management, even at conferences on this topic, can react defensively or punitively towards new ideas. In this example, we can see how organizational creativity involves an interaction between the individual, the group, and the organization in terms of an interplay between authority from within, representative authority being withheld by the group and delegated authority supposedly withheld by management (Obholzer & Roberts, 1994, p. 39). In such a situation, an individual would be left only with authority from within to support a creative proposal. This example not only illustrates the operation of envy but also highlights the importance of management in setting a culture of participative creativity or of commissioning creative initiatives in order to counteract the fears of group rivalry and punitive authority. In an organizational context, creativity and authority have to engage with each other in a reciprocal relationship that is both supportive and challenging. Even then, all styles of creativity may be accompanied by some degree of internal persecution arising from one's own internal envy or fear of other people's envy, imaginary or real.

In conclusion, psychoanalytic ideas about creativity form themselves into three clusters around three different needs; the need to be potent, the need to repair, and the need to develop. This chapter has illustrated some links between these three clusters and organizational creativity. Initiatory creativity creates something that previously did not exist; reparative creativity restores something damaged to a well-functioning state; evolutionary creativity disrupts a well-functioning state to achieve further development. These three aspects of organizational creativity, in their turn, can be linked to different styles of leadership. In the initiatory style, the organizational leader may be seen as a prophet with a compelling vision but who finds adaptation to changing circumstances more difficult to manage. In the reparative style, the leader may be seen as a carer with a capacity for reparation but who fears that organizational development may cause pain or produce casualties. In the evolutionary style, the leader may be seen as a flexible and open-minded catalyst but who could put current viability at risk by not allowing time for ambivalent responses to be resolved. Evolutionary creativity is not a destructive attack but the new idea may give rise to a manic–depressive or a paranoid–schizoid response. In a manic–depressive response, contrasting views about loss and gain based on concern for the organization need to be voiced and worked through. Even when the new idea is accepted as a necessary development, there still needs to be a process of mourning and assimilation, not to be mistaken for rejection of change. In a paranoid–schizoid response, the new idea is seen as wholly destructive, giving rise to implacable opposition. A process of mediation or divorce may be required before the impasse can be overcome. Although evolutionary creativity is necessary for survival, envy of creativity and fear of envy are ever-present emotions that also need to be managed. Creativity is uncontrollable, anxiety-making, and envy-provoking. Ultimately it arises from unconscious sources—but with whose permission and by what authority?

SECTION III
WORKING RELATIONS IN A NEW ORGANIZATIONAL ORDER

Introduction

David Armstrong

Many, if not all, of the organizations we engage with as consultants no longer fit neatly within the paradigms of the past century. On the one hand, external relations between the organization and its environment can be increasingly fluid, flexible, and unpredictable. The rapid growth of partnerships, strategic alliances, or mergers, cutting across conventional organizational boundaries and domains; the outsourcing of many traditional functions; and the associated revolution in the transmission and exchange of information, are eroding the model of a relatively stable open system, managing well-bounded processes of import, transformation, and export. On the other hand, and relatedly, internal boundaries within the organization are subject to attrition and continuous renegotiation, as settled work groups are replaced by shorter term project teams, employment contracts are time limited and work roles more ambiguous.

The two chapters in this Section examine and discuss the impact of these new and emerging organizational and business environments on people's relatedness to the "organization" and their own work. Andrew Cooper and Tim Dartington chart ways in which, notably within the public sector, organizations are being subsumed within "networks", dissolving traditional boundaries of autonomy and control while simultaneously generating increased complexity and instability. In turn, they suggest, the latter both feeds and is exacerbated by a societal and political culture preoccupied with the management of risk. They illustrate how this shifting context links to a withdrawal of psychological investment in the work organization, altering the nature of the psychological tie between professionals and managers, employees and the organizational unit.

Contrasting the "new organizational order" with "orthodox psychoanalytic theories of organizational functioning and dysfunctioning", they challenge how far such formulations now fit the realities of people's experience in organizations. At the same time, they describe and emphasize the continuing need for framing new forms and processes of "containment"—shared practices of reflective thinking—as a precondition for human psychic and social health in work.

Sharon Horowitz presents a case study of the process of adaptation to new structural and procedural models, as this emerged during consultancy to a senior executive heading the IT division of a multi-national enterprise. She describes how, in an organizational setting that appeared structurally chaotic and ambiguous in terms of the locus and boundaries of formal authority, her client developed the metaphor of a "compelling space". This drew on and informed his way of creating a pattern of dyadic relations across the business that could influence and sustain the design and delivery of innovative technological solutions to business opportunities, while simultaneously building and strengthening his and his colleagues' leadership capability. She shows the way that this, in turn, impacted on and influenced the consultancy process and she outlines the conditions that both promoted and supported it, only to be subsequently lost as the business cycle moved into recession.

The concluding sections of the chapter review and speculate on broader processes of adaptation and " pseudo-adaptation" in the new business environment. In a similar vein to Cooper and Dartington, but in relation to a different organizational domain, Horowitz spells out the attendant risk of losing modes of collaborative working that allow the anxieties inherent in the process of learning and innovation to be used creatively, and the dilemmas this presents for the theory and practice of organizational consultancy.

CHAPTER SEVEN

The vanishing organization: organizational containment in a networked world

Andrew Cooper and Tim Dartington

T here are worldwide networks that cut through geographical, political, and cultural frontiers; art, science, or technological discoveries and, increasingly, the internet and communications in general. But there is also trafficking—in drugs, arms, currency, power, women, children, organs—and the malignant implementation of globalization. It seems that where there was a border, now there is a network. In its luminous aspect, it is a symbol-generating and containing fabric that modulates, diversifies, and expands. In its ominous aspect, it spells dislocation, disintegration, and degradation (Abadi, 2003, p. 223).

Introduction

In recent decades organizations have changed in important ways, and, as part of these changes, the experience of working and managing in organizations is also significantly different. Because it is grounded in experience, the practice of organizational consultancy has necessarily also absorbed awareness of these changes. New concepts and theories of organizations as social and cultural entities have emerged to make sense of change at the level of social process, and psychoanalytic thinking about organizational experience is also addressing new questions about autonomy and dependency and the management of personal, professional, and systemic boundaries. None of us fails to register the differences in our experience, but we all struggle to understand fully their meaning. How local or global is the significance of any particular trend we encounter? Which is fashion, jargon, or spin and which is of more enduring and substantive moment? Are our theories and methods still pertinent, or do they stand in need of revision? In the end what is surface and what is depth in the world of modern organizational life? In this chapter we try to understand the meaning of some of the new features of modern organizational experience from the consultant's point of view, and articulate some of the practical and theoretical tensions and dilemmas inherent in the world now encountered by the consultant as part of his or her daily engagement. Thus, we address four inter-related questions:

- What are the sociological and psychological characteristics of this new organizational "order"?
- What might it be like to work within it, and what are the psychic pressures and rewards of doing so?
- What is it like to consult to organizational groups inhabiting these new environments, and what new dilemmas does this pose for the consultant?
- What implications do these experiences and trends have for our theory and practice?

The new organizational order

As systems, organizations are less bounded than they were and the boundaries that exist are more permeable. This is true whether one thinks in terms of their capacity to control the exchange with their environments, their degree of interdependence within networks of commercial, governmental, and professional influence, their openness to information flow, and their need to engage in rapid information exchange, and so on. Partnership, collaboration, outsourcing, secondment, are all contemporary reflections of the trend towards "networked" organizational functioning. As Manuel Castells (2000) argues in his compelling analysis of modern socio-economic trends, the rise of the "network society" cannot be traced to a single, unifying, developmental trajectory in corporate functioning but the different strands

> [all] are different dimensions of a fundamental process: the process of disintegration of the organizational model of vertical, rational bureaucracies, characteristic of the large corporation under the conditions of standardized mass production and oligopolistic markets. [Castells, 2000, p. 167]

The unit of economic organization, he argues,

> is the network, made up of a variety of subjects and organizations, relentlessly modified as networks adapt to supportive environments and market structures . . . It is a culture, indeed, but a culture of the ephemeral, a culture of each strategic decision, a patchwork of experiences and interests, rather than a charter of rights and obligations. [*ibid.*, pp. 198–199]

Networks and networking may be fashionable terms and activities, but in Castells' view they *are* the new social structure.

In most western industrial societies, the boundary between public and private sector organizations is far less clearly defined than it was in the immediate post-war period, which witnessed the foundation or consolidation of liberal democratic welfare states in these societies. The demarcation of values and practices associated with these domains has weakened accordingly, and the great ideological oppositions that underpinned them (e.g. labour vs. capital) have also been significantly dissolved. Commercial values, practices and management methods have penetrated the public sector in a major way and some argue that the welfare state project is now driven by an overriding concern with "fitness for labour" rather than social justice or collective well-being (Hoggett, 2000). Political desire for flexibility and adaptability on the supply side of a capricious world market may largely account for the introduction of a national educational curriculum, less obviously for competency frameworks as the instrument of training for occupational groups such as social workers, but in both cases we see the subordination of "creative" pedagogic principles to rational instrumental ones. In the British National Health Service (NHS) and social care sectors, the logic of "outcomes", "evidence based practice", and "best value" in the context of strategic partnerships and clinical networks prevails, and attests to a culture of commodification in human services undreamed of fifteen years ago.

A number of these trends are gathered in a tendency towards "externality" in the methods framing occupational and professional training, and methods of assuring the quality ("fitness for purpose") of the worker, his or her work, and the organization itself. Reliance upon traditions of craft or apprenticeship training with their associated institutions of self-regulation is increasingly eschewed in favour of "transparent" methodologies of skills development, assessment, deployment, and public scrutiny. There are many indices, some shallower and some deeper, of the impact of these changes upon the psychological orientation of individuals with respect to their work. One is the appearance of new cultures of *curriculum vitae* emphasizing "key skills" and "key achievements" rather than a developmental history of accumulated expertise, and debts to mentors, supervisors, and teachers. Because organizations, including traditional sites of professional learning such as universities, are no longer assumed to produce workforce quality on the basis of an unbroken historical or developmental continuum of doing so (or at least having a reputation for doing so), the test of an individual's employability is no longer "Where did you work or train?" but "Can you evidence your fitness for the role we require of you?" The PowerPoint presentation and the observed task replace the personal interview.

In the course of a research project into European child protection practices, Hetherington, Cooper, Smith, & Wilford (1997) describe a young British social worker saying "How would we manage without the child protection procedures?" They contrast this state of mind with both the prevailing "relationship based" practice of child protection staff working in the era before the spate of public enquiries into child deaths that transformed the landscape of British child care work, and the practice attitudes among continental groups in the research study that reflect a concern with relationships and social solidarity. But there is evidence that the more solid welfare states of other European countries are moving the way of Britain and America; that is, towards individually-focused, procedure-based, and legalistic responses.

This connects to the ubiquity of risk awareness and risk management in the life of modern organizations and in the consciousness of workers and managers alike. Anthony Giddens (1990), one of the two great sociologists of risk in modern society (Ulrich Beck (1992) is the other), observes that we have moved from a social preoccupation with scarcity, and hence justice and redistribution, in the direction of deep concern about survival. A crisis in trust has been linked with the pressures of living in a risk society (O'Neill, 2002). If the power and vagaries of nature once dominated our awareness, now it is "manufactured uncertainty", the threats we have created for ourselves and our natural environment. This preoccupation extends right to the heart of the systems we have for trying to insure ourselves against social and personal risks and dangers. These proliferate, but so do their weaknesses and failings, and thus so do efforts to insure against failure to prevent failure. Collapsing pension funds, endowment mortgages that will not deliver, "failures" in the child protection system, dangerous personality disordered people who are "untreatable", "failing" schools and hospitals, unregulated alternative medical practitioners, family doctors who are serial killers—all these phenomena now gather under the single umbrella of actual or potential "failure" in our risk prevention strategies. In consequence there is almost no area of life, and especially no area of organizational life, which is not profoundly shaped by methodologies and responsibilities associated with risk prevention.

The dominant model of risk analysis in all spheres of social life is actuarial (Power, 1994), raising profound and difficult questions both about whether such methodologies can ever deliver what they promise in many domains, and the broader human significance of trends towards the quantification of all human processes of living. Habermas's (1987) general thesis concerning the invasion of the "life world" by the rational instrumental concerns of the "system" is sociologically pertinent here, while a few commentators have discussed the "audit explosion" phenomenon in terms of the social anxieties that it might be understood to be managing or defending against (Cooper, 2001; Cummins, 2002).

We may hypothesize that there is a central tension emerging between complexity and control in all forms of life, with organizations and institutions functioning as important "hubs", which both generate increased complexity (through their networks of connectedness) and simultaneously experience a dissolution of boundary, autonomy, and control (because of their subordination within networks). Governments and other agencies of national or global influence contribute to the complex, ephemeral, mutating character of socio-economic processes through increasing deregulation of many spheres of activity, while simultaneously attempting to claw back control through increased regulation of socioeconomic actors and the outcomes of their work. As complexity in deregulated, networked environments threaten to escape central control mechanisms, so "risks" and risk management strategies proliferate. Organizational instability is experienced as continual ("change fatigue" ensues), and individual dependency needs cannot be met within organizations. New forms of privatized self-reliance and defences against anxiety evolve in the workforce. Castells has his own way of articulating this:

> Identity is becoming the main, and sometimes the only, source of meaning in an historical period characterized by widespread destructuring of organizations, delegitimation of institutions, fading away of major social movements, and ephemeral cultural expressions. People increasingly organize their meaning not around what they do but on the basis of what they are, or believe they are ... *Our societies are increasingly structured around a bipolar opposition between the Net and the self.* [Castells, 2000, p. 3, original italics]

We are now becoming used to living "beyond the stable state". As Donald Schon observed in 1971,

> The loss of the stable state means that our society and all of its institutions are in *continuing* processes of transformation. We cannot expect new stable states that will endure even for our lifetimes. [Schon, 1971]

Our aim in this chapter is to think also about states of mind and relationship. We are accustomed to thinking about the "institution in the mind" (Armstrong, 1997) but what does it mean to live and work in a world of unstable institutions, and unstable organizational relationships? Must we embrace instability of mind to be capable of working *with* such conditions of life? Or can "containment" assume some new meaning and psychic location?

What is it like to work within the new organizational order?

The changes described have passionate advocates to defend them. Those who are uncomfortable with these trends are sidelined; many were and continue to be taken out by early retirement. The consensus is that whatever one thinks of these changes, they are inevitable and represent, in some post-Newtonian or post-modern way, "progress".

Work and employment—a psychological rift

The work organization has ceased to be experienced psychologically as a safe place, in an anxious culture of "failed dependency" (Khaleelee & Miller, 1984; OPUS, 1980–1989). Accordingly there has been a withdrawal of psychological investment in the work organization (Miller, 1993, 1997). At first, blue-collar workers were the main sufferers, then the service industries were also seriously affected, and then the professions began to feel the squeeze. Managers at all levels have found themselves equally affected by the down-sizing, delayering, and business failures. Permanent employment began to be experienced as temporary, and employees chose or were forced to accept short-term and part-time contracts. Changing work patterns were accompanied by a changing balance in the workforce, with the increased significance of female wage-earners encroaching on the traditional male domination of workplace culture. Individual survival stratagems were encouraged, with further growth in the numbers of self-employed with their own businesses, and of contract workers operating through agencies or as individuals. The instrumental relationship—an exchange of money for services rendered—has become the norm for employees too, as the loss of societal containers threw people back into positions of radical individualism (Dartington, 2001).

Correspondingly, the nature of the psychological tie between workers and management, and all employees and the organizational unit, has altered. Organizations no longer provide actual or potential sites of secure dependency for employees as they once did, and the traditional hierarchy of authority relations that accompanied the assumption of a dependable "job for life" has weakened in favour of "flatter" authority structures in which more employees are required to be more actively creative and responsible (as well as directly accountable) for their functioning. Some social analysts have detected a clear shift in consciousness and expectation among young people—the so-called Generation X—who now think in terms of the autonomous self-management of their "portfolio" careers, in which they build a repertoire of skills and experience that they sell to successive employers in pursuit of self-advancement as much as personal security. Others declare that "The career, as an institution is in unavoidable decline" (Flores & Gray, 2000). If relations of dependency have become weakened under these circumstances, they have done so in a reciprocal fashion, and with an associated relocation of risks as well as responsibilities. Trends towards "agency" working in the social care field, as well as portfolio careers among investment analysts, seem to reflect this development.

This is unsurprising given the name of the "age of anxiety" by some commentators, where omnipotent fantasy is all the time threatened by fear of annihilation (Dunant & Porter, 1996). While it has always been true that you are only as good as your last sale, there used to be some countervailing influences. A good salesman built up relationships over years. No-one can work at maximum performance all the time, but there is no longer a cultural consensus about what might be optimal, ensuring consistency of performance over time. There will always be informal practices and employee protection agreements to frustrate the management desire to see organization as a clean machine (Ackroyd & Thompson, 1999). This is one aspect of the issues explored in the fire service dispute in Britain at the end of 2002.

Arguments for the "horizontal organization" organized around "core process groups", are advanced because of the overwhelming need to be more customer-focused, delivering maximum value to the customer (Ostroff, 1999). This process exposes a dilemma; putting the customer first puts the employee second. Adding value leads to downsizing, wiping out non-value support systems of middle management and business expertise in the organization.

Shareholder value means that a slowing down of the rate of increase of profits is seen as failure and leads to a crisis of confidence. Nevertheless, in a 24/7 economy, where we are living with communications at the speed of light, we try to see ourselves as efficient machines, which then break down with stress-related diseases, depression, heart disease, strokes, cancer, diabetes. We become trigger-happy in the face of frustration, experiencing desk rage, road rage, air rage. This is "a world in which every available minute becomes an opportunity to make another connection" (Rifkin, 2001).

Commitment and alienation

Here it is useful to distinguish between two kinds of commitment, or its obverse, alienation. There may be commitment or alienation in relation to the work itself and/or in relation to the employing organization. These are not necessarily correlated. "Scientific management" ensured that work was often more repetitive and unsatisfying than it needed to be, but the organization met the individual's dependency needs both materially and psychologically by providing a sense of attachment and belonging. In what is also now called the Information Age, there are fewer unskilled jobs and an increasing number of roles that require specialized skills, are satisfying in themselves, and are often critical to the effectiveness of the organization. The psychological investment is in the work itself while the employing organization is little more than a convenient, and often temporary, location for practising one's professional competence. We are seeing a trend, where employment is primarily about survival only; integrity is linked to professional identity or other wider societal associations (Miller, 1999). We are into the world of transportable skills and portfolio careers—traditionally the strength of the more marginal in society.

Other features of the new century have been an escalating divergence in the remuneration of those at the top of the organization and those at the bottom, and the numbers of apparently indispensable managers and professionals who work excessively long hours and have little time left to invest in family and social life. This is linked to environmentally blind individualism; what's best for me is assumed to be for the general good. The popularity of executive coaching is symptomatic of this trend. This reflects an individualistic culture where the unit of production is "Me & Co", the title of one of the many "help yourself to happiness" manuals on sale in bookstores. We have a pervading societal culture that is preoccupied with stress and yet avoids looking at the causes of stress, and in particular stress at work.

Dependence and fallibility

Alongside the inadequacies resulting from the failure of magical solutions, managers are accountable to those who believe that the implementation of their policies should not be problematic. Essentially, there is a profound distrust of human endeavour and its propensity for failure. But this severely compromises any reparative project to do with human weakness and vulnerability.

Taking an example from social welfare, we see a shift from the human to the mechanical, from judgement to procedure. Social workers, rather than getting into a therapeutic relationship with clients become experts at assessment. The human element is downgraded to the (heavily policed) work of care assistants, who then cannot enlist the voluntary help of relatives or neighbours because of health and safety regulations. This is consistent with the need for written policies on everything, whether or not they are likely to be followed. While we expect human fallibility in ourselves, we do not tolerate it in the professions on whom we continue to rely to meet our dependency needs. This helps to explain the pressure to make them mechanical, not expected to fail.

Having moved so far in this direction, there has been recently a sudden recollection of the importance of human fallibility. Learning from the airline industry, the idea is to record "near-misses" or mistakes and to learn from them. However, this runs counter to the audit culture, where the pressure is to cover up short-comings in the service. The response of Haringey Council in the Victoria Climbié enquiry is a tragic current case study. This contributes to an organizational culture where there is a splitting of potency and responsibility. Political leadership has projected its own uncertainties (will it be re-elected or thrown out?) into the operating system that it exists to govern. To be potent is not so much to get a good job done as to do well in a complex game of snakes and ladders, winners and losers, beacon status, or no stars. Responsibility becomes a question of risk assessment, legal accountability, and scapegoating.

Finally, we may observe a culture of comparison, which creates performance anxiety in governments and individuals. One impact of the European Union in the wider context of globalization has been to introduce league tables for government performance, just as governments have introduced league tables for schools and hospitals. Public services like the NHS and education have to be watched carefully, or they might act as if they have minds of their own. If they are to be "given" resources they are then controlled through increased surveillance. So we see more performance management and systems of inspection. This is the price of greater local autonomy. But can true autonomy be conditionally granted?

So what is it like to work in the new organizational order? "Exciting", is the requisite reply, and certainly there are individuals and organizations who thrive in this culture. But is there room for the expression of concomitant elements of depression and despair, for an understanding of "failure" as an aspect of the systemic whole?

Consulting in the new organizational order

Resistance, uncertainty and control

As consultants we often sit in a room full of people. During the time we have been thinking about this chapter, they have included the staff of an in-patient service for disturbed adolescents, a multi-disciplinary community mental health team, a clinical team working with anorexic patients, university academics with a multi-cultural intake, and a social work team fearful of being held responsible when a parent kills a child. One thing they have in common is that they cannot predict the outcome of their work. It follows that they don't want to be constrained by rules and procedures that have to be enforced with unthinking rigidity. When they are so constrained, then they know that this is defensive against the threat of suspension, disciplinary procedures, internal and external inquiries, when something that is outside their control goes wrong.

We hear the weary observations of people who do not want to be told who they should give time to and for how long; what they should take account of and what they should ignore. They do not want to record their observations in tick boxes. But their resistance to the discipline of externally imposed procedures is seen as pathological and they are uneasily aware of this. They are the victims of the belief, introduced in the context of manufacturing, that what is significant is what can be straightforwardly measured.

We experience them, in addition to their protestations of excitement and challenge, as depressed, or even as despairing. They get angry with each other in ways that are both covert and predictable. In such systems, those lower in the hierarchy, with low levels of remuneration, have the longest exposure to the clients/patients/students, who project into them their own anxieties about failure. Those that use their services are almost by definition inefficient in their self-management. Collectively, these public sector workers are likely to develop a siege mentality, where their sense of community is reinforced by their sense of not being understood from outside. This means that they are suspicious of any external assessment of what they do. This is explored, for example, in the protracted negotiations of government with doctors, both consultants and general practitioners. In group relations terms, we may say that they are wanting to take their authority from the task, as long as they can define what that is, and not from those who refer their clients or control their budgets.

From an outside perspective, they may at times be thought to hold on to restrictive practices worthy of the old print unions, and to be facing a similar fate from a new managerialism. They are resistant to changing their practice in response to budget and staffing cuts, resistant to closing cases, to making brief interventions even briefer, or developing more economic ways of delivering their service. They are the forces of conservatism that the modernizers of public services see as getting in the way.

Trust, autonomy and the failure of trust

These staff occupy a quasi-closed system that in the past has allowed unacceptable abuses and has also made all the innovative and creative advances that we now see as the tradition of good professional work. Mostly they are happy to be left alone by outside authority, and they are allowed this, because the complexity and the messiness of their work is not something that outsiders to their system really want to know about. Systems such as Quality Protects, clinical audit, and Health Improvement, are accepted and absorbed, but they are also thought of as a waste of time, because they do not address an underlying professional and vocational dynamic that is fiercely autonomous. However, whenever there is a critical incident, this collusive contract is broken and they are likely to find themselves castigated for the appalling inefficiency of their systems.

As consultants working in systems with a therapeutic task, which can only function on a basis of trust, we are finding also that we are not easily trusted by the senior managers who authorize us to do our work with them. And this in effect turns us into contract workers; we experience for ourselves how the added value of our professional enthusiasm and integrity goes unrecognized and how our enthusiasm is then diminished. We begin to see a link between manic activity and mental passivity in managers, who no longer feel that they can be leaders. The professional identity of the individual, secure in her values, is overwhelmed by imperatives, which the manager experiences as imposed from outside. All the manager can then do is engage in manic activity to achieve increasingly demanding targets. Customers and clients are demanding in their own right, but these targets are not theirs. The targets are imposed in their name, but those delivering services may feel at times that these get in the way of responding to the real needs. Nevertheless, this manic activity is projected throughout the system, from top to bottom, with greater resistance as the personal rewards become less.

By the use of counter-transferential data in this way, we are exposed to an "organizational darkness" where we see "ordinary brutality at work" (Stein, 2001). We are experienced simultaneously as sentimental, "touchy-feely", by drawing attention to the emotionality inherent in working relations, and at the same time unbearably rigid in insisting on showing respect for the ordinary clarities of task, territory, and time. By offering a containing presence, where thinking is always possible even if it is not happening at that moment, the consultant becomes a punitive figure in a managerial world. At a meeting to review the end of a difficult project, a manager irritably asks "What is the meeting *for*?"

Elation and exhaustion

Both consultants and clients need a more integrated picture of the consultant, who is certainly able to draw on expertise and experience, but is also able to take a reflective stance in relation to the dynamics and pressures of the organization and its culture. The independence of thought and action of the consultant who may actually be useful may be subject to an envious attack from managers, whose material and perhaps psychological rewards come in significant part from their ability to turn a blind eye to the more uncomfortable realities of their situation.

Let us take the example of a social services department in a large local authority, itself inevitably moving from an old to a new organizational world. After consulting to four senior managers through a series of monthly meetings, we discovered that these were the only two hours in the month that the four managers met together. This limited opportunity to think together about what was happening in the organization was only made possible by the consultancy, as the organizational structure was no longer important enough for them to have a continuous management relationship. Increasingly, they had to rely on keeping each other in mind, even though they were not in direct communication, trying to maintain a relatedness to each other that had to compete for mental space with other kinds of relatedness and accountability.

We experienced at second hand the tiredness and lack of sense of direction of the managers. The targets are not their targets, and the relentless pressure undermines any sense of achievement they may have. They seem forced into a passivity of mind, while at the same time having to maintain the appearance of manic activity, as we have described. They seem to take a masochistic pleasure in making the consultant feel inadequate to the task of helping them to think. When we said, in response to a recent development, "That must be maddening for you", we got the jolly but dismissive retort, "It's bonkers."

How should we expect them to respond differently? Within the service they were managing, they could discern two kinds of responses among their staff. There were those who doggedly kept on going, providing the service they had always done, surviving various reorganizations until finally their own service was cut, contracted out, or closed down. And there were those who entered into the spirit of continuous revolution, working with enthusiasm, enjoying the hike in their salaries and the extra responsibility. In social services, there were those who were excited by the closer association they now had with what they perceived as a meet-your-target-or-clear-your-desk world of health management.

During our time with them, three of the four managers were competing with each other and external candidates for a new post. One got the job and six months later was facing a yet more uncertain future, as he waited to hear when he would have to apply for a yet bigger job since his new post was to disappear. His two colleagues, disappointed at losing out to him, now continued in their existing posts with greater security, for the time being.

One way of coping was to give up the attempt at control over their diaries. They would arrive at meetings not knowing if it was a "one-off", or part of a series, or who or what to expect—they have become slaves to their schedules. Meetings were prioritized according to the hierarchy of those that called them, rather than according to the importance or relevance of the work.

As organizational consultants, we like to think that our reflective work with clients is important, but find it is always likely to be undermined by the demands of what is urgent. It is through our understanding of role and task that we hope to survive in this fluid environment. But our expectation of how people manage themselves in role has to change. One temptation is to identify with that superego function in the organizational client, which is saying, "This is a mess, get it sorted". Instead, as we attempted to engage with the state of mind of the managers, as described above, we had to learn to live with the mess, not tidy it up like a punitive nanny. We may think that the situation is "bonkers" but we can still ask; how can I help here in a way that is not going to put additional pressure on someone who is struggling to survive?

We admit that our immediate response at times is to feel very tired. The consultant does not usually have a management authority to rail against in the same way as the client, and so he or she must cope in a different way with the feelings of aggression and hate that are engendered, and work with the resulting feelings of vulnerability within the professional role.

The vanishing organization

It is not at all straightforward to think of "consulting to organizations" in these days of endless reorganization. If traditional organizational structures, with uncluttered lines of authority and clear boundaries, continue to exist in our minds as knowable entities, this is because they are in part historical containers of values and professional identity. In this sense they are the country we were born and brought up in, from which we are now living a life of exile. As such they are a powerful influence on us, a source of creative strength in facing an uncertain future, but also of nostalgia and resistance to current realities.

In a "networked world", we should not think of organizations as complete in themselves, but even now they provide structure of a kind, around which networks and alliances of workers can cluster. However, the networks do not have clear boundaries—those on the periphery of one network are at the centre of another. In these circumstances, rather than talking about consulting to an organization, we have to think of ourselves as working with what is at best a creative tension between, for example, the formal structures of successive NHS Trusts in uneasy partnership with changing local government, and the resistant/emergent nomadic alliances of those who have the task of making it all work. David Armstrong talks of "working with clients who are wrestling with the challenges and fears, both for survival and identity, around the nature and pace of change" (Armstrong, 2003).

Psychoanalytic theory in a networked world

The orthodox psychoanalytic theory of organizational functioning and dysfunction is rooted in a series of central metaphors that are either increasingly challenging or increasingly irrelevant to their time, because the times have changed the nature of organizations. One dominant image in systems psychodynamic thinking is of the open but well-enough bounded organizational system, structured and ordered by the conceptual trinity of role, task, and authority, transforming inputs into outputs. At root it owes much to that most deeply cathected and difficult to relinquish psychoanalytic image, the nurturant and protective relationship of mother and infant (Miller & Rice, 1967).

According to this image, faced with the inchoate and primitive terrors of infantile emotional life, the mother is either herself sufficiently emotionally available to experience something of these terrors, and, drawing on her adult capacity for thoughtful endurance and suffering, to facilitate their transformation into states more tolerable for the infant—or she is not. Likewise, organizational processes are subject to distortion, disruption, and dysfunction in response to the anxieties and conflicts evoked by the primary task. In turn, the organization may succeed in providing forms of relationship and thoughtfulness for employees exposed to these anxieties, thus enabling the work to proceed effectively and efficiently—or it may not.

In both infant and organization, the presence of these conditions for the transformation of experience is understood as the precondition for growth, healthy adaptation to the environment, mastery of developmental challenges, and depth of moral, emotional, interpersonal and social engagement. The preponderance of attention within this schema to disturbance or "toxicity", and the task of managing it, is somewhat counterbalanced by recent ideas about the importance of emotional "aliveness", in both parental and leadership roles, for the development of creative capacities, whether in childhood or organizations (Armstrong, 2002). This perspective reminds us that understanding the pain or conflict that accompanies work does not in itself deliver us into a creative or "animating" relationship to the task. Efforts to rescue psychoanalytic organizational theory from an excessive preoccupation with the defensive management of anxiety, by, for example, reframing conflicts and anxieties as necessary tensions situated at the heart of the "idiom" that constitutes the unique character of the organization (Hutton, Bazalgette, & Armstrong, 1994) are valuable. But they are not by themselves an adequate language for the predicaments and conundrums of organizational forms as they are now present in our lives.

As organizational life is now configured and experienced, there is frequently no longer a *structure* of "parenting" either for organizations, or for those working within them, that can perform the kind of psychic work assumed to be necessary by traditional theory. At the broadest level, the founding conditions of the British welfare state entailed a kind of national "family consensus" as to its desirability, represented in government by each family member being securely housed within a defined ministry, governed by a single minister. Today, with cross-cutting ministerial agendas and pooled budgets overseen by cabinet style (networked) local government structures, there is no longer a nuclear family organization presiding over our affairs.

Essentially the same points apply to another hallowed set of conceptual foundations for organizational thinking—the basic assumptions underlying work group behaviour. Bion's model of a work group and its various modalities of defensive distraction from "task" presupposes an image of the group as both bounded and more or less functional, depending on its capacity to manage its conscious and unconscious need for leadership. The brilliant and extremely funny opening sections of Bion's (1961) *Experiences in Groups* concern the struggle of groups to manage when the group leader refuses to be the group leader. Evolution in the direction of an autonomous "work group" is achieved once members relinquish the fantasy that they can rid themselves of responsibility for knowledge, hope and thought on to the leader (BaD), a pairing of group members (BaP), or displace the impediments to their struggle on to some external group (BaF). All this privileges intra-group relationships as the key to "autonomy" and successful execution of the primary task. But the new preconditions of organizational life, in which the site of autonomy is persistently decentred, cast a long shadow of doubt over the contemporary relevance of these presuppositions. It is consistent with our argument that later thinkers came up with further basic assumptions—of "oneness" and "Meness" (Lawrence, Bain, & Gould, 1996; Turquet, 1974)—in an effort to adapt to emergent organizational and cultural conditions.

If this old theoretical order is dying, is something new struggling to be born? It does seem possible that we stand on the threshold of a genuine paradigm shift that will help make sense of the new experiential order through the articulation of new principles for understanding the production and reproduction of social life, psychic states, and organizational forms—a revised logic of living systems. This is Sonia Abadi discussing the shift from a language of frontiers to a language of networks in her keynote address to the 2003 Congress of the International Psychoanalytic Association:

> Little by little the idea arises of a potential being, virtually incommensurable. Thus in clinical practice models appear that speak of crises and ruptures, of undoing knots that had traumatic origins, of dissolving splits, re-establishing the continuity of existence. It is no longer a matter of making the concept of the border flexible but of entering the paradigm of the network—the true epistemological turning point that has materialised in recent years. And it has been precisely in Freudian theory where this paradigm has been implicit from the beginning, in harmony or discordant with the paradigm of the frontier. [Abadi, 2003, p. 226]

The new sciences of complexity foreground the self-organizing properties of systems, which is to say their capacity for the generation of qualitatively new properties once a certain level of dynamic complexity has been attained, their nature as "structured processes" (Watson, 2002). Possibly "strange attractors", the underlying pattern of inherently unpredictable ordering in such systems, will transpire to be their site of "containment", but we have no experiential analogue for such an idea. Perhaps Hutton, Bazalgette and Armstrong's (1994) notion of "X generated management" approaches this thought, with its emphasis on the uniqueness of each organization's "idiom" or central tension that generates the particular character of work and hence management required within the organization

Conclusion: rethinking organizational containment

Many of us now have direct experience of working in a "networked" organization in which hierarchies are not so much "flat" as complex, intersecting, and fluid. Here is an account of one woman's managerial experience in a traditionally well-bounded but internally complex public sector organization, where the intersection and overlapping of tasks and responsibilities within the wider departmental, professional, and administrative structures, gives rise to an experience of continual uncertainty about the actual ownership of authority. In this account *any individual's authority must be continuously negotiated in relation to the current task.*

> I enter work on a particular day with a mounting sense of trepidation. By the end of the previous day I had discerned a familiar process gathering pace, a steady but invisible whirlwind of anxiety, rivalry, tension, forming among a knot of colleagues, but also implicating me. While I believe this state of mind to be located among my colleagues, and not just in myself, I am also not wholly convinced it is not a "projection" of my own, the mobilization of my own competitive anxiety. I am the "lead" in an important decision-making process, where I know the views of the Chief Executive and support the stance he is adopting. Or do I? How do I know exactly? I feel I need to "know" for myself, because I allegedly "lead" this overall process of decision-making. To know, I must have clearly separated out my own view of organizational needs from any influence exerted on me by the CE's authority over me.
>
> So why has he involved himself in the decision-making process? Does he not trust me to exercise effective authority and judgement? Is he keeping me under his watchful eye? I fantasize that a colleague, who is also a rival for my leadership functions, thinks I should challenge exactly this point. I am anxious that he perceives me as "weak". Am I? Or am I just a good, inclusive "team player" who exercises authority through consensus? The CE says we are taking these decisions through "teamwork", but how do I know when the CE's liking for "teamwork" is genuine, and when it's a cover story for the exercise of his centralized power? Or when and whether I am myself using the ethos of "team work", "collaboration", "discussion" as a way of evading disagreements?
>
> I have certainly worked hard to keep everyone involved in this process of decision-making as much as possible (but I seem to overlook the same people more than once—why, I ask myself?) By the time I complete these consultations with my network of about twenty colleagues, some of whom are peers, some senior and some junior, I feel emptied of all significance, all authority. I have become accountable to all of them, not they to me. My "authority" has been entirely dispersed into the intricate web of capillaries of power in the organizational nexus—or so it seems to me. I walk around in a fury telling myself (and everyone else in my head) that I am just a "gofer". My narcissism is threatened, injured. Or is it my genuine potency that is being subtly challenged? Have I given away authority or have I

demonstrated maturity, inclusiveness and organizational sensitivity?? Am I paranoid? Am I clear-sighted? Or have I capitulated and failed my followers? I have no idea. All I do know is—there seems to be nobody in overall control, no single, graspable, principle of organizational conduct to reassure me either externally in the organizational structure, or inside myself.

What can we learn from this story?

The psychological experience of operating as a manager in these circumstances is one of remorseless uncertainty, not only with respect to the status and meaning of relationships with others, but also within oneself. The need for perpetual negotiation of her authority and influence over matters requires the manager to constantly assess whether she is behaving too adaptively or too obdurately. The answer, if there is such a thing as a certain answer, is always context-dependent, and context shifts ceaselessly, not least as a result of her own changing perceptions and constructions. Correlatively, the meaning of her own feelings is continually uncertain—is an experience of "weakness" or humiliation evidence of an inappropriate narcissistic eruption, or of a painful but helpful submission to the reality of interdependence? Adequate functioning in these circumstances requires the manager to patrol continuously the shifting internal boundary between fantasy and reality, and to accept feedback from others about how her actions are being interpreted, actions which are themselves grounded in her own interpretations of the meaning of her feelings and of the meaning of others' behaviours. This is about as much as she can do, without descending into madness. The organizational "script" is being continuously rewritten, via a process of continuous interactive negotiation. The organization produces and reproduces itself in an unceasing turmoil of change, but somehow remains stable, and well-bounded in its overall identity and patterning.

In *Reworking Authority: Leading and Following in the Post-Modern Organization* (1997) Larry Hirschhorn writes:

> Building the post-modern organization is thus like walking across a trapeze. Facing greater market risks, the enterprise asks its employees to be more open, more vulnerable to one another. But in becoming more vulnerable, people compound their sense of risk. They are threatened from without and within. . . . Thus the stage is

set for a more primitive psychology. Individuals question their own competence and their ability to act autonomously. In consequence, just when they need to build a more sophisticated psychological culture, they inadvertently create a more primitive one. [1997 p. 27]

This more "primitive" psychology results from a nakedness in the individual organizational ego. Where once role, task, and authority in the context of a bounded system were the guarantors of the possibility of organizational sanity, the employee or manager now struts naked in the open-plan, hot-desking office of interorganizational vulnerability. Vulnerability is painful, shaming, and potentially maddening—as well as being endearing, democratic, and potentially empowering. We have all had this bad dream—of inhabiting or discovering ourselves undressing in a house without walls, or with walls made of glass. Once again, the thesis of "failed dependency" with respect to traditional organizational forms helps to account for the sense of collective disorientation, disappointment, and cynicism in the face of lost certainties of organizational hierarchy and job security.

Now, it would seem we must face the fact that something has *replaced* the assumptions and expectations of dependency. It is as though we have been transported through time and space and set down in a distant culture where family forms and norms are quite unfamiliar. Perhaps there is a partial analogy with the "reconstituted" family, the family arising from the making, breaking, and remaking of affectional and matrimonial bonds among adults who live lives not until death do them part, but of serial monogamy—gathering and dispersing sibling groups of children along the way.

Interdependence and failures of interdependence are the new watchwords. This is true of the intra-group dimension, and most importantly of the intergroup relationship. But as the requirement for interdependence grows, so also will defensive retrenchments against this demand. Customers and users of welfare services are no longer servile or passive recipients, but themselves expect to negotiate their own expertise in relation to that of the expert. This places new demands on the capacities of service providers for interdependent functioning—how much to concede, how much to hang on to (and who, by the way, is *right?*)—and these demands cause strain and stress, and above all take time. One response is to interpose some form of technology between provider and user, obviating negotiation while sustaining the illusion of "choice". Another is to instrumentalize relationships in the effort to eliminate the uncertainty that ensues in a culture of interdependence and negotiation.

Hirschhorn asks: "What is the evidence that the wider culture values the feelings of interdependence and the behaviours associated with bringing these feelings about?" (1997, p. 88). This is one key question, but there are others. The very real social optimism and creative potential of the "new interdependence" is offset by the reduction in relationship time and psychic energy available for its fulfilment. This is a central factor in the decline of relationship-based practices in welfare, and the corrosion of commitment to depth engagements in the new organizational cultures. At the same time, there is a critical question about how, if this potential were to be released, we would manage at the level of psycho-social functioning. The experience recounted above, of the daily psychic pressures involved in working in a fluid, networked environment, is moderated and rendered creative by the continuing availability and strength of an overall institutional container, left over from previous organizational forms. This container allows the intra-psychic and interpersonal tension and uncertainty to be continually processed *through the medium of relationships*. Not perfectly, to be sure, but "well enough".

Because we hold a capacity for relationship to be the precondition for human psychic and social health, and because containment (in the very particular sense it has in psychoanalytic thinking) is a precondition for the growth and sustenance of relatedness (as well as itself being a particular form of relationship), the profound impediments that modern organizational forms pose for "containing practices" constitute a considerable threat to our capacity for social and psychological cohesion. We stress that this is an open, rather than a dystopian, conclusion. The shift towards a culture of fluidity, flexibility, and negotiated interdependences in social life contains new possibilities for new forms of depth engagements, but in the absence of a *function* to do the work of containment these are as likely to be risky, volatile, enervating, destructive, and unpredictable as they are to promote solidarity, creativity, purpose, and growth rooted in a sense of security. The big question facing psychoanalytic theory and practice is "How can this function, congruent with the new conditions, be elaborated and made real?" We do not know the answer, but we hope that by formulating the question, we will contribute the process of discovery required for answers to emerge.

CHAPTER EIGHT

The discovery and loss of a "compelling space"

A case study in adapting to a new organizational order

Sharon A. Horowitz

Setting the scene

D r Johnson, in his famous eighteenth-century dictionary, defined "job" as: "petty, piddling work; a piece of chance work." In the late nineteenth-century Garment District of New York City, "job work" meant "piecework." (Fox, 1994) While much has changed over the centuries, it appears that this earlier "piecework" description of jobs resembles emerging features of contemporary organizations, which, in their adaptation to changing technological and global competitive forces in the marketplace, have had to reinvent many aspects of their business models.

This adaptation process has shortened the length of most business time frames and changed the length of today's employee contracts. These structural and procedural shifts have, by extension, required a parallel adaptive function in the workforce in that people have had to alter how they take up their authority as well as their relatedness and attitudes towards their place of work. One unintended consequence of the new employment contracts has been the untethering of the psychological contracts that contain the multitude of unconscious themes around individual attachment to the organization. Previously, employment contractual relationships had helped foster and maintain an organizational containment function that offered a certain level of psychological safety to individuals, enabling them to take professional challenges and creative risks that, in turn, helped nurture innovation. With the advent of ubiquitous short-term employment contracts, existing structures in which it is psychologically safe enough to take the challenges and risks of learning and creativity are vanishing. Yet, there remains a pressing need to tap into and release learning and creativity in order adequately to respond to external challenges and still achieve goals, targets, and performance criteria. This then presents a dilemma; how do organizations remain competitive and innovative when they can no longer provide their employees with the creative space in which to produce the innovations so vital to their survival? How do they resolve the dilemma of both needing to be creative in order to adapt and innovate while, simultaneously, meeting productivity needs within a short business cycle?

The chapter explores this dilemma in detail based on emerging theories as well as a client case study, and concludes by suggesting some potential ramifications it may hold for both individuals and institutions as well as for the organizational psychoanalytic consulting community.

Case study

The consultation process originated in 1996 in New York City with a senior executive, Robert, in the information technology (IT) division of an international investment bank. After a transitional period, it eventually expanded to include organizational development and role consultation to his direct reports who were located in Europe, Asia, and the United States. Partnering with colleagues in these different countries to provide one-on-one consultation to each of the clients, the consultants worked collectively as a team to identify common as well as differing overt and covert themes and dilemmas that emerged within the client system. The consulting team reported these themes back to the clients, who in turn either built upon their hypotheses or, in some cases, rejected them outright. The consultation, over an eight-year trajectory (1996–2004), helps capture a number of emergent developmental phases within organizational life during the past decade and demonstrates some of the ways in which contemporary global organizations are evolving.

Phase 1: Initial themes

Some of the themes which the consultation initially worked with included ways in which structural defences were mobilized against intense interpersonal and collective expressions of competitiveness, envy, rivalry, fear, and greed between and within teams and within the larger Wall Street culture. A recurring theme focused on the vicissitudes of IT's alignment with the bank's business units; specifically, the management of dependency dynamics that were built into the structure of these business relationships. On the one hand, the clients were astute and adept at anticipating the business' agendas and worked feverishly to build and maintain platforms and products vital to the functioning of business units. On the other, there were expressions of resentment and envy centring on the inequity of the reward system that resembled the dynamics of wanting to bite the hand that feeds you. There was always a longing for recognition, a longing to have "a seat at the table" and great difficulty in accepting IT's role and place within the business model. Their fantasies included the wish by the senior managers to be recognized beyond what was generally offered in return for their having gone "above and beyond the call of duty". Statements such as "I built the systems that made him successful!" were commonplace. Some of the major events that occurred during this phase of the consultation and that fed such fantasies included systems integration for a global bank merger, the millennium (Y2K), and the Euro conversion. All of these events necessitated IT's active planning and engagement with the business units, but also seemed to feed their grandiose strivings in that they frequently saw themselves as the "saviour" of the organization. These fantasies were often followed by resentment and disappointment when bonuses and promotions did not mirror managers' internal and collective wishes and needs. Through the unearthing and naming of these fantasies, the clients were able to gradually develop a more realistic "management of 'self in role'" and position themselves more effectively in the workplace.

Although the initial role consultations proved beneficial on an individual level, in that they facilitated clarity and insight into the senior managers' strategic choices and motivations for business decisions, the broader organization development consultation on a systemic level did not seem as fruitful. In fact, one of the themes that emerged within the consulting team itself was a pronounced counter-transferential feeling state of ignorance as to "what was going on". Despite repeated and detailed description from the clients, the system appeared chaotic and unstructured, replete with poorly defined roles, diffuse boundaries, and a loosely managed senior management team. How different parts of the system linked together was a mystery, and it seemed impossible to get a sense of the whole. The organizational structure was also quite puzzling in terms of reporting lines and decision-making processes. There seemed to be few, if any, meetings and little formal time devoted to longer-term planning. New divisions, structures, and other expansions appeared like mushrooms and there seemed to be no cohesion and integration. Furthermore, based on the lens used to interpret the system, group and team building interventions were offered and repeatedly rejected by the clients.

In response, the consulting team began a process of re-examining its basic underlying hypotheses and hunches about the system, suggesting that the team's limitation was in trying to conceive of the organization within traditional organizational theories and paradigms. With this awareness, the team began to reframe the question for analysis; in lieu of traditional formulations what are the new interpersonal constructs that are emerging? How is work getting done in this seemingly chaotic work environment?

An important clue to this inquiry came shortly thereafter with the synchronized discovery of the phrase "compelling space."

Phase 2: The concept of the "compelling space"

Robert, who has worked in IT in the financial services sector for over twenty years, started out as a computer programmer and rose to become a managing director in 1993. In the late 1990s, when mentoring one of his direct reports, he reflected on the strategies of his own success and advised his direct report to find himself a "compelling space" within the organization to develop and mature as a leader. How he came to the concept and what it meant to him involved a series of speculations and hypotheses. To the consultants working within a psychoanalytic framework, this phrase had great emotional and cognitive resonance.

Robert's explanation of the concept was more of a metaphor in his mind than a specific description. It seemed to capture and describe adaptive responses to challenges and dilemmas facing organizations at that point in time. On one level his work within this "space" reflected his own self-initiated opportunities for professional development. After realizing he was no longer learning anything from his boss, he strategically positioned himself within new key one-on-one relationships within the organization where he was not an expert. By putting himself in a place of "not knowing" and tolerating the anxiety generated by this situation, he was able to engage with another person to learn something new. He thought that engaging in numerous self-initiated and self-authorized risk-taking projects across the organization was the best way to strengthen one's learning for leadership.

On another level, Robert's concept seemed to capture a niche whereby individuals could best position themselves for business opportunities. It reflected his partnerships with the key business users he supported. Within these partnerships, new and innovative technological solutions were designed and delivered. Thus, from this perspective, the notion of "compelling space" did not refer to creative engagements of groups and teams, but rather to the organizational growth and development that was taking place within the immediate, unpredictable, and mutual engagement of working pairs. These pairs were not defensive in nature, but rather seemed to reflect peoples' creative attempts to connect with one another and work together within a vast, sometimes anonymous and diffuse organizational structure.

Once named, the term had an important impact on the consultation process. It clarified the value and significance of organizational dyads. It gave an appreciation of how the client explained his own career advancement and his effective leadership style within IT. Additionally, it led the consulting team to re-examine and question the hypotheses they were themselves using to interpret the systemic dynamics. They concluded that, during the transitional period of the late 1990s, the client and system at large were functioning effectively within a series of partnerships or dyads. As an initial adaptive response to the forces of globalization, the client system was not trying to take in or attend to the whole. Hence, the consultation had to adjust its theoretical notions of systemic thinking and change its theoretical framework accordingly.

Phase 3: The bubble bursts

In 1999, as the organizational and individual role consultation with this client system continued to evolve, Robert left the bank to become chief information officer (CIO) of another global financial service firm.

During his transition, he requested organizational and individual role consultation in this new system. Having assumed his new duties near the height of the "irrational exuberance" of the "bubble economy" followed quickly by the deep recession of 2000–2001, the emphasis of the consultation began to vary, reflecting both the culture of the new organization and the rapidly changing economy. The boom and bust of this business cycle made for an exceptionally challenging and exciting work environment in which Robert flourished.

Phase 4: A need to adapt

In early 2003, the consultation process seemed stuck. Robert began to complain of chronic boredom. Numerous attempts were made to analyse the boredom as a defence against the psychological and emotional repercussions of the extreme downward trajectory of IT's role and business importance in the post-bubble economy. (It bears noting that between 2001 and 2002 over 560,000 IT-related positions were eliminated in the United States alone (Platzer, 2003).) A much discussed and hotly debated *Harvard Business Review* article entitled "IT doesn't matter" (Carr, 2003) seemed effectively to capture the zeitgeist. Along similar lines, Robert offered the following assessment:

During the pre-bubble and bubble phase, IT was at the top of the heap. As a profession we were considered artisans. Having an IT person in one's household became something akin to having a doctor in the family. But when we finally got a chance to sit at the table, what did we do? We overspent and overcommitted. We did not know how to handle our newly achieved strategic business role over the long haul. And now, all of a sudden, IT is back to merely being a service provider. People in IT are only now coming to terms with that realization. It's a painful pill to swallow. But, everything is cyclical, even this, so hopefully next time around, as a profession, we will get it right.

However, focusing on the diminishment of the profession itself, or what he experienced as a narcissistic injury, did not seem altogether to capture what Robert was trying to name or understand. One consultation meeting in particular was very challenging. There was almost no conversation between the client and consultant. There was nothing to build upon. After the meeting, the consultant felt filled with feelings of loss and sadness, sensing that there was no work to be done. But this loss was not about termination. Rather the work had been stopped dead in its tracks. The next day, Robert sent the following e-mail:

It was nice to see you . . . However, after you left, I had an anxiety attack, I think. I got this terrible feeling all over, like dread, and felt flush and wanted to cry. I kept feeling all sorts of bad feelings about the situation at work. . . . It lasted for maybe an hour. I felt all knotted up. I went through each thing that was bothering me afterwards and tried to address them. It's the same stuff . . . boredom at work, lack of direction . . . feeling I have no choices . . . bummer, because it was nice to see you but I was rattled by what happened afterwards.

After several meetings attempting to analyse and explore the boredom/panic sequence, it occurred again. In a subsequent e-mail communication, Robert wrote:

The revenue units have gained all the power, so to speak and there is little room for the functional units like IT . . . while running IT here is a good job, I'm afraid that I've outgrown it. Thus, more fuel for the boredom. The challenges have moved to subtle politicking.

Robert's experiences of boredom and panic were multi-determined. For one, they could be understood as reflecting the dramatic decline of IT's importance in general, which he described as "a humbling, crushing blow". In this, his identity had primarily been defined through climbing, aspiring, reaching, and scheming. Now there was apparently nowhere to go and nothing to climb. Yet, the timing and organizational context of these emotions also served to reveal some potential intelligence about the adaptive, and in some ways, maladaptive, processes that had evolved since the concept of the compelling space first emerged in the consultation process. Eventually, one explanation seemed to make sense: Robert had lost his own compelling space.

For Robert's concept of a "compelling space" to exist, certain organizational conditions were present. First and foremost, in spite of the emotions that were stimulated, there was always enough containment within the structure of pairs to enable a certain amount of psychological security to prevail for work to take place. Indeed, the pairs interacted and related to one another over a long enough period of time for trust and loyalty to develop. Thus, the individual was not simply as good as his or her last performance. Mistakes or disagreements could be seen in context. Within such a relationship, people could experiment, take risks, rely on hunches and intuitions and, by extension, co-create and gain new knowledge. It was from these vital components of a compelling space that personal, professional, and organizational developments were able to take place. In this context, Robert's boredom and panic could be understood as an expression of the lack of the possibility for creativity to occur. Because there seemed to be few conditions in which the prospect of new ideas could take root, he was no longer able to experience his work as providing opportunities for innovation and mental development.

"Pseudo-adaptation" as a mode of survival

Robert's experience is indicative of the consequences of changing global organizational structures in which few, if any, stable, long-term work relationships are able to exist. The pressures and uncertainties of global competition have resulted in such cost-saving measures as international outsourcing (coupled with its attendant lay-offs) as well as a profound shift in the underlying nature of the employment contract itself. New employment contracts are now increasingly structured to be short-term, extending only for as long as the particular project or skill set is needed. In this context, employees are no longer treated as assets, but rather as commodities. Within such contractual arrangements, the new credo has become "loyalty is dead".

Arguably, this commoditization of the workforce has had numerous benefits for the organization. One positive outcome is that workplaces are now viewed as more honest, in that unreasonable expectations and wishes from both sides are quickly eliminated. Workers receive financial reward in return for a specific type of work for a specified amount of time. Additionally, individuals are no longer free to rest on their laurels or coast on the job. And previous loyalties among team members and immediate supervisors are being replaced by competitive rankings and 360° appraisals of competencies and value added. Not surprisingly, these new contractual arrangements require increased self-reliance and self-sufficiency. Each person has to take responsibility for his or her own career.

However, within a culture of no long-term employment resides a job experience of "dull continual worry" (Sennett, 1998). While the new global organizations may be more nimble, lean, and efficient, the compelling space construct is being lost. This has primarily unfolded in two ways; first, the new structures do not address or provide for people's basic aspirations for security and mental development. Second, they not only lack containing functions, but the new organizational design serves to inflict continual anxiety on to the workforce. If one is only as good as one's last performance, if one is routinely subjected to "ranking and yanking" via 360° performance evaluations, and if one's job can be outsourced, then one is always living on edge, maintaining a survivor mentality in the face of colleagues and friends getting laid off. The reality of international outsourcing means working in a chronically uncertain work environment where the only predictable element is to be self-protective, keep one's skills updated, and build as many relationships as possible outside of the place of employment because those contacts will offer better security towards the next job opportunity. Perhaps this is also the reason for the growing emergence of work–life balance issues in that people are seeking real, as opposed to pseudo, connections outside of work in their home lives because they are not available to them in the workplace.

As such, the new organization can no longer be considered a vehicle through which unconscious anxieties and fantasies can be effectively contained. Rather, organizations can now be seen as being a primary source for fuelling and heightening the anxieties of annihilation, resulting in uncontained anxiety levels that are "inhibiting, eroding, and even paralysing our capacity to function effectively" (Gutmann, 1989).

In such a highly charged environment, it appears that the pairings and partnerships which form the basis of "compelling space" construct have now been replaced by the crystallization of an organizational culture utilizing the basic assumption of Me-ness (baM) (Lawrence, Bain, & Gould, 1996). In baM an individual eventually determines that engaging and connecting with the group or organization as a whole is too threatening and, on an unconscious level, retreats. In such a defence, perceived workplace vulnerabilities are no longer experienced as anxiety-producing and potentially overwhelming because the identification with the organization has been withdrawn. The growing prevalence of baM can correspondingly be understood as a defence against the loss of identification with the institution. In this context, self-reliance emerges as an adaptive defence against the anxiety and rage associated with the loss of dependency on the organization. But what is most striking about the baM culture, is that baM, by its very nature, means there is no "institution-in-the-mind". There is no acknowledged relatedness to the organization as a whole. Rather, people work in isolated formats and retreat into a "socially schizoid withdrawal". In baM, even the basic elements of a compelling space, which were so much in evidence in organizations during the 1990s, are vanishing.

Since baM does not foster notions of attachment and connectedness to others, what becomes central to people's motivation towards the organization is how the relationship will advance their self-interest and their employability. The motivation is "take care of oneself". Thus, what appears to have emerged is a "pseudo adaptation". Since the notion of professional security is now perceived to be located within the marketplace, rather than the workplace, employees find themselves, as Robert noted, "caught in a game of subtle politicking". In other words, one relates to the organization solely as a source for self-advancement.

In addition to the potential for exploitative situations to occur, "pseudo-adaptation" in turn poses challenges for organizational longevity, which rests on the possibility for creative processes to unfold. Within baM cultures, "there cannot be a joining with others to create something new" (Lawrence, Bain, & Gould, 1996). No true learning can take place because there is no true reaching out and internalizing, as there is no corresponding recognition and acknowledgement from the other. Without the conditions for reaching out and connection, organizations are highly vulnerable because innovative ideas cannot come forward. Innovation relies on the exchange of ideas, hunches, intuitions, that unfold between and among people and that are built upon, negated, fought against, and added to within collaborative and cooperative processes (cf .Chapter Six). Collaboration and cooperation, in turn, require shared history between and among people who have been around long enough to take risks and expose their "not knowing" to one another. In other words, they can allow the anxiety inherent in the process of learning to be used productively (cf. Chapter Five).

Hence, the dilemma for organizations is how do they continue to adapt productively? How do they remain competitive and innovative when they can no longer provide their employees with the creative space in which to produce the innovations so vital to their survival? How do they resolve the dilemma of both needing to be creative in order to adapt and innovate while, simultaneously, meeting productivity needs within a short business cycle? The solution seems to lie within a new structure or form that has yet to fully emerge or take shape, but which must successfully allow for mutual contractual negotiations that acknowledge the shared dependency between employer and employee.

One association is to Menzies Lyth's description of the butterfly phenomenon (Menzies Lyth, 1991). This reference is to the behaviour of children in a day nursery who, as a result of the discontinuity of care, exhibit a "discontinuity of attention". A follow- up of these children observed that they formed a series of episodic and discontinuous relationships with their world, and had difficulty sustaining continuous attention in school. Menzies Lyth goes on to say that, fortunately, such situations are not inevitable and that consultation at the right level can influence personality changes in the individual children.

Implications for organizational consultants

All professions will ultimately have to adapt to these changing institutional structures. It is likely that this will initially be met with great resistance and opposition. People cannot simply adjust to new economic conditions overnight. Rather, such adjustments require a process in which the individual has to alter dependency dynamics, de-cathect from libidinal attachments, mourn the relationship, their group memberships, and their own identity before ultimately reconnecting to other forms of relating so that new work can get done. The process of adaptation involves a series of non-linear developmental shifts in which the individual might eventually realign his or her skills and competencies with the new work required.

Specifically, these shifts within the client systems and the larger economic environment will have significant and long-lasting implications for the profession of organizational consultancy. Historically, the central paradigm of psychodynamic consultation has been based on long-term engagements in which process, reflections, and insights are key components of the consultation process. But over the years, the client needs have changed. Moreover, the contracts for consulting work have gradually been relegated to gatekeepers such as HR, procurement departments, and supply chain management. People external to the experience of the consultation process itself are making decisions about the efficacy and applicability of organizational change initiatives. In addition, they are under increasing pressure to apply criteria for evaluating success and viability according to short-term business models. Metrics, then, become a part of the contracting phase. How does one measure and quantify behavioural changes or psychological and systemic changes? In short, the profession may have to mirror the adaptive processes of the clients to whom they consult. They, too, are being required to redefine and adjust their own identity as well as their skills, interventions, and theoretical paradigms.

These shifts are not dissimilar to the changes the psychoanalytic profession had to make with the advent of managed care systems in the United States, when medical decisions along with appropriation of costs and treatments were routinely "outsourced" to managed care agencies that were authorized to make decisions about treatment protocols. In efforts to save costs, clinicians were forced to justify, and demonstrate the effectiveness of, treatment to people who were not trained in the field of psychodynamic psychotherapy. Moreover, clinicians had to adjust their interventions to a new population who wanted shorter, briefer treatment. In that environment, the theoretical paradigms adjusted accordingly. New short-term treatment techniques emerged. While the long-term analytic treatment modality was still offered to patients, it became the exception, rather than the norm.

The consulting profession's primary challenge is to assist clients in designing structures that provide some positive adaptive features that can contain anxiety states. But this does not mean a return to the past. It is a future construct that allows for emotional security so that connection and trust can be present to work with—but in a shorter business time frame that contains the conditions in which individuals can support organizational goals amid a new awareness about the psychological contract with reciprocal rights and obligations. Management consultants have already begun to explore what these options may look like in, for example: Prince's (2001) "Employability security", Clancy's (1999) "Product loyalty" and Bridges' (1994) "Dejobbed workplace". What these models all seem to have in common is respect for the psychological contract and a form of acknowledging the mutual need and dependency between employer and employee.

One option may be to provide a mixture of psycho-educational training and role consultation to leaders, to enable them to provide the containing functions for short-term or transitory groups and teams. In fact, in case examples of adaptation that have unfolded, employees report feeling increased loyalty to a product or their unit. While these attachments are transitory at best, in that as the product is completed or the unit is re-organized, so is the attachment lost, nevertheless, the work production still requires some form of containment. Leadership insight and ability to handle "emotional" expressions within the workplace may provide enough containment to allow the work to get done efficiently and effectively.

Such a process holds out the opportunity for society to revisit the eighteenth-century definition of "job" as "petty, piddling work; a piece of chance work" and the nineteenth-century definition of "job work" as "piecework" and, while acknowledging the continuing similarities stemming from this heritage, offer the world a new definition of "job" for the twenty-first century.

SECTION IV

WORKING WITH THE EXPERIENCE
OF VULNERABILITY

Introduction

Linda Hoyle and Jane Pooley

R elationships in organizations and in wider society are changing from apparently stable and predictable patterns to more fluid and potentially chaotic formations. Chapters Seven and Eight have described some of the dilemmas and opportunities this presents to organizations and their consultants. The new landscape raises both anxiety and desire. For example, competition, performance management, and target-setting provide both an opportunity for individuals to reach their potential and also raise the fear of failure. Sometimes this climate means there is limited space for reflection and individuals are increasingly seeking "safe" forums either to work on their individual development or to resolve conflicts with others, or organizations are seeking these opportunities on their behalf. It is noticeable that organizations are increasingly asking for help for individuals, or pairs, or groups in conflict rather than larger scale organizational interventions, training programmes, or group facilitation. This may illustrate the fragmentation of organizations and the difficulty they have in developing a systemic view of the needs of the whole organization. As Sharon Horowitz pointed out in Chapter Eight, leaders in organizations may no longer be "trying to take in or attend to the whole".

Section III vividly illustrated how difficult it can be to work with clients struggling with a "new organizational order". This can face consultants with feelings of uncertainty, confusion and impotence about how to assist clients to make sense of the organization and their relatedness to it. Often it can involve helping clients to continue to relate to what can feel like a "lost object", in that the organization in any recognizable sense has disappeared.

In this Section, two chapters explore ways of providing "safe" forums to attend to the tensions between anxiety and desire. Interestingly, they both deal with relationships between a working pair. Chapter Seven described how the search for meaning in an anonymous and diffuse organization can lead people towards mutual engagement via working pairs. In the case of executive coaching, this is between a client in an organization and a coach who is outside it, perhaps because the client has been unable to find this kind of relationship within the organization. In the case of mediation and conflict resolution, the pair in question is a conflictual pair of people in the same organization, who have become disabled by personal and organizational tensions.

The approaches described in Chapters Nine and Ten offer ways of consulting to individuals and organizations by making the links between individual, group, and organizational dynamics. This idea is derived from applying concepts from systems thinking to consultancy practice and involves the search for patterns and connections between different contextual levels of analysis, i.e. the individual, group, and organizational level. The approach draws on the consultant's counter-transference to understand and explore the emotional aspects of people's experience in organizational life as a source of intelligence about the challenges they are facing. In this way, the coach or mediator enables the client to make the links between the experience at individual or pair level to wider organizational dynamics.

Both chapters also illustrate the tension between providing a "safe" space for an individual, or a pair of individuals having difficulty in the organization, to work at their experience of vulnerability, at the same time as resisting the development of a dynamic in which the coach or consultant colludes in protecting the individuals and the organization from addressing "failed dependency" (Miller, 1993).

Chapter Nine, by Jane Pooley, "Layers of meaning; the coaching journey", begins with an exploration of why the current organizational climate is contributing to an increased use of coaching as a management tool. Theoretical frameworks are used to explore different stages of the coaching journey and the emergent issues to understand the individual and organizational dynamics that clients bring into the coaching relationship.

Chapter Ten, by Linda Hoyle, "The clash of the Titans: conflict resolution using a contextualised mediation process", focuses on the mediation process used as an intervention when there is conflict between individuals and groups. It shows how applying a process consultancy approach widens the issues beyond individuals into the broader context of the organization. This approach makes it possible to think about the conflict not just as a personal problem but as a symptom of something that needs attention within the organization as a whole.

CHAPTER NINE

Layers of meaning:
a coaching journey

Jane Pooley

I ndividuals at different levels within both public and private
sector organizations are increasingly employing coaches who
work outside their organizations. This chapter explores the
author's way of developing a coaching relationship, viewing
it through different lenses. First, the lens of experience is used to
explore how coaching relationships unfold to offer insight into the
client's situation. Second, the theoretical lenses of systemic, psychoanalytic, and attachment theories are used to examine the dynamics at work during this development. The life cycle of a coaching
relationship is offered as a framework to demonstrate how the
relationship can release leadership potential and resources.

Setting the scene

There are many different approaches to coaching. This chapter
focuses on a coaching style that has grown out of systemic and
psychoanalytic traditions. The elements that are primarily examined with this style of coaching are the client in role and the client in
his/her organizational context. An understanding of the presenting

issues comes about through examination of the client's personal and work history, organizational dynamics, task and role clarification, and the primary task of the organization, together with its history and context. The experience and feelings that are generated between client and coach, together with dreams and free associations, are used to enhance understanding. The insights gained and the connections made between these layers of meaning are used to design actions and strategies that link the person, role and organization together towards productive outcomes.

The reasons for the growth of the coaching industry are no doubt as various as the types of organization and individuals that seek this kind of help, however there are some underlying themes. The growth of the global village, together with the ability to travel, to communicate across the globe in real time, through to changes in electronics, computing and e-mail, have brought with them a quickening of change in all organizations. This brings with it anxiety and pressure as well as opportunity.

There is more overt pressure to perform in most, if not all, organizations than existed even five years ago. The manifestation of this is the ethos of performance management with more frequent appraisals and shorter judgement cycles. Some organizations have recognized the pressure and have offered their employees access to external coaches. It is important to understand the particular nature of the organizational context in which the coaching relationship is positioned.

The client's search for meaning

So what is it that clients are looking for? Clients often express a wish to reflect on ways of working with complex and, for them, fast-moving organizational systems. There is a concomitant need for them to take account of their own needs and those of their colleagues. They are looking for a neutral space where judgement is absent, risks can be taken, and connections and thoughts considered and understood, sometimes when the loneliness and isolation of their task has become apparent to them. These feelings invariably increase when boundaries and role become uncertain and are also driven by the fact that workplace performance and assessment have become increasingly public acts.

Requests for coaching can also arise when the client wishes to establish and achieve clearer goals in a wider sense of role and professional effectiveness and, indeed, simply to look at ways that the business can be changed and developed. Sometimes these issues have been clarified through feedback based on appraisal systems and have been built into development plans.

Clients invariably seek a "safe place" to consider questions of work–life balance. Clients also seem to be looking for ways to connect their personal and workplace cultures, beliefs, and ethics, perhaps looking for the *existential primary task* (cf. Chapter Five) to give them meaning.

Looked at in this way, it is clear that clients enter the coaching relationship with hope; hope that is born out of a wish that something new or different can emerge that will relate to all aspects of their lives and enhance their functioning and prospects. This need to work with hope (and its bedfellow, despair) is at the core of the coaching relationship. Put another way, the mobilization of a paired relationship, in which hope and despair can be contemplated, is the basis on which the coaching relationship is built. The task of the coach is to work in this paired relationship without colluding in flight, fight, or dependency (Bion, 1961). Holding the "home" organization in view is therefore essential to the task.

The demand for coaching can also be understood as a request for dependency from clients who feel they need an anchor in what they experience as fast- moving organizational waters. They are often unaware that rapid movement and change has disturbed their capacity to create for themselves, and for the people they manage, a containing environment. While clients often present with a list of issues on which to work, the coach's role is to understand what may be behind these issues so that both the obvious and the hidden can emerge during the coaching relationship. The task is to develop the process of making meaning in order to heighten the capacity to address presenting issues more accurately. Clients increasingly appear to need an environment where their anxiety can be held in order for them to create a containing culture for their staff. In such a culture, fantasies can be explored without prejudice, and creative thought, work satisfaction, and heightened productivity can emerge. However, it is important to see the dependency on the coach within the paired relationship as a stage in the development of the relationship, not an end in itself, or this would be a retreat from organizational relatedness.

The following case study illustrates a key principle in this method of coaching; that is, to encourage clients to forge new understanding in order to make choices based on greater clarity about themselves, their role, and their environmental context. Reed and Bazalgette (2003) succinctly describe this in their work on role consultation as "finding, making and taking role".

> A client, Helen, who was a director in a US based multi-national company that has UK and European bases, had responsibility for managing large production systems. She reported that she had "got wind" of the fact that there was to be a restructuring of the European arm of the business and that she might be made redundant. She became angry and upset and believed that there were many reasons why this would be a mistake for the company. Hadn't they (the US parent company) understood the importance of her work in the company's global market lead and her level of innovation?, she mused. She was temporarily in a "me versus them" frame of mind in which her colleagues and fellow Board members were repositioned as the enemy.

Here we can see the fight–flight dynamic emerging and the need to work with it as part of paired coaching relationship.

> Helen had temporarily lost her capacity for collaborative thought and how she might influence key decision makers. For a while she found herself unable to focus on her work or to even care about it. In my judgement, this was wholly out of character as this individual had been very diligent in all she did. She became childlike. The metaphor that came to mind was one of throwing her toys out of the pram. She was in a great deal of distress and inner turmoil. During this period Helen agreed with me to work through her anger by bringing the experience into the coaching room.

> We focused on ways that she might have contributed to having been placed on the outside and how she might develop her working relationships in the future so that she did not need to resort to omnipotence as a defence against her anxiety. Helen and I were able to explore this through my experience with her during the coaching relationship. I, the coach, had often felt incompetent in her presence, with a sense that I was being tested out and would not live up to her expectations. I found that I had lost my ability to think anything other than inconsequential

thoughts. I reflected this back to Helen and together we began to consider what happened when she felt under the spotlight and how the current experience of her organization was being registered in her and was being represented in the room (Armstrong, 1997). She reported that she had an abhorrence of any situation that she thought showed her up as inadequate. She associated her feelings about this current major event to being sent off to boarding school, aged seven, with a learned need to survive by cutting herself off from any anxiety. Thus, she experienced the restructuring at an unconscious level as the break-ing up of the family, reactivating her childhood experience of going off to boarding school. After making these links to her past, she was more able to think about what this might represent in the organization. She began to see that colleagues who were also affected by the prospective changes were manifesting similar responses to her own, and she related these to a wider level of anxiety in the organization. This general level of anxiety was linked to the prospective removal of key leaders who had shaped and managed the organization. It was under-going a major restructuring programme and key leaders who had been in charge for many years were leaving, "breaking up the family". Helen could now see her responses as not only individually generated but also systemically driven. She was then able to think about how she might influence the form that the reorganization might take and began to work on strategies to do this. She undertook the strategy-forming part of her work with visible energy and vigour and began to enjoy the political aspect of the work, networking with colleagues and working "off line" in preparation for crucial management meetings.

This case example illustrates the level of anxiety that can be experienced through changes to the environment and to working relationships and demonstrates how, in this situation, changes can trigger earlier life experiences that lock the client into a cycle of personal distress, preventing them from seeing a more systemic view. Taking into account the "here and now" data between coach and client and biographical information, the client is supported to work with the "out there" situation in their working life. In this case, the client was able to move from feeling vulnerable and being predisposed to blaming and criticizing others. She became more curious and optimistic about other views on her situation and in options that were open to her in terms of responses. Work in this way can move clients' thinking from linear causality (victim/blame thinking) to circular causality ("what I do affects him and what he does affects me and we are all part of other teams and systems that influence each other and each other's behaviour"). Working with the contextual ripples (Cronen, Pearce, & Tomm, 1985) both from within and outside the organization adds a dimension of enquiry that has the potential to open up possibilities that would not have been available for her consideration.

Imagine, for a moment, the experience of moving into a new team or taking up a new role. First impressions dominate, then questions arise about how am I doing? Are they going to value me? What sort of person do I need to be? What can I uniquely bring to this role? What sort of working relationships do I need to build? How can this team or company be developed and what is my role in this? Do I have the kind of relationship with colleagues that enable us to give and receive good feedback to and from each other? How will we have differences and create something from them? Will I get feedback about how well I am doing? Will I be remembered at all? How will I be valued? Will my skills transfer? All these questions are ones of identity and come into sharp focus in the "new organizational order" (cf. Section III).

Executive coaching, like any other relationship, goes through stages in its development; it has a life cycle. At all stages, anxiety is aroused in relation to the connection being formed; issues of judgement, concerns about the trustworthiness of the space. Will I be changed? Do I wish/need to change? How can I leave? At each stage in the here and now of the coaching relationship, different experiences are available for examination and thought that throw light on organizational development issues. Let us now examine in more detail aspects of three key stages; beginning, mid-life, and ending.

The beginning stage—establishing trust

A client, David, came seeking advice on whether or not he should stay in the high profile job that he was not enjoying, or whether he should join another employer, having been headhunted on several occasions. In the introductory meeting, he talked about difficulties with a peer and how this relationship was preventing him from developing his department's work. He had formed a judgement that a colleague "had it in for him".

In such a situation, an introductory meeting is set up to give clients space to talk about the concerns they have, and for them to gain information about the coaching relationship. Time, frequency of meetings, ways of working, confidentiality, and the background of the coach are some of the issues that are typically discussed. At the end of the introductory meeting, the client either decides to set up four initial appointments or to consider the meeting in their own time, making contact when they have decided how, or whether, to proceed. This open-ended exploration sets a tone for the working relationship between client and coach; a relationship of respect and equality and with openness about how the work will be conducted.

In the first four sessions, the presenting issues are discussed in the light of the obvious connections and meanings and with a curiosity about those that are not so obvious. Sometimes the coach will ask for a personal/professional biography which will often throw light on the patterns of events and relationships in the past that may be informing the "here and now" work relationships.

> In his introductory meeting, the potential client, David, was more than usually interested in the coach's background, issues of confidentiality, whether he could be seen outside working hours, and how his organization would be invoiced. These, of course, are necessary preoccupations. However, the intensity with which they were probed was unusual. David seemed more interested in them than in issues that had brought him to seek coaching. This alerted me to the need to be both transparent and robust in explaining the ways I worked and to clarify my expectations of clients as well as theirs of me. Accordingly, we discussed terms and conditions in detail as well as the possibility of working with biography as a way of illuminating the presenting issues. In the face of a client whose state of mind was highly anxious and suspicious there was clearly a need for me, the coach, to create a containing environment in which boundaries could be set in order for my client to move into a more enquiring state of mind. He decided to have four initial sessions and that progress should be reviewed in the fourth session. However, I was also made aware by the lack of trust that this could be a particular issue in his organization, as indeed it is in many organizations today (cf. Chapter Seven).

The ritual of allocated sessions and regular reviews creates a sense of purposefulness and a structure in which to set and measure progress against the agreed aims and objectives. An active framework is created, which embodies the coaching relationship and gives the client a message of autonomy as opposed to one of dependency. In the early stages of a coaching relationship, coaches are creating a framework for a working relationship which would normally include listening, offering feedback, and challenge. Each client has different preferences and tolerances in these respects and it is the coach's responsibility to "tune into" their client and create an environment that is safe enough for risks to be taken, paying particular attention to language and to the context of the clients working environment.

It is imperative for the coach to hold in mind the organizational culture and specific context in which clients are working. This helps to consider the presenting material as not just personal but as an explanation of some aspect of the organization that is being played out through the client's experience.

> The client (David) held a senior role in the prison service. In a prison, secrets and lies, corruption and suspicion, are evitable dynamics. These are some of the dynamics that underpin criminal activity and are bound to be brought into a custodial context. It was not surprising therefore that such a state of mind was also presenting in David and thus needed the attention of the coach.

> David talked of a disciplinary process that he had gone through in a previous job when a prisoner had accused him of bullying. This had resulted in him being suspended from work for over a year while an investigation took place. I set and held tight boundaries until David felt contained enough to explore this issue and to separate his present experience from his past experience. There was much material that left him feeling vulnerable. It was particularly important to David that his coach was able to witness his experiences and make careful links with them and his current reality. In this way he could begin to consider what belonged where from past and present. He was also able to identify what was part of the organizational dynamic that was being pushed into him, so that he could understand and use these insights in his work. He began to be able to think more clearly. David then found that he could hold multiple realities in his mind, leaving him freer to make choices and consider options. Using the idea of time past, time present, and time future was a useful way of enabling him to move from an apparent rigid of mind.

The notion of time introduces movement into the system of mind and therefore access to new possibilities (Pooley, 1994). Traumatized people often become stuck in time, not able to access memory of the past or dream about their future. This state of shock, literally holding breath, presents itself in smaller measure when clients experience a difficult event or are under great strain. Finding ways to activate both memory and desire frees the mental system. Very simply, this process can begin by paying attention to rituals such as the ritual of the coaching session. Certainty about the behaviour and reliability of the coach begins these stabilizing ritual processes. The experience of an earlier session that the coach remembers, of the coach's availability in the here and now of the present session, and the image of a session planned for the future, begins the process of freeing a conceptual space. This is particularly useful for clients who experience themselves as being lost within their organizations, often experiencing them as chaotic (cf. Section III).

The question of where the line is between coaching and therapy is an important one to ask but it is not easy to answer straightforwardly. The word therapeutic means healing art. Coaches might be said to be working with "dis-ease". That is, with a client who has identified something in their professional system that is not fitting or working as well as they could wish. They enter coaching to "heal", mend, or in some way or another address the presenting issues. If the coach's task is to address underlying, often unconscious, dynamics in individuals and in organizations in order to build sustainable systems with the capacity to adapt and change, then it is essential to use knowledge about people, groups, resistance, defence mechanisms, emotional worlds, and so on. In this sense it is a therapeutic relationship.

There are some basic parameters and frames in the coaching relationship that draw a useful boundary around both task and role. As already stated, the starting point of a coaching relationship is that it sets out to extend and widen understanding and identify the fields of vision that clients are using to understand their situation. At the same time, self- realization comes about through working with the emerging relationship between client and coach. From such new awareness comes the possibility for the client to improve an aspect of their work, to change something in order to enable themselves, their team, or organization to become more effective.

It is, therefore, part of the coaching process to agree desired outcomes that are specific and measurable and to specify how this will be checked, for example via 360° feedback interviews. The coaching journey has a focused end point. This is about work, about the client's role, and about developing the client's understanding of the organization. Personal material is not off limits and is worked with in so far as it affects work performance. Objectives are reviewed and new outcomes agreed, but the testing and measuring of progression in relation to the "back-home" business context makes a clear distinction from most other therapeutic interventions, which are not primarily aimed at improved work performance but have more diffuse goals such as greater insight or well-being. Nevertheless, the coaching relationship is a journey of discovery, where unexpected thoughts or connections are always waiting in the wings. The distinction comes about in the testing of these new insights in the workplace, and using the feedback from this to develop further understanding.

Attachment research can be of help to the coach on this question (Main, 1996). Research in this area focused on infant–parent relationships and highlighted how, through these early experiences, people develop templates for relating to adults and peers. The research shows that repetition is likely to occur in adult relationships when the person has been unable to consider how their early relationships impacted on them. People can be helped to see *how* and then to reflect on *why* those patterns may be repeating in adult life. These early attachment relationships inevitably reappear in the context of the work setting as well as in the home setting. For some clients, coming to terms with this kind of material can free them to understand why they often get stuck in unproductive, and often repetitive, relationships of power by responding in habitual ways. It is also what Bion (1961) describes as "valency", and Obholzer refers to this in Chapter Two. It offers the coach an understanding of the role that they could take up in relation to the client in order to counterbalance projections from previous relationships.

As organizations change, attachment relationships can often become transient. In Chapter Eight, Sharon Horowitz describes these as the "butterfly phenomenon". Individuals do not tend to stay in one role for long as they used to do and frequent changes in reporting relationships will inhibit the development of group working relationships. A secure base (Bowlby, 1988)—a place where both physically and emotionally people experience consistency and safety—is often unavailable to them. The creation of such a base requires attention to the physical—availability of a quiet room, suitable furniture, agreement to switch off mobiles, clear time boundaries, etc.—and attention to the emotional—a non-judgemental approach, a reliable and consistent attitude, etc. When people feel confident in having such a base, they know that the relationship is trustworthy and robust enough to manage difficulties and differences and can contain strong feelings of anger, anxiety, and other arousals. Clients are then much freer to behave in ways that are less defensive, open to opportunity, creativity, and exploration. There is, however, a danger that coaching may be sought out to replace the secure attachments lacking in many modern organizations and that inappropriate dependency on coaches and, for that matter, consultants, can often develop. In such cases the coach–client relationship could become encapsulated or "walls off" the individual from the "toxicity" of the organization and prevents the development of new ways of relating to others in it. It is important to keep the relationship of the client to the organization open and lively. Thus, an appropriate degree of challenge and constant reflection on the meanings to the organization of particular dilemmas under consideration is vital.

This first stage, therefore, is about setting a scene, creating a space in which to think. This is not just a neutral environment, it is a space and a relationship from which new ideas and meaning can emerge and, while "safe", it is not wholly comfortable. Attention to this level of engagement sets the tone for what follows.

The mid-stage—the search for perfection

Having established the basis for a working relationship, this next phase is characterized by an engagement with, and exploration of, what is being presented and what is being experienced both by the client and by the coach. This widening and deepening of the discourse is at the heart of this stage of development.

This approach to coaching works from, and respects, the human dimension of the organizational experience as opposed to the technical or financial dimensions. The focus is to bring to the attention of clients how their personal feelings and responses in themselves may be influencing decisions and actions. The ownership of both the problem and the solution stays with the client. In this respect the coach is taking up a position of "not knowing" and using that frame for a competent exploration of the unsaid and unthought (cf. Chapter Six and containing the "uncontainable"). This apparent paradox is fundamental, in that the coach is working through interest and influence rather than hierarchical authority and knowledge. The coach is not necessarily an expert in the technical issues of workplace; clients can teach the coach what they need to know. Indeed it is important that the coach sees the world as the client sees it, or the "organization-in-the-mind" of the client (Armstrong, 1997) The coach will, however, have expertise in understanding and working with human processes. Within this framework the client is more likely to retain his or her own sense of influence, identity, and purposefulness.

Once the environment is set and the client is both comfortable enough, and anxious enough, to engage in exploring some of their preoccupations, play becomes possible. It is important that this is not taken as being frivolous or as a flight from complexity. That is not the intention and a watchful eye needs to be kept on these defences both in the coach and in the client. However, when fantasies, dreams, and nightmares are taken seriously and invited into the relationship, dialogue and exploration at new levels can commence. Shifting the register in this way gives clients another framework in which to find expression and new ideas. Clients who are supported in their ability to daydream, to try out possibilities and explore flights of fancy, to externalize hopes and anxieties, are in a truly playful space. The capacity to symbolize inner thoughts and feelings through play is as vital in adulthood as it is in children. Unconscious conflicts and dilemmas can safely emerge in this space and the drive towards concrete thinking and total clarity, where the solution is idealized perfection, is avoided.

A finance director, Jack, was preoccupied with the inability of the board on which he sat to address the, to him, obvious demise of one arm of his company. He had not been able to convince his colleagues that radical steps needed to be taken if the company was not to be threatened by this failing directorate. Why, he wondered, could they not see what was blindingly obvious to him? I, the coach, felt Jack's stuckness and was aware it was important to stay with his preoccupation. (In this stuck space the coach will not only experience some of the dilemmas that the client is holding, but also some of the emotional responses to the situation. These can be a clue to both the underlying causes of the dilemma and its solution.) I knew that Jack enjoyed playing chess so invited Jack to imagine that the company's balance sheet was, in fact, a chessboard. Using this analogy, which parts of the company would be represented by which pieces and why? Where would they be placed? What moves in the game would represent the current situation? What moves could be made in order to arrive at a different end point? And so on . . . Coach and client "played" with these ideas for some time and were both quite engaged in the "game". Jack suddenly said, "If I were the bishop and moved next to the knight (representing Andrew his colleague in strategic planning) I could show him that we need a new angle on this. I need to work with the knight (Andrew) so together we can get a handle on this and get our moves co-ordinated. I was standing on the outside looking in and felt as if I was knocking on a door and no one was listening. I will go and talk to him and do some work outside of the boardroom to prepare the way."

While this insight seemed obvious to me, it was only available to Jack by his move into a different, yet familiar, mind space. It was by drawing on his knowledge of and joy in chess that he was enabled to explore options in a playful way and recognize that he could take action and move from his sense of hopeless impotence.

Here the notion of "good enough" is relevant. A risky concept to introduce in a world that is searching for perfection and "total win", but none the less a useful reminder of the personal power that can be unleashed from raising to consciousness that which is unconscious. Winnicott taught, from his extensive observation of infant and parent early relationships, that being a "good enough parent" *is* more than good enough (Winnicott, 1965). In fact the search for perfection paradoxically works against creating an environment where a child can learn to take risks, get things wrong, survive being left alone, learn that despair and hope go hand in hand, and come to think for themselves and about others. It is only in an environment that can accept mistakes that people learn to tolerate and digest their experiences and to think and reflect without being compelled into knee-jerk reactions.

This idea can be translated organizationally through coaching clients. For example, helping a client who felt she had been given an impossible task (Roberts, 1994).

A head of a science department in a large comprehensive school was due to go off on maternity leave within six weeks. She had been asked by the head teacher to create a timetable and work sheets for her classes for the next six months. She had willingly accepted, as she was passionate about her work and keen for her pupils to do well. As the time drew nearer for her to leave, she realized that she had taken on an impossible task. She was in despair about having to go off and abandon her pupils and failing to meet the head's expectations of her. In considering how this situation had arisen, it became clear that the school had been in "special measures" until this new head had arrived five years ago. Together, under the head's leadership, the senior team had turned the school around. At the time of discussion, the school was oversubscribed. The coach and client began to consider that there might be some residual anxiety in the client and in other senior staff in the school; a fear that the success was not sustainable and the school could easily slip back into failure. The coach and client understood the level of commitment many had put into turning the school around, and recognized that it was early days for them to believe that the change was permanent. So, coach and client hypothesized that impossible tasks may be set in an unconscious attempt to "keep ahead of the game". With this insight, the head of department went back and talked to the head teacher, openly addressing the question of why impossible tasks might be being set. As a result, the head of department was relieved of the task of preparing six months' timetables and worksheets. She was also asked by the head teacher to join her in facilitating an in-service training day with staff and an external facilitator to take stock of their successes and to address the (now understood) anxiety of slipping back in time and practice. Addressing the anxiety in the system freed them to celebrate their successes and to plan for a different future.

The coach is *not* primarily concerned with the psychopathology of the client. The coach *is* concerned with identifying the factors in the organizational system in which the client is working that are eliciting particular experiences and patterns (cf. Chapter One). Are there particular dynamics around the function and task of the organization that heighten certain defences and ways of doing things?

Are there particular current constraints or challenges to the business function that push the organization's culture into particular ways of delivery? Are there significant issues in lines of authority and accountability that require unpicking to free the client's capacity for thought and subsequent action?

In order for clients to feel safe enough to take risks, to think about what they are presenting, they need to experience their coach as someone who not only has the capacity to listen and be present, but is also able to understand what is often not being said in words or actions or to reflect back and move into different layers of understanding. The coach needs to demonstrate a capacity to wonder about the meaning behind the obvious. Naming the un-nameable gives clients an experience of being understood at quite a deep level. For example, looking beyond the obvious reasons for the client who is systematically late, or who regularly leaves their mobile switched on, or who brings gifts, recognizing that these all have possible and multiple meanings that are worthy of exploration.

> An MD, Peter, who had grown up with an excessively critical and chastizing mother, had managed life by determining to be "the best" at most things he took on and he had, in great part, succeeded. He began to bring the coach bags of chocolate from his factory on each visit. These were kindly given and the coach was happy to receive them. However, when the coach and client looked at his motivation for these gifts, they began to see that Peter was ensuring that the coach would not turn on him and chastize him; his hope was, in this seeming act of kindness, to keep the coach "sweet". In understanding this, and recognizing consciously his need to be best, and to keep relationships "sweet", he was able to harness his energy and enthusiasm for the business in ways that were less driven by unconscious anxiety. Peter was showing how his organizational culture related to its people. This insight was valuable in later work, when the coach and client recognized that the giving and receiving of gifts was militating against working with resistance and allowing differences to emerge in the corporate culture.

Creating a safe space, with clear boundaries is only part of enabling containment. Awakening to the fact that thinking can only take place when the client experiences in the "helper" the ability to accept projections, without turning them back, and to understand fear without belittling the experience is also vital (Klein, 1955; Segal, 1991). A useful coach is one who has the capacity to accept that clients will have feelings and emotions that they are not ready or able at that moment to own for themselves. The coach's task is to hold this, reflect on the experience, and hand it back when an appropriate moment emerges. In order to be adept enough at working in this way, coaches need to have a good degree of insight into their own inner worlds, so that client's and coach's material do not get confused.

The coach can see these dynamics most acutely at points of transition, as when clients are moving job or working through a re-organization, possibly making changes in their personal lives at the same time. Each person has different thresholds for tolerating change and different ways of managing these life events.

> Henry had been working with me (his coach) for five months. He had recently gained a promotion and was about to move from heading one arm of the business to heading another larger European division. He was in his late thirties, and had been very successful in his career. He was worrying about how he would take up his new role and start off on a good footing with his European management team counterparts. Henry was preoccupied with data about parts of the new role and responsibilities and found it difficult to stand back and look at the whole picture. He was in the state of disorganization very common in staff working through a significant transition. The coach's role at this point was to recognize the turbulence and work with Henry to find anchor points in transferable skills and insights that he could take from one role to the other. His sense of fragmentation was augmented by the challenge that the new role would make to his home life, as he would need to travel more. Understanding that temporary disorganization and high arousal is part of a transitional pathway allowed me to avoid particularizing; to hold the fragments of the role that Henry was concerned with and consider them in relation to the whole picture, and so help Henry to connect with his complete experience of this change. Reminding Henry that how he would leave his current role was as important as how he expected to arrive into his new one seemed to calm him and enable him to attend to the tension between closing down and opening up. It was clear that some of the issues about the new role that Henry had been preoccupied with were important in understanding the dynamics of the move, but to have focused on that particular issue in this session would have exacerbated his situation.

Towards the end of the session, when Henry was in a more reflective state of mind, it was possible to open discussion on this, and agree a return to these preoccupations in our next meeting if they still seemed relevant.

This mid-stage of the coaching journey is characterized by the creation of a working relationship between coach and client that tolerates the capacity to both know and not know; to find answers to questions in surprising spaces, and to work with the idea that there is often new meaning to be found underlying the presenting issues in the client and in their sphere of influence. Searching for these meanings and journeying in this way raises the clients' capacity to work with complexity and to find strategic solutions that attend to all parts of the system in focus.

End stages of coaching: termination and evaluation

Working towards termination of the coaching relationship also links to issues that clients will have to negotiate in their organizations. Anger, regression, yearning for what was and what might have been, are all themes relating to loss that can be relevant to gaining insights into how change and endings affect clients and their colleagues and how they can be better managed in an environment of rush and pressure.

Shelia, an HR professional, came into coaching to explore why she was not being successful in interviews for new roles outside her company. Among other things, the coach and client worked on her interview strategy. She began to understand how important it was to meet prospective employers and consider what they might need her to understand about them. As well as selling her skills, she needed to enter into a relationship with them by being interested both in them as people and in the company's history, strengths, and dilemmas. Shelia had been so overwhelmed by her own sense of failure and her personal preoccupations that she had retreated into self-absorption. The coaching sessions were used to help her become more curious and less introverted. Shelia soon gained a promotion and became global HR director of a large pharmaceutical firm. However, when she was in the process of leaving she retreated into her self-absorbed state. She was not going to have any kind of leaving party and just wanted to walk out of the door saying goodbye to no one. This after twelve years in the company! Coach and client looked at this urge and understood the dangers she felt in facing the rituals of leaving. In that moment she would not only be facing the warmth and goodwill of her colleagues, but also facing the things that were left undone or that were not tied up in some way. She came to recognize that, by working openly with her handover and with the leaving process, she would be supporting her colleagues to take on some of the aspects of inter-relatedness that this company was struggling with. Shelia had understood that her self-absorption was also inherent in the culture of the company, where individuals were privileged over teamwork. This move had come about following a number of investigations into the company due to malpractice. Part of the aftermath of this was that a defensive, individualized culture had developed where all employees were "watching their backs" and protecting their territory.

This example illustrates how the avoidance of proper endings which is part of the chaos of the "new organizational order", can be worked on in the coaching relationship.

One of the ways that this approach to coaching differs from other models is its basic tenet that to emphasize and work only with the positive is counterproductive and unrealistic. Approaches that focus solely on success, without considering the potential blockers to success, both conscious and unconscious, individual, group, and organizational, are at best oversimplified and naïve, at worst dangerous. The complexity of the client's situation requires the consideration of both apparently positive and negative features. As Argyris reminds us (1985), failure to recognize and work with resistance can have disastrous consequences (cf. Chapter Five). Skilled leaders do not push harder when they discern resistance, but they attempt to understand its meaning as a source of data from which organizational change can be posited. Retaining this spirit of enquiry and curiosity enables clients to find pathways that create opportunity rather than build up defensive systems. A crucial aspect of coaching is the ability and sensitivity to discern where resistance to change is sited. If clients are to bring about change in their organizational system, they need to understand where the anxiety lies, and what structures or resources are needed to contain it in order that it will not overwhelm or incapacitate the change programme. Understanding these issues helps clients create their own containing environment, and to develop insight into the human systems in their organization. Strategic planning can then take account of these matters.

Evaluating coaching takes the form of reviewing what has been achieved against the agreed aims and objectives. This process is worked on at review points throughout the coaching relationship and new objectives are set as the clients' capacity to think deeper and wider grows. This dialogue goes on in tandem with the experience of the relationship between coach and client. Feedback is invited and given both ways. At the end point the total picture is in view, an evaluation of what has emerged during the coaching work can be made, together with discussions as to how new insights can be worked with in the workplace.

One expected outcome would be a shift from problem and obstacle focus to opportunity focus; a move from blame to curiosity; an ability to understand that the dilemmas may not only, if at all, reside in the individual but in an aspect of the organizational culture. As a result of working in this way, clients are able to consider the specific role that they hold in the organization with greater confidence and clarity and a have a clearer sense of how to approach issues of both personal and organizational change.

Another less obvious but crucial outcome would be an increased capacity for clients to play with ideas. The loosening of the constraints of anxiety helps clients to take hold of agendas, and to be more dynamic and proactive in how they work with them. Clients and coach often use 360° feedback to measure some of these movements and to throw light on blind spots that may need further work. It often happens that clients gain promotion, or take on additional responsibilities, or develop their insight and sphere of influence, over the coaching period.

Coaching can build the client's capacity to use his or her own emotional intelligence (Goleman, 1998). It brings them into the strategic frame as people with passions and desires alongside the organizational system and the context in which it operates. By bringing person, role, and system together so that each informs the other, the client is able to infuse their role in the organization with more rigour and focus.

This approach enables clients to move between layers of meaning to understand presenting issues, hence to diagnose more accurately where to intervene.

Final note

It wasn't an easy road but I am so glad I took it. I can now see my role and my company with fresh eyes. I can see things that I would not have noticed before. I respond differently to challenges and use my feelings to guide me in my planning.

My company has benefited from the coaching work that I have done because I have been able to pass on some of the insights I have gained to my colleagues and I have started to work more collaboratively with them.

Because I understand my own responses to issues better and because I can now analyse what this is telling me about parts of the company that need attention I use my energy much more efficiently. My family as well as my job have benefited.

My coach was very tough on me at times but I needed her to be. Her insistence that I look over the fence and not at the fence has helped me open my practice and troubleshoot before the crisis. Our sales have increased as a direct result.

Each journey a coach travels with a client is a new journey of discovery. There will be rocks and hard places on the way, there will be oases, there will be turbulence and joy. There will be joint satisfaction in finding and making connections and, finally, for the coach there is energy in watching teams and organizations develop and flourish. Who could ask for more?

CHAPTER TEN

Clash of the Titans—conflict resolution using a contextualized mediation process

Linda Hoyle

Introduction

Earlier chapters (One, Three, Four, Seven, and Eight) described how changes in organizations and leadership have created uncertainty and ambiguity around everyone's roles and, in particular, around the power and authority that can be exercised by those in leadership roles. This can be heightened during change processes and creative potential can be lost (cf. Chapter Five). External forces create the need for more relatedness between people in organizations through requirement for more corporate working, involvement of staff in decision-making, and greater skills in collaboration. At the same time, pressure on individual performance and the experience of personal vulnerability can militate against the negotiation of adequate relatedness between individuals to cope with and contain the tensions associated with continually changing roles, accountabilities and contexts.

One of the central challenges in organizations today appears to be the degree to which it is possible to acknowledge and manage some of these uncertainties without the explosion of more personal dynamics between colleagues or between leaders and their followers "in which the tensions around the location of leadership get played out in accusation, hostility, and recrimination" (Chapter Four). The evidence of this lies in the increasing requests for mediation and conflict resolution received by TCS in recent years.

This chapter explores how it is necessary to keep the organization in mind (Armstrong, 1997) through a process which is initially presented as a problem of a pair or small group of people in an organization, in order that negotiation of a more adaptive relatedness can take place.

The increased demand for conflict resolution and mediation interventions within organizations, as well as a rising interest in training in mediation skills for managers and human resources professionals, indicates that there are more incidents of conflict between individuals and groups in contemporary organizations that require an intervention by a third party. Many of the conflicts arise from allegations of bullying and harassment, which lead to a grievance being raised by one of the parties, and often mediation is seen as an informal intervention to resolve the situation rather than formal disciplinary procedures.

The use of mediation to resolve the grievance situation seems to be a positive step forward in that this requires a process of inquiry and negotiating a resolution rather than investigation and blame. However, the question that remains is, why are there so many incidents of bullying and harassment that lead to grievances being raised? As mentioned earlier, the landscape of organizations has changed significantly from traditional, hierarchical structures where it was clear who were the people in positions of authority. With flatter hierarchies and increased competition between organizations, there is more pressure for people to improve their individual performance, take responsibility for their own personal development, and to manage themselves. The relationship between managers and employees has changed. On the positive side, this means that individuals feel more autonomous and take more responsibility for their careers and development of their role in the organization. They are more likely to challenge and question the status quo and stand up to people in positions of authority. However, this means that the management role requires the capacity to be able to tolerate being challenged and questioned. No longer do managers acquire the automatic followership that used to come from the authority of the role they took up. The nature of containment has changed in that managers need to be able to tolerate the tensions and conflict situations that arise from difference, challenge, questioning the status quo, creativity, and ideas for change. It may be that the lack of containment from managers in these situations means that the conflict escalates and eventually grievances are reported, bringing the situation to a head. It is interesting that, at this point, an independent third party is often brought in to help resolve the situation and to provide the much-needed containment for the situation.

The aim of this chapter is to examine organizational situations where difference between individuals and groups has led to conflict involving individuals in powerful positions and to explore the role of the process consultant in providing an intervention. Two case studies are presented in which TCS was contacted for help with negotiating difference between individuals who were in conflict. The cases were similar in that they involved individuals in powerful positions in the organization. However, the first case study illustrates a situation where both the individuals were in equally powerful positions, whereas the other case study involved one individual in a more powerful position than the other. Another similarity was that, in both cases, the human resources director made the initial contact with TCS and a "mediation" intervention was requested.

These cases raised several challenges and dilemmas for the work of a process consultant, which will be discussed after presenting the case studies. Before doing this, the terms "workplace mediation" and "process consultancy" will be clarified.

Workplace mediation

It is only recently that formalized approaches to workplace mediation have been established in the UK. According to Reynolds (2000), in 1996 the first organizations to set up formalized mediation in the UK were a local government authority, Lewisham Council Housing Department, and the Department of Health. As Reynolds points out, the terms mediation and conciliation are often used to mean the same thing and he continues by making the distinction that:

> Mediation is used to mean the intervention by an impartial third party. Mediators do not offer advice or solutions; their skill is in

facilitating parties to come to their own solutions. A mediator in this sense is concerned with the process, not the content, of the dispute. [Reynolds, p. 166]

This definition is similar to one put forward by Legum (2001) who outlines the difference between three types of third party intervention:

Facilitation: The facilitator's role is strictly confined to promoting communication between parties in conflict. Facilitators do not suggest solutions or make proposals to help the parties reach agreement; their role is primarily technical; the improvement of communications as a means of promoting understanding and of conveying to each side what the other actually intends. [Legum, 2001, p. 206]

Conciliation: The conciliator usually plays an active role in facilitating exchange, by suggesting possible solutions and by assisting the parties to reach a voluntary agreement. [*ibid.*, p. 205]

Arbitration: A form of adjudication in which the third party decides the issues dividing the disputants, whereas in mediation the intermediary helps the disputants to reach voluntary agreements. The arbitrator is required to reach a decision binding on both sides; the mediator has no such authority. [*ibid.*, p. 205]

The definition of workplace mediation put forward by Reynolds (2000) above and the facilitator role described by Legum (2001) above are similar, and for the purposes of this chapter will be referred to as the "facilitator role". This chapter explores the distinction between the facilitator, conciliator and arbitrator roles that could be taken up when a client asks for a third party intervention.

Process consultancy

The facilitator role outlined above is similar to the model of "process consultancy", which was defined by Edgar Schein as:

a set of activities on the part of the consultant that help the client to perceive, understand, and act upon the process events that occur in the client's environment in order to improve the situation defined by the client. [Schein, 1988, p. 11]

This approach involves the consultant being less concerned with the content of a problem and more with the process by which the individual, group, or organization identifies and solves problems. This model of consultancy focuses on helping clients to form their own diagnosis and then allows the client to generate, select, and implement any associated solutions. The main advantage of using a process model, therefore, is that the client maintains the ownership and responsibility for the diagnosis and solution of the problem. The consultant is also able to pass on some of their diagnostic and intervention skills to the client. In Schein's words, "helpers must help their clients to learn how to learn" (1990, p. 60).

Schein also states that process consultants "must have a model of how to improve the situation" (1987, p. 29). What he means by this is that the focus for the consultant is towards concepts of health, change, and improvement, which requires them to hold an underlying theory of "system health" (Bennis, 1962). He continues by giving examples of underlying theories such as psychoanalytic theory or sociotechnical theory. He points out that the interventions of consultants with different underlying theories may be similar, and it tends to be the written analysis of different theoretical perspectives that professional colleagues may have a reaction to. The theory of "system health" that underlies the process consultancy approach used for the case studies in this chapter is an integration of psychoanalytic and open-systems thinking.

It is clear from the definitions of facilitation and process consultancy that there are strong similarities. Both approaches emphasize that the consultant is focused on the process of enabling clients to resolve their own conflict rather than making decisions for them or solving the conflict, which would be the role of an arbitrator. With this in mind, the two case studies presented below illustrate some dilemmas that arose for the consultant working with clients who requested a mediation intervention to deal with individuals in conflict.

Case studies

The names and details of the people involved in these cases have been altered to ensure that they remain anonymous and that their cases are confidential.

Health service case study

The HR director of a hospital contacted TCS and requested mediation for two senior doctors who were in conflict. One of the doctors, Rachel, had instigated a grievance procedure against the other doctor, Paul. The grievance was about a clinical incident, which had been investigated and was not upheld. The consultant was asked to conduct a mediation between them so that they could continue to work together after a harrowing grievance investigation that had lasted two years.

It was agreed that the format for the mediation would be to interview each individual and then to bring them together to facilitate a process where they would find their own solution to the conflict. In other words, the initial contract was that the consultant would take up a facilitator role for this piece of mediation work.

However, the individual interviews with the doctors revealed that the situation was more complex than had been initially presented by the HR director. It emerged that there were conflicts within the department and within the hospital as a whole. The doctors refused to meet together for the joint mediation session because they both felt that the problem was wider than a conflict between them as individuals. Paul was on study leave and therefore not currently working in the department. However, he was due to return soon and Rachel was adamant that he should not be allowed back into the department because they could not work together.

This was fed back to the HR director and it was agreed that the next stage of the process would be to conduct interviews with other members of the department and with key individuals throughout the hospital. The intervention had now become a piece of organizational development (OD) work using a process consultancy approach. Some important issues came out of the wider interviews that provided a context to the conflict between Rachel and Paul. Several working hypotheses were developed as a result of the OD work, which were presented to the management of the hospital:

- It could be seen that the conflicts were a defence against the anxiety evoked by potential changes to the system. First, there was the possibility that the hospital would merge with other hospitals, which could mean the closure of several departments. Second, newly qualified senior doctors, such as Paul, were bringing in ideas about different clinical procedures, working practices and work–life balance initiatives.

- It seemed that Paul, Rachel, and their department as a whole were acting out the conflict on behalf of the whole system. The conflict between Paul and Rachel could be seen as different responses to change. Rachel represented resistance to any changes to the system, whereas Paul represented potential change to the system. People formed camps within the department and throughout the hospital in support of either Paul or Rachel, which could be seen as "splitting" as a defence against the anxiety evoked by potential changes to the system.
- The interpersonal relationship between Rachel and Paul could be seen in terms of the unconscious process of projective identification. This meant that the behaviour of each individual reinforced the behaviour of the other. The nature of this reinforcing cycle of behaviour meant that it was difficult to make a judgement as to who was right or wrong in this situation.

When these ideas were presented to a meeting of the management of the hospital it was perceived that they were in a state of high anxiety and paralysis. The powerful Medical Council, which is made up of all senior doctors, was split, with one camp putting pressure on management to support Rachel and the other camp urging support for Paul. The source of the management inertia seemed to be a fear about making the wrong decision and facing a vote of no confidence from the Medical Council. The power in the system seemed to be clearly held by the body of senior doctors and the fight about whether there should be change in the system was acted out by two of these powerful people who were seen to represent the different camps. This fight seemed to have rendered the management paralysed and impotent to act or take any management decisions.

What was interesting during this case was that the consultant felt constantly pressured by management to take up an arbitrator role rather than a facilitator/process consultancy role. For example, during the meeting with the hospital management the consultant was asked to make the decision for them. This was constantly pushed back to the client and it was said that these were management decisions and that the consultant's role was to provide more contextual information to help their decision-making process. It took a lot of energy to continually maintain a neutral role and not to pass judgement on any of the people involved in the case. The consultant's experience of the consultancy project was that they had to contain their own anxiety about being drawn into an arbitrator role as well as managing a process to contain the anxiety for the client.

Engineering case study

The HR director of an engineering organization contacted TCS. A conflict had occurred in the administration department of the organization between the departmental director, James, and a junior member of staff, Jenny. The incident described by the HR director was that Jenny had made an allegation of bullying against James. Jenny and James had agreed to take part in a mediation process to resolve the conflict rather than go through a formal grievance procedure.

The HR director requested that the mediation was conducted using the "shuttle mediation" format outlined in *The Workplace Mediation Manual* (Findlay & Reynolds, 1997). This form of mediation required the consultant to take a facilitator role. The process began with a meeting of the consultant and both individuals, where the consultant presented the ground rules and the format of the mediation. The individuals then went into separate rooms and the mediator took it in turn to meet each of them. In the first meeting, the mediator asked them to describe their perspective of what happened during the incident and to agree what they would allow to be communicated to the other person. They were also asked to set out what they wanted from the other person and what they would offer in return. The process continued with the mediator shuttling between the individuals to relay an account of their perspective of the incident, a list of wants, and a list of offers.

This process of shuttle mediation lasted a whole day. The mediation seemed to become stuck because James refused to discuss anything other than the one incident that had occurred. In contrast, during the meetings with Jenny the context around the incident was discussed, including the history of the relationship between Jenny and James, other relationships between staff in the department, and relationships between the department and other parts of the organization. From discussions with Jenny the mediator gathered the following contextual information surrounding the incident:

- Jenny had worked in the organization for five years and had never had a performance appraisal from her line manager.
- James was the director of the department, but was not Jenny's line manager.
- Stuart was Jenny's line manager, who she described as being more like a friend than a manager. Jenny said that Stuart had never criticized her work, but did tend to make sarcastic jokes about her being late or taking time off sick, which Jenny described as usual "office banter".

- Jenny described the office environment as being "us and them", with the junior members of staff down one end in an open-plan area and the managers in smart offices overlooking the workers.
- She also described an "us and them" culture between the engineers and the administrative staff in the organization, which meant that junior admin staff like her felt like they were the "bottom of the heap".
- Jenny described the incident where she alleges bullying. James had called Jenny into his office and reprimanded her on the quality of her work, lateness, and sickness record. Jenny had made the point that Stuart had never given her an appraisal and had never complained to her about these issues. Jenny thought this comment seemed to make James very angry and he raised his voice at her. During a heated exchange Jenny was given a verbal warning by James. After the meeting Jenny went straight to the HR director to make the allegation of bullying.

Jenny asked for these contextual issues to be communicated to James during the shuttle mediation. When this was done James became angry with the mediator, and said that he did not see the relevance and would only focus on the one incident that happened in his office. He refused to answer any questions that would have provided contextual information to understand what happened during the incident. James' account of the incident was similar to Jenny's. However, James was adamant that he did not bully Jenny, but did admit that he became angry during the meeting. James was offended that he was being called a bully and wanted an apology from Jenny. On the other side, Jenny felt offended by the manner in which James conducted the meeting and wanted an apology.

The difficulty with this case was that there were no witnesses and both parties were certain about their perspective of the incident. After many shuttles between the individuals, the mediator asked them to meet together. The turning point came when it was agreed that neither side was prepared to apologize and they would only ever be able to agree to disagree. They were then able to focus on the purpose of the mediation, which was to agree on how they would continue to work together. They used the handwritten notes that the mediator had been using to relay the agreed information between them and they set about negotiating a way forward. It was a heated discussion, but it only took another hour to reach an agreement of how they could work together.

On a positive note, part of the agreement was that James said he would review the management and appraisal systems in the department, which seemed to be the underlying source of the conflict. The media-tor found it frustrating to work on this case because the contextual information was not fully brought into the mediation and therefore the focus was on two people with different perspectives of the same inci-dent, which was irresolvable. It was also interesting that the power difference between the two individuals meant that the director was able to block the uncomfortable contextual information from being part of the mediation.

Conclusions

In both these cases there was valuable contextual information surrounding the conflict between two individuals. Although the consultant began each project by taking up a facilitator role to medi-ate between individuals, it emerged that there were problems of difference and conflict within the organization between different groups of staff. In both cases it seemed that the two individuals were representing different aspects of intergroup relations within the organization. The dilemma faced by the process consultant was whether to continue in the facilitator role or to move into another role where the contextual information about the wider organiza-tional dynamics could be used, thus keeping the organization in mind and attempting to help its members work differently at their relatedness to it.

In the health service case study, the consultant did move from a facilitator role to a process consultancy role, where the underlying theory of system health was an integration of psychoanalytic theory and open-systems thinking. However, the impact of the shift from facilitating a process to providing contextual information was that the client attempted to move the consultant into an arbitrator role. It may have been that this was a way for management to avoid addressing some important contextual issues that are present across the whole of the health service. For example, it is quite common for senior doctors to be on the same level as each other, which can result in unclear lines of authority and power struggles between doctors. This can also lead to power struggles between doctors and management, who find it increasingly difficult to manage senior doctors. The contextual information also provided evidence of resistance to change, which could have been used more creatively to understand the underlying anxieties and impact of proposed changes across the whole organization.

In contrast, the engineering case study illustrated a situation where the consultant was attempting to bring more contextual information into the mediation process, but the individual in a more senior position blocked this and pushed the consultant back into a facilitator role. Again this could be seen as a way of avoiding some issues that were uncomfortable for the director. For example, the mediation uncovered that the line manager had not addressed Jenny's performance issues about the standard of her work, lateness, and sickness record. It was unclear how it came to be that the director was meeting Jenny to confront these issues rather than the meeting being between Jenny and her line manager. According to Jenny, it was her mentioning this issue that triggered the director's anger, but as he was unwilling to discuss the context, it never became clear what the real source of his anger was. It may have been that the director became aware that he had been left to sort out a performance management situation that another manager should have dealt with. In any case, the director seemed unable to contain the emotional tension of the situation, particularly when Jenny began to raise some uncomfortable contextual information. This case also illustrates that in both the private and public sectors performance management has become increasingly important, and what can happen when managers avoid the difficult job of confronting performance issues of a staff member.

In both cases, the role of the mediator was to provide containment for the individuals in conflict and it could be argued that the conflicts arose because there was a lack of management containment in the organization. The findings of these case studies also present a challenge to ideas about the role taken up when a client requests mediation for a conflict between two individuals. The role taken up in these case studies was not to be a conciliator or an arbitrator. The consultant did not suggest any solutions to the clients or add any options to resolve the situation, which would have been a conciliation. They clearly did not take up an arbitrator role, although at times the health service client wanted the consultant to make a judgement about who was in the right. However, the consultant did not take up a pure facilitation role, which in Legum's words would be "strictly confined to promoting communication between parties in conflict" and is "primarily technical" (Legum, 2001, p. 206).

Both cases illustrate the pressure placed on the consultant to provide the containment lacking in the organization, as if the client's request for help represents simultaneously an outsourcing of the containment needed to facilitate organizational change but without the necessary legitimization for the consultant to perform this role effectively, even if this were to be appropriate. This can create considerable anxiety and frustration for both consultant and clients. It also reflects the position many people in leadership roles find themselves in—unable to find and use power and authority to act effectively within their roles.

In conclusion, a solution to the dilemma is the use of a psychoanalytic and open-systems thinking theory of system health during mediation. This means that the process involves gathering contextual information during the mediation, which is then reflected back to the individuals to help them to understand and find their own solutions. This method of mediation comes somewhere between a facilitator role and a conciliator role, which is represented in Figure 3.

In addition, conducting a contextualized mediation does raise a certain amount of anxiety for the mediator. This anxiety arises when the process moves away from facilitating an exchange of communication about the one incident that has been stated as the source of the conflict. By contextualizing, the mediator is taking a more active role in the process but does not offer any solutions or

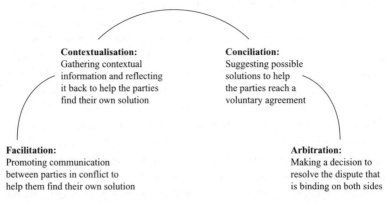

Figure 3. Types of third party intervention in a conflict.

options for resolution. Taking this more active role seems to encourage the client to try to draw the mediator into a conciliator or arbitrator role. However, as Legum points out:

> To strip a conflict of its complexity is to falsify it. One function of the facilitator, therefore, is to help participants to acknowledge that they are enmeshed together in a complex and multidimensional problem. Helping conflicting parties to "acknowledge" the complexities of the situation in which they are "enmeshed" with others is clearly important to the opening up of channels of communication. [2001, p. 207]

There was also evidence in the two case studies to suggest that sometimes the client might try to avoid working with the contextual information that is uncovered during the mediation, possibly because it raises some uncomfortable issues. This may be why the client at times tried to move the mediator away from taking up a contextual mediation role.

Finally, it is important to say something about negotiating with the client in the initial phase of the assignment to decide what would be the most appropriate type of intervention. From the experience of the case studies, it is crucial to be absolutely clear about what role the consultant is taking up in relation to mediating the conflict. The case studies above illustrate the impact of power relationships during a mediation process. In one case the two powerful senior doctors refused to engage in a face-to-face mediation. This act seemed to block them from understanding the context of the conflict between them, which might have enabled them to find a resolution. In the other case, the director blocked the contextual information being brought into the mediation, which in a similar way meant the underlying issues within the department were not understood as being part of the conflict. In conclusion, it is important to emphasize during the negotiating stage with the client that using a contextualized approach to mediation will involve gathering contextual information that will be reflected back to individuals to enable them to find their own solutions to the conflict.

Endword

Clare Huffington

The experience of consulting to organizations and leading TCS as its director over the past ten years has mirrored that of our clients over the same period. It has involved a process of self-examination and of questioning of our identity as a consultancy organization, in terms of both our conceptual platform and the approach to consultancy that this conceptual platform informed, as well as the services that we then offer. Changes in the context around us have presented us with both a challenge and an opportunity in that, while they sometimes felt like a threat to our survival, the contextual changes have also promoted an ongoing process of review and debate that has ultimately been developmental and continues to be so.

The struggle has been partly due to a reduction in the type of consulting work we were used to. Large organizational intervention projects, training and team consulting assignments were thin on the ground; clients seemed resistant to interventions that encouraged greater relatedness across the organization. Instead, they were asking for individualized approaches like coaching, mediation, and conflict resolution, or research and evaluation projects. Many of these involved competitive tendering. There was also the challenge to offer interventions, workshops, and training in much shorter time frames. All this mirrored changing work patterns that were emerging in organizational life.

Another aspect of our struggle was that the experiences clients presented were confusing and difficult to understand and did not fit with the conceptual frameworks we had to hand. At times, this made us feel impotent and useless. It faced us with a challenge. We could see a clear need to respond differently to client needs. But how could we develop new conceptual frameworks? Colleagues told us we should not mention the unconscious any more or it would alarm clients and lose us work. We did not agree.

As we saw it, we had to adapt our ideas to a new context rather than collude with the pressure to abandon them altogether. We would have to do the hard work of letting go of some ideas and being open to evolving new ones. This meant facing our own anxieties about the "uncontainable" unknown, and trying to contain and work with it creatively. We would stay close to our clients' needs, while keeping focused on our mission to improve the mental health of society through addressing the mental health of people in their workplace. And we would not "lose" the unconscious!

So we took on the challenge of offering clients what they asked for, evolving new services and new ideas where old ones would not do. We have used the experience of doing this as an opportunity for action research on the emotional life of contemporary organizations. The result has been the subject matter of the book.

Through all the changes, not only have we held on to the core concept of the unconscious in all human relations, "working below the surface", but we have also retained a focus on relatedness in organizations. This is to counter the nightmarish, but also unfortunately real, scenario of each member of an executive team consulting his or her coach before, during, and after team meetings—a highly perverse and simultaneous version of basic assumption Meness and pairing and in service of nothing beyond organizational fragmentation. The question we are now asking ourselves is, "What is the nature of the relatedness that can contain what organizations now need to do?" Another question might be how far creativity needs a safe place to flourish, since we know some of the core concepts in our consultancy approach evolved in wartime. Can creativity emerge in dangerous places such as the global marketplace?

Other areas coming into view include working in and with networks, addressing the political dimension of organizations, developing group relations events that will examine virtual dynamics in organizations, experiential approaches to leadership development, and strengthening organizational relatedness through individuals so as to "in-source containment".

In writing this endnote, I feel reassured that our struggle to continue to work at the mental health of organizations using a "below the surface" approach has not been an impossible or "uncontainable" task, although sometimes it has felt that way. We are part of a process in which we are co-evolving with our clients in a search for new adaptations to ever-changing circumstances. It is this experience that excites us in our journey into the future.

Notes on consultancy approach and techniques

W e have described the contextual shifts that have challenged both our conceptual framework and consultancy
practice over the past ten years. We have found ourselves working on particular themes, some of which we have
described in this book. The challenges and opportunities offered to
us by our clients in the changed environment have forced us to
change some of our thinking and to develop new ideas. It has been
important for us to hold our conceptual framework quite loosely so
as to be open and receptive to new experiences that might challenge
them, but might also be an opportunity for creativity and learning.
In this respect, we feel we are in the same uncertain but receptive
state of mind as our clients are and need to be. The tensions that
flow from this position need not be resolved but continually
explored and worked with, or the risk is of decoupling from the
changing environment, becoming too fixed in our thinking and
potentially stagnating.

In parallel and in relation to the themes we have been addressing with clients, we have also found ourselves engaging with them
in quite different ways. This has led us to evolve new methods and
techniques in working with them. An example would be the way

we now think of containment as less about finding ways to manage conflict and disturbance and more about stimulating exploration and curiosity. This is more likely to lead to organizational reframing and creativity and we have called this "pro-tainment" This is described in the chapters on women's leadership and on distributed leadership (Chapters Three and Four). This has led to the development of some specific methods of working with clients that allow them to explore this theme; for example, "Organization-in-the-mind" workshops (see below).

The shifts in the context have led to the use of existing techniques in different ways; to the relative importance of some techniques over others; and also to the creation of wholly new methods of working with clients. In this section, we offer examples of some of these changes in our approach and techniques.

Changed ways of thinking, changed ways of working

"Organization-in-the-mind" workshops

"Organization-in-the-mind" refers to the mental constructs of the organization that are determining one's decisions and actions, both unconsciously and below the surface; and to the more unattended world of feeling, imagery, language, and relationships that constitute the "implicate order" of the organization—its particular way of being as this is registered "in the mind".

The aim of these workshops is to create a frame of individual and group reflection, analysis, and dialogue, through which leaders and managers, from the same or linked organizations, can draw on and use a wider range of experience and exchange as a source of "intelligence" into the particular organizational dilemmas, challenges, and opportunities they encounter and the implications for their own exercise of leadership and management.

Workshops are held residentially, over three days. Their design is built around examining working experiences of participants from three linked perspectives; person, role, and system. One senior civil servant expressed this in a short report on her experience during a workshop:

The guiding principle was that everyone who works in an organization works as a part of the organization (*the system*) and as someone with a certain *role* (eg Deputy Director) and as an *individual*. These three fields (system, role and individual) are combined in yourself. The three fields of course do not overlap each other completely; outside your work you exist as an individual and the organization also exists outside you. And you take on more than one role in your life. In the group discussions and assignments, the idea was to gain as much insight as possible into how these three forces influenced each other in concrete work situations and to recognize when one force was dominant. So that you do not attribute behaviour to an individual if it is inherent in his or her role or in the organization, and vice versa.

The methods used include:

- working with imagery and associations, where members are invited to share and respond to pictures they draw of "the emotional world of my organization and myself within it"
- role analysis, where they offer and examine "critical incidents" from their current work situations, in a structured, small group setting
- an intergroup event in which members form sub-groups around sensed affinities in their approach to leadership that are explored and tested through interaction within and between groups
- dialogues around particular themes in understanding and exercising leadership that are emerging in their own or the wider context of the organization
- reflections at the start of each day to share overnight thoughts, dreams, or associations that may link to experiences within the workshop and outside.

Used in-house, one outcome from these workshops has been decisions taken by members to develop a continuing process of reflection and analysis amongst themselves:

> I have noticed that I now look at some things within the organization in a different way and deal differently with others. A few of us who attended the workshop have decided to take this further ourselves.

Old wine in new bottles; changes and
adaptations to existing techniques

Open space technology

Open Space Technology is a way of bringing together and engaging with large groups of people from all levels across an organization or network to work at issues of whole system learning and change. Originated in the USA by Harrison Owen in the early 90s (Owen, 1992), it revolutionized ways of thinking about and designing methods of "harnessing large group forces in a non-hierarchical way" and in the service of organizational or cross-organizational agendas for change (Glouberman, 1995). Open Space Conferences aim to create a setting and an infrastructure in which there is maximum opportunity for participants to address such agendas, organizing themselves through convening meetings on topics of concern to them and recording their conclusions and recommendations within the "real time" of the conference itself. The latter, in turn, becomes a vehicle for "moving the process of change forward" (*ibid.*).

In our own work, we have drawn on and designed Open Space Events during assignments where the primary focus has been on bringing about cultural change, the evolution and implementation of new strategic directions, the development of partnership working, or the implications of organizational restructuring. While such events have proved their value in mobilizing collaborative approaches to organizational innovation and development, our experience has also highlighted the need to frame such events within a broader process of intervention, both prior to and subsequent to the event itself. In particular, without attention to preparation and follow through, the risk is of generating a cycle of expectancy and disillusionment within which the momentum found during the event itself is lost.

Mediation and conflict resolution

We have developed our approach to mediation through our experience of providing interventions to help individuals and teams resolve conflict situations. Requests for these services have increased in recent years and Chapter Ten, "Clash of the Titans—conflict resolution using a contextualized mediation process", provides details of our understanding of why there has been more demand and outlines our approach. The central tenet of our approach is that we use process consultancy skills to help the clients understand the context in which the conflict situation has developed. For example, the request for mediation may be to address a tension between two individuals but exploration of the wider situation may reveal that these individuals are representing a conflict that is present throughout the whole organization.

Senior executive coaching

The Tavistock Consultancy Service offers senior executive coaching to senior people in organizations. This takes the form of a series of confidential meetings in which those in leadership roles can think about their leadership style, the experience, knowledge, skills, and attitudes they bring to their work, areas for development and planning for their own futures and that of their organizations. Coaches can also act as a sounding board to leaders as they work on ideas about developing the organization and offer expertise where it is needed, for example on managing resistance to change. The distinctive TCS competence brought to senior executive coaching is in "working below the surface"; helping clients to bring into focus the less apparent feelings and responses in themselves and in others that may be influencing their decisions and actions.

Clients are offered an initial exploratory meeting, free of charge, to identify issues that they wish to work on. The approach to coaching is a collaborative one and this exploratory meeting helps to identify appropriateness of coaching as well as develop a productive working relationship with the coach or a coach in our team with the particular expertise or skills required.

Four sessions will be offered to begin with, after which there will be a review to evaluate effectiveness and plan further meetings if desired. The average number of meetings is approximately ten, but some clients meet for longer than this. The spacing between sessions is negotiated between the client and coach. Each meeting generally lasts for two hours and can take place at TCS offices, the client's offices, or another location of the client's choice. Clients are given frequent feedback, review, and evaluation, which serves to maintain momentum and a goal-directed and focused approach.

At the first meeting, ground rules about confidentiality and openness are established. Objectives and expected outcomes from the coaching are clarified and agreed as well as methods of evaluating progress, which could include contact with the client's chair/chief executive, colleague directors, or direct reports. Decisions on how to communicate between meetings and whether additional initial information is required such as CVs, psychometric reports, Myers Briggs assessments, appraisals or other feedback on performance from the organization is also discussed at the first meeting. We do not routinely use psychometrics within coaching but are able to do so if this would be helpful to the client.

Coaching plus

Figure 4 illustrates the additional elements that can feed into the coaching process, such as formal or informal 360° feedback interviews conducted by the coach on the client's behalf; or other concurrent interventions alongside the coaching process, such as observation of meetings at the workplace, work shadowing by the coach, individual or team development and training. As a result of

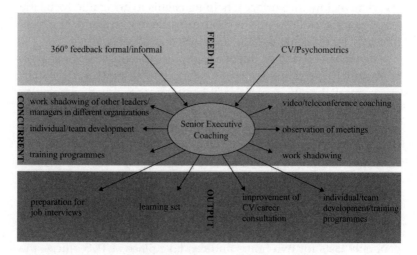

Figure 4. Additional elements that can feed into the coaching process.

the coaching process, the output might include learning sets, individual and/or team development, and career consultation.

Methods from family and systems psychotherapy

The drive towards individual performance and consequently the possibility of fragmentation in the organization has made it difficult for individuals and teams to conceptualize the organization as a system. This is important if those working in the organization are to perform their roles effectively in relation to other parts of the system and, in particular, to influence it or bring about change. Therefore, some of our work with clients has focused on helping them to develop the capacity for systems thinking. In doing this, we have been greatly assisted by work family/systems therapists have done in developing techniques to help therapists and family/system members to understand what a system is, how it works, and what to do to change it. Methods we have found helpful are described below.

Reflecting teams

A reflective discussion is a way of giving feedback to members of a system that allows them to move towards an observer position in relation to the system as a whole (Andersen, 1987; Campbell, Draper, & Huffington, 1989). A reflecting team can be composed of two or more consultants or even clients. They talk in front of clients about the way in which their thinking about the experience of the consultation so far is affecting their ideas or hypotheses about the issue being worked on (team development, culture change in the organization, for example). It is important that the discussion represents different points of view. Participants are asked to listen and observe but not join in. After about ten minutes, the team invites participants to comment on what they learned from listening to the discussion.

The effect on participants, both those in and out of the reflecting team is that it breaks the usual patterns of interaction and allows them to see their organization in a different way. This potentially allows them to connect to it differently and thus behave differently in the future. Used as a rhythmic punctuation in a workshop over several days, it can be a powerful method for the organization to learn about itself.

Sequential discussion

A sequential discussion is a good method for enabling clients to deepen their thinking about an issue by creating a "team mind" (Campbell, Draper, & Huffington, 1991).This can change the team interaction from the expression of different unconnected, potentially conflictual points of view to more of a shared dialogue or coherent story, revealing deeper shared connections or differences. The method involves the team addressing a topic one by one, with each subsequent member connecting their contribution to the previous one, only speaking if a connection can be made between the two. There can be several rounds so each participant can have more than one turn. The experience is not only of a series of "stories" but of the whole dialogue forming a "story about the stories", which can be strikingly revealing of the team about itself.

Circular questioning

Circular or systemic questioning (Penn, 1982, 1985) refers to particular kinds of question asked of a client and the potential for the asking of these questions to bring about change in themselves, in a process sometimes called "interventive interviewing" (Tomm, 1987, 1988). The nature of these questions, their purpose and effects have been intensively studied and taxonomized by family therapists (e.g. Tomm, 1988).

In general, circular questions are about helping the client discover the "patterns that connect" people, ideas, situations, and so on, in the system as a whole and to encourage them to mobilize their own problem-solving resources as a system. Linked to the consultant's hypotheses, they are a powerful tool for simultaneous diagnosis and intervention around client issues in coaching and other situations (Hieker, 2002).

Other methods and techniques from family therapy are described in Draper, Gower and Huffington (1990), and Campbell, Draper and Huffington (1991).

Play, fantasy, and reverie

In response to the increasingly performance driven culture in all sectors, our clients appear to have less and less time to reflect on what they do and learn from it, but there is increasing pressure to innovate and be creative to ensure the organization stays ahead of its rivals. Some of them are experiencing considerable stress and conflict at work and feel the organization to be increasingly psychologically intrusive. Approaches which emphasize fun, playfulness, fantasy, and reverie seem to be more important now to help people free their thinking and access preconscious and unconscious material to aid creativity. Therefore, we have found it useful in working with individuals and teams to use drawing, sculpting, and other drama therapy techniques, model and picture making, outdoor work, creative writing, guided imagery, and the use of dreams.

Social dreaming

Social dreaming is a method of working with dreams and dream images in a social or organizational context. Pioneered and developed by Gordon Lawrence over the past ten years (Lawrence, 1998, 2003), it has shown how sharing and associating to dreams collectively can offer fresh insights into the concerns and feelings of people in organizations and communities; what they signify or foreshadow. As a client who has made use of the method in working with her own group of senior managers puts it, dreams "give suitable expression to something already in the air".

In our recent practice, we have drawn on and adapted the concept of social dreaming in role consultancy, in workshops, and as a method of exploring our own organizational experience and context.

New ways of conceptualizing development and training

TCS runs a portfolio of development programmes to help individuals develop process consultancy skills. These are designed for people who are practising consultants and those who are considering making a transition into consultancy work. Based on feedback from participants on the programmes and those who were interested but did not attend, we have reconceptualized and redesigned these programmes.

The main feedback was that pressure of work limited the time people had available to attend, so the programmes were restructured into a series of three-day workshops. In terms of content, participants valued the experiential nature of the programmes and wanted a blend of practical skills development plus depth of insight about their personal style and feedback about the impact of their behaviour in role.

In response to this feedback, the portfolio of process consultancy programmes was relaunched as Change Agent Development Programmes and these have been redesigned in several key ways. First, each programme has a specific focus for applying process consultancy: one-to-one situations, group facilitation, and managing the process of change. Second, each has elements of practical skills development. This involves participants taking up the role of a process consultant and receiving feedback from participants and TCS workshop staff, and also receiving input from TCS workshop staff on conceptual frameworks and models appropriate to the theme of the workshop.

Third, the unique aspect of these programmes is that the practical skills development is blended with intensive experiential events and regular review sessions to focus on the "here and now" experience of working together on the workshop. This element enables participants to learn about group dynamics in real time, so that the evidence of what may be happening below the surface in the group is accessible to work with and understand as the workshop progresses. The integration of experiential work and skills development also enables participants to receive valuable feedback about the impact they have in groups and the impact the group has on them as an individual.

The Advanced Process Consultancy programme is the fourth in the portfolio; it enables participants to consolidate their learning from the short workshops and offers further observational and process skills development and supervision of a team consultancy project with an organizational client.

The integration of skills development and learning from the "here and now" experience of the group dynamics on the workshop has also been applied to new TCS programmes: Mastering

Leadership, Excellence in Leadership Performance, and Executive Coaching Skills Programme.

Developments in group relations

- The Resource Management Event
- The Marketplace Event

The origins of group relations can be traced to a 1946 Kurt Lewin workshop, commissioned by the Connecticut Interracial Commission to improve intergroup tensions between different religious and racial groups (Marrow, 1969, p. 210). Studying the conscious and unconscious dynamics of group membership and of representative leadership between groups remains a core element of group relations training. It came to England in 1957 with the first Leicester Conference organized by the Tavistock Institute. This conference had an emphasis on training change agents to influence their own organizations. In 1962, A. K. Rice redesigned the programme to include the large study group and the institutional event. Rice now saw the conference itself as an object for study with its own management, leadership and political processes. This continues to be the focus of the Leicester Conference today, namely the study of authority and leadership in the conference as an organization. The experiential method means that members participate as students who manage their own learning.

From the context of this relatively unchanging tradition, other group relations events have developed in response to new social needs. Some have focused on deeper contact with unconscious processes, such as social dreaming, which accesses the creative potential of the unconscious organizational matrix (Lawrence, 1998). Others have responded to the increasing need for collaboration across boundaries, such as the small study group visiting exercise, or by using the small study groups as the basis for an intergroup event, challenging their silo-like isolation. The resource management event and the marketplace event are a response to changing organizational structures.

The resource management event has evolved through several formats. It began with an event designed by Jon Stokes in the late

1980s in collaboration with Marilyn Pietroni in response to the introduction of the purchaser–provider split into public sector organizations, when senior clinicians found themselves in new purchaser roles, functioning as assessors rather than providers. Requests from Tavistock Consultancy Service clients to make experiential training events more relevant to their needs has led to the further development of this event. It now has a corporate task of creating a programme of events designed to meet members' needs, using members' own resources. Management of the event is delegated entirely to members and the staff are only in consultant role. In this way it explores an element of organizational authority that is missing in the Leicester model with its historical roots in representative and personal authority, i.e., authority over others delegated from above (Obholzer & Roberts, 1994, p. 39). The corporate task highlights the interdependency of managers and managed-for task performance. It often happens that every group shares the belief that it can blame other groups for failure to achieve the task. In this event the delegated aspect of authority and the interdependency of sub-groups enable participants to make more obvious connections with organizational experience.

A second development at the Tavistock Consultancy Service has been the marketplace event. In recent years the boundary between public and private sector organizations has given way to public–private partnerships and the introduction of market mechanisms into public sector resource allocation. The clash of values arising from these new organizational forms has been acute. These differences crystallize around the notion of competition. In the private sector, competition with other providers is a key organizational driver. In the public sector, competition between providers is seen as a foreign element. The marketplace event is based on competition. Members break into small groups representing independent organizations. Each group devises an event and a marketing strategy for attracting customers. Then, moving into the marketplace plenary room, each group competes to attract enough customers to put on its event. The ownership of anxiety about failure triggers an outburst of energy, sexuality, excitement, physical pushing and pulling, seduction, bullying, mistrust, deal-making, and cartel-forming behaviour. In the review session a common response is one of shock when it is recognized that the pressure of competition and fear of failure has led to a dumbing-down of the events on offer and a lowering of expectations about what will attract others. On the other hand competition also stimulates some creative responses; thereby questioning the assumed link between creativity and safety. The new aspect of this event that is different to the Leicester model is that it incorporates competition as an on-task driver. In this way it connects directly with private sector organizations and challenges public sector ones. These developments show the flexibility of the group relations tradition of experiential learning that can be adapted to new social needs while maintaining its emphasis on unconscious processes and personal and group responsibility.

Research as consultancy; consultancy as research

We have developed an action research method that integrates process consultancy skills and applies principles from psycho-analysis and systems theory. The unique nature of this model is that it provides a means of conducting a consultancy intervention in an organization at the same time as conducting research. In this way the roles of researcher and consultant are intertwined.

Action research evolved from the work of social psychologist Kurt Lewin in the 1940s (e.g. Lewin, 1946). He advocated that in order to gain insight into a process the researcher had to create a change and then observe the variable effects and new dynamics (Banister, Burman, Parker, Taylor, & Tindall, 1994). Lewin empha-sized the cyclical process of action research, his own approach being a cycle of planning, action, and "fact-gathering". We have integrated this model of action research with process consultancy skills, which are based on the model described by Schein (1990) as an approach where the consultant is less concerned with the content of a problem and more with the process by which the indi-vidual, group, or organization identifies and solves problems (Huffington, Cole, & Brunning, 1997). This model of consultancy focuses on helping clients to form their own diagnosis, and to generate, select, and implement any associated solutions. Used as a research model this means that individuals in the client organiza-tion are involved in all stages of the research process; that is, diag-nosing the situation, planning action, taking action, evaluating the impact of making a change, and specifying learning from the intervention. This cycle is then repeated by returning to the diagnostic phase. We also apply ideas from psychoanalysis and systems theory during the diagnostic and evaluation phases of the cycle and enable clients to develop the capacity to understand their organization using this approach. An example of this integrated action research/process consultancy approach is described in Chapter Five, "From sycophant to saboteur—responses to organizational change".

Glossary

Action research: research model derived from the work of Lewin where insight into a process is gained by creating a change and then observing the variable effects and new dynamics.

Attachment Theory: theory pioneered by John Bowlby (1907–1990) studying infants' instinctive responses to separation from their primary care-giver and the nature of their tie to them.

Authority and power: power is an attribute of persons or of groups. It refers to the ability and readiness to act upon others to achieve a given result. Authority is an attribute of systems. It refers to the right of persons or groups to make and accept accountability for decisions which are binding on others, without reference back. Power without authority raises questions of legitimacy; authority without power raises questions of effectiveness.

Basic assumption: term introduced by Bion (1961) to refer to one of two omnipresent modes of mental functioning in groups, in which members behave as if they shared unspoken and unconscious assumptions about the group, its task, and leadership. Bion identifies three variants of basic assumption functioning:

Dependence: the group is dependent on a leader, experienced as the source of all knowledge, health and power.

Fight–flight: the group is in fight or flight from an "enemy" (object or idea) and the leader's role is to mobilize fight or flights so as to preserve the group.

Pairing: the group looks to the pairing between two members (or equivalents) to generate the new "saving" idea.

Later authors have added other assumptions to these three, e.g. One-ness (Turquet, 1975) and Me-ness (Lawrence, Bain, & Gould, 1996).

Complexity theory: a systems theory of organizations that draws on the idea that interacting components of the organization will self-organize to form evolving structures and an emergent set of organizational properties

Container–contained: a highly generalized concept formulated by Bion (1962, 1970) to designate a state of integration in terms of a reciprocity between two functions; a containing function and a contained function; for example, between a baby (contained) and its mother (container) or between an individual (contained) and the group/organization (container). Catastrophic anxiety about survival is stirred up if the containing function breaks down or when it has to be substantively transformed through a forceful explosion of growth in the contained.

Defence against anxiety: a phrase implying that a mental mechanism, and by extension an organizational configuration or behaviour, is being used to keep anxiety at bay.

Depressive position: a term introduced by Klein to refer to a state of psychological integration of love and hate towards another person or object seen realistically as having good and bad aspects.

Ecological perspective: term used to refer to understanding the impact of the social, political and economic environment on an organizational system.

Enactment; Inactment: enactment refers to the projection (placing) of internal needs and defences on to an external environment that

appears to mirror them. Inactment means unconsciously responding in feelings or behaviour to stimuli coming from the external
environment. The difference lies in the point of origin.

Envy, jealousy and rivalry: envy refers to the desire to spoil something good simply because it is good but does not belong to the self.
Jealousy is a hostile feeling at being excluded from a relationship
with a loved person. Rivalry is a feeling of competition with
another person for a desired object.

Failed dependency: a state of mind in which individuals and/or
groups feel let down by the failure of an institution to meet their
needs.

Force field analysis: analytic technique developed by Lewin to
understand what forces will enable change to occur and what forces
will be barriers against change

Generativity: term used by Erikson (1963) to refer to the middle
stage in life where there is an active participation in productive and
creative areas of life, particularly showing concern for the welfare
of ensuing generations.

Good and bad objects: a shorthand way of referring to the separation of conflicting aspects of objects in the paranoid–schizoid position, as if good and bad aspects belong to different people or
objects.

Group relations model: the theory and method developed by the
The Tavistock Institute and associated bodies, including TCS, for
understanding and exploring the dynamics of intra- and intergroup
behaviour, drawing on the pioneering studies of Wilfred Bion
(1948–1951).

Holding: an environment that is experienced as emotionally containing. One where significant others are able to accept and consider
intense feelings without being compelled to act out a retaliatory
response.

Idealization: a mental mechanism of the paranoid–schizoid position that unrealistically exaggerates the good aspects of an object to the exclusion of any deficiencies.

Identification: a psychological mechanism for assimilating self and object. It can operate by introjection or by projection: introjective identification by which the object's characteristics are ascribed to the self and projective identification by which the self's characteristics are ascribed to the object.

Inner world: a Kleinian concept of an unconscious internal psychic space in which internal objects interact with each other.

Input–conversion–output model: the model used in open systems theory to refer to the processes on which the organization and its component parts depend to maintain their viability in a given environment.

Institutional or organizational transference and counter-transference: a variant of transference and counter-transference (cf. below) where the relationship transferred and elicited has an institutional significance or meaning; e.g. a consultant experiences the feeling of being placed in a role in the client's organization-in-the-mind.

Interpretation: The act of giving a meaning different to the intended meaning or literal meaning of thoughts, words or actions.

Large group process: the conscious and unconscious patterning of behaviour in large groups, usually related to the preservation of identity (Turquet, 1975).

Learning organization: an organization that learns and encourages learning among its people. It promotes exchange of information between employees, hence creating a more knowledgeable workforce. This produces a flexible organization where people will accept and adapt to new ideas and changes through a shared vision.

Leicester conferences: a series of residential educational conferences held at Leicester University by The Tavistock Institute since

1957, designed to explore group dynamics and leadership through experiential learning (Miller, 1990).

Narcissism: a concept with a complex technical history that broadly means being in love with oneself at the expense of relationships with others.

Oedipal phantasies: phantasies derived from the Oedipus complex in which the self feels like a child excluded from the parental sexual relationship.

Organization and enterprise: an organization is a collection of individuals organized into a social arrangement where they interact with one another in pursuit of common goals. An enterprise is a distinctive practice or set of practices that embody an organization's implicit or explicit concept of the work it does.

Organization as system: refers to ways of understanding how organizations function as systems and how what happens in any one part cannot be separated from what is happening elsewhere.

Osmotic boundary-keeping function: the system is dependent on the wider environment for its needs to be satisfied and in order to survive and keep its function the system has to constantly adapt as it interacts across a boundary with an environment that may be continuously changing and increasing in complexity.

Paranoid–schizoid position: a term introduced by Klein to refer to a state of psychological splitting in which conflicting emotions are kept apart and good and bad aspects of people or objects are also kept separate.

Person–role–system model: term used to understand the interrelatedness between the individual as a person, the individual in their role, and the organization as a system.

Phantasies/fantasies: phantasies is a term used to distinguish unconscious imaginings from conscious fantasies and daydreaming.

Primary process: the emotional undercurrent elicited by the nature of an organization's work that may interfere with its performance.

Primary task: term used by Rice to mean the task that the organization "must perform to survive", which was later developed by Lawrence and Robinson (1975) to distinguish between the normative primary task (what the organization ought to pursue); the existential primary task (what members believe they are doing) ; and the phenomenal primary task (hypothesis about what members are engaged in and of which they may not be consciously aware).

Process consultancy: style of consultancy described by Schein as being less concerned with the content of a problem and more with the process by which the individual, group, or organization identifies and solves problems

Pro-tainment: a term used to refer to a neglected function of "containment": establishing a sense of lively engagement with an "object" person or thing.

Psychotic anxiety–paranoid/persecutory anxiety: psychotic or paranoid anxiety is part of the paranoid–schizoid position in which the principal anxiety is the destruction of the self by imaginary bad objects. Persecutory anxiety may also refer to painful feelings in the depressive position about damaging or losing good objects.

Reframing: technique used by consultants when giving feedback to the client in the diagnostic phase to reframe a problem or issue so it can be seen from a different and more positive perspective.

Resistance: resistance implies a conscious or unconscious refusal to accept reality for emotional reasons.

Secure base: concept developed from Bowlby's work on physical separation that focuses on the primary care-giver's availability (sensitivity and responsiveness) to the infant. A child that experiences this emotional availability (secure base) is able to venture out appropriately and explore their environment.

Selected fact: term used by Bion to describe a sense of discovering coherence through an emotional or cognitive synthesis of disordered elements.

Social systems as a defence against anxiety: a theoretical perspective that highlights the way in which organizational structures and patterns of behaviour are designed to protect the individual against anxiety. The anxiety may arise from the nature of the task, the patterning of the environment, the gradient of change, etc. (cf. Enactment: Inactment).

Super-ego: an internal parental function that can be experienced as helpful or punitive.

System: activities and relations with a boundary. Systems may be open or closed. Open systems are those that are dependent for their survival and growth on continuous exchange with their environment, across their boundary. (Note: open systems, however, may on occasion behave *as if* they were self-sustaining.)

Transference and counter-transference: transference occurs when the client brings into a relationship with a consultant something that belongs elsewhere. Counter-transference is the response in the consultant, which may take the form of a feeling, or of a pressure to take up a particular role, that gives the consultant information about the emotional state of the client or of the client's organization.

Valency: an individual's propensity to take up a particular role in a group or to adopt a particular type of basic assumption

Work group: the counterpart to basic assumption functioning (cf. above), in which members cooperate around an overt task with due regard to external and internal realities and a capacity to learn from experience.

REFERENCES

Ackroyd, S., & Thompson, P. (1999). *Organizational Misbehaviour*. London: Sage.

Abadi, S. (2003). Between the frontier and the network: Notes for a metapsychology of freedom. *International Journal of Psychoanalysis*, *84*(2): 221–234.

Andersen, T. (1987). The reflecting team: dialogue and meta-dialogue in clinical work. *Family Process*, 26: 415–428.

Argyris, C. (1985). *Strategy, Change and Defensive Routines*. Boston, MA: Pitman.

Armstrong, D. (1995). *The Analytic Object in Organizational Work*. London: Tavistock Consultancy Service.

Armstrong D. (1997). The "institution-in-the-mind: reflections on the relation of psychoanalysis to work with organizations. *Free Associations*, *7*(41): 1–14.

Armstrong, D. (2002). Making present: reflections on a neglected function of leadership and its contemporary relevance. *Organizational and Social Dynamics*, *2*(1): 89–98.

Armstrong, D. (2003). The work group revisited: reflections on the practice of group relations. *Free Associations*, *10*(1: 53): 14–24.

Baker-Miller, J. (1986). *The New Psychology of Women*. Boston, MA: Beacon Press.

Banister, P., Burman, E., Parker, L., Taylor, M., & Tindall, C. (1994). *Qualitative Methods in Psychology: A Research Guide*. Milton Keynes: Open University Press.

Bateson, G. (1973). *Steps to an Ecology of Mind*. St Albans: Paladin.

Beck, U. (1992). *Risk Society: Towards a New Modernity*. London: Sage.

Bennis, W. G., (1962). Toward a "truly" scientific management: The concept of organizational health. *Industrial Management Review (MIT)*, 4(1): 1–27.

Bion, W. R. (1961). *Experiences in Groups and Other Papers*. London: Tavistock Publications

Bion, W. R. (1962). *Learning from Experience*. London: Heinemann.

Bion, W. R. (1970). *Attention and Interpretation: A Scientific Approach to Insight in Psychoanalysis and Groups*. London: Tavistock.

Bowlby, J. (1988). *A Secure Base: Clinical Applications of Attachment Theory*. London: Routledge.

Bridges, W. (1994). *Jobshift: How to Prosper in a Workplace Without Jobs*. New York: Addison-Wesley.

Britton, R. (1998). *Belief and Imagination*. London and New York: Routledge.

Brooks, L. (2000). Just what do you think about life in Britain today? *Nova*: June.

Burns, P. (2000). *The Silent Stakeholders: Reforming Workforce Consultation Law*. London: The Work Foundation.

Campbell, D., Draper, R., & Huffington, C. (1989). *Second Thoughts on the Theory and Practice of Milan Systemic Family Therapy*. London: Karnac.

Campbell, D, Draper, R., & Huffington, C. (1991). *A Systemic Approach to Consultation*. London: Karnac

Carr, N. (2003). IT doesn't matter. *Harvard Business Review*, 3–10 May.

Castells, M. (2000). *The Information Age. Vol 1, The Rise of the Network Society*. Oxford: Blackwell.

Caulkin, S. (2000). Politics, be proud of it! *The Observer*, 3 September.

Civin, M. (2000). *Male, Female, Email: The Struggle for Relatedness in a Paranoid Society*. New York: Other Press.

Clancy, J. (1999). Is loyalty really dead? *Across the Board, The Conference Board Magazine*, XXXVI(6): 15–19.

Coffey, E., Huffington, C., & Thomson, P. (1999). *The Changing Culture of Leadership: Women Leaders' Voices*. London: The Change Partnership.

Cooper, A. (2001). The state of mind we're in: social anxiety, governance and the Audit Society, *Psychoanalytic Studies*, 3(3–4): pp. 349–362.

Covey, S. (1992). *Principle-Centered Leadership*, London: Simon and Shuster.

Cronen, V., Pearce, W., & Tomm, K. (1985). A dialectical view of personal change. In: K. Gergen & K. Davis (Eds.), *The Social Construction of the Person* (pp. 203–224). New York: Springer-Verlag.

Cummins, A.-M. (2002). "The road to hell is paved with good intentions": quality assurance as a social defence against anxiety. *Organizational and Social Dynamics*, 2(1): 99–119.

Damasio, A. (2000). *The Feeling of What Happens: Body, Emotion and the Making of Consciousness*. London: Heinemann.

Dartington, T. (2001). 'The preoccupations of the citizen—reflections from the OPUS listening posts. *Organizational and Social Dynamics*, I(1): 94–112.

Denis, J. L., Lamothe L., & Langley, A. (2001). The dynamics of collective leadership and strategic change in pluralistic organizations. *Academy of Management Journal*, 44(4): 809–837.

Dentico, J. P. (1999). Games leaders play: using process simulations to develop collaborative leadership practices for a knowledge-based society. *Career Development International*, 4(3): 175–182.

Doyle, J. (2000). *New Community or New Slavery: The Emotional Division of Labour*. London: The Work Foundation.

Draper, R., Gower, M., & Huffington, C. (1990). *Teaching Family Therapy*. London, Karnac.

Drucker, P. (1999). *Management Challenges for the 21st Century*. New York: Harper Business.

Dunant, S., & Porter, R. (Eds.) (1996). *The Age of Anxiety*. London: Virago.

Equal Opportunities Commission (2004). *Sex and Power: Who runs Britain?* Manchester: Equal Opportunities Commission.

Erikson, E. H. (1963). *Childhood and Society*. New York: Norton.

Findlay, Z., & Reynolds, C. (1997). *From Stalemate to Synergy: The Workplace Mediation Manual*. London: Hill Top Publishing.

Flores, F., & Gray, J. (2000). *Entrepreneurship and the Wired Life: Work in the Wake of Careers*. London: Demos.

Fox, M. (1994). *The Reinvention of Work*. New York: HarperCollins.

Freud, S. (1921c). Group psychology and the analysis of the ego. *S.E.*, 18: 69–134.

Fukayama, F. (1995). *Trust: the social virtues and the creation of prosperity*. London: Hamish Hamilton.

Giddens, A. (1990). *The Consequences of Modernity*.Cambridge: Polity.

Giddens, A. (1999). *Runaway World: How Globalisation is Shaping our Lives*. London: Profile Books.

Glouberman, S. (1995). The psychoanalytic implications of Open Space events. Unpublished paper.

Goleman, D. (1998). *Working with Emotional Intelligence*. London: Bloomsbury Publishing

Gould, L. J., Stapley, L. F., & Stein, M. (Eds.) (2001). *The System Psychodynamics of Organizations*. New York and London: Karnac.

Gregory, M. (1996). Developing effective college leadership for the management of educational change. *Leadership and Organizational Development Journal, 17*(4): 46–51.

Gribben, R. (2001). Grey power offers bright future for over 50s. *The Daily Telegraph* 14 August.

Guest, D. (2000). We've never had it so good: An analysis of what workers want from work. Paper presented to Institute of Public Policy Research, "The Future of Work Seminar", 23 October.

Gutmann, D. (1989). The decline of traditional defences against anxiety. *Oxford International Symposium Proceedings, 1988*. Washington, DC: A. K. Rice Institute.

Habermas, J. (1987). *The Theory of Communicative Action*, Volume 2: *The Critique of Functionalist Reason*. Cambridge: Polity.

Hayes, N. (1997). *Doing Qualitative Analysis in Psychology*. Hove, East Sussex: Psychology Press.

Heifetz, R. A., & Laurie, D. L. (1997). The work of leadership. *Harvard Business Review*, January–February, *75*(1): 124–135.

Hieker, C. (2002.) Reflexive questions in a coaching context. Unpublished paper.

Helgesen, S. (1995). *The Web of Inclusion*. Doubleday: New York.

Hetherington, R., Cooper, A., Smith, P., & Wilford, G. (1997). *Protecting Children: Messages from Europe*. Lyme Regis: Russell House.

Hipple, J., Hardy, D., Wilson, S., & Michalski, J. (2001). Can corporate innovation champions survive? *Chemical Innovation, 31*(11): 14–22.

Hirschhorn, L. (1997). *Reworking Authority: Leading and Following in the Post-Modern Organization*. Cambridge, MA: MIT Press.

Hirschhorn, L. (1998). The Psychology of Vision. In: E. B. Klein, F. Gabelnick, & P. Herr (Eds.), *The Psychodynamics of Leadership* (pp. 109–125). Madison, CT: Psychosocial Press.

Hirschhorn, L. (2003). Politics, strategy and passion. Paper presented at ISPSO Symposium, Boston.

Hirschhorn, L., & Gilmore, T. (1992). The new boundaries of the "boundaryless company". *Harvard Business Review*, May–June: 104–115.

Hite, S. (2000). *Sex and Business*. London: Pearson Education.

Hoggett, P. (2000). *Emotional Life and the Politics of Welfare*. Houndsmills: Macmillan.

Huffington, C., Cole, C., & Brunning, H. (1997). *A Manual of Organizational Development*. Karnac.

Hutton, J., Bazalgette, J., & Armstrong, D. (1994). What does management really mean? In: R. Casemore, G. Dyos, A. Eden, K. Kellner, J. McAuley, & S. Moss (Eds.), *What makes Consultancy Work— Understanding the Dynamics* (pp. 185–203). London: South Bank University Press.

James K., & Clark, G. (2002). Service organizations; issues in transition and anxiety containment. *Journal of Managerial Psychology, 17*(5): 394–407.

Jaques, E. (1955). Social systems as a defence against persecutory and depressive anxiety. In: M. Klein, P. Heimann, & R. E. Money-Kyrle (Eds.), *New Directions in Psychoanalysis* (pp. 478–498). London: Tavistock Publications.

Jaques, E. (1995) Why the psychoanalytic approach to organizations is dysfunctional. *Human Relations, 48*(4): 343–349.

Kabacoff, R., & Peters, H. (1999). Leadership and gender: a comparison of leadership style. Management Research Group Paper.

Khaleelee, O., & Miller, E. J. (1984). *West Yorkshire Talks about the Future of Work*. London: OPUS and Work & Society.

Klein, M. (1940). Mourning and its relation to manic-depressive states. In: *Love, Guilt and Reparation and Other Works*, Volume1, *The Writings of Melanie Klein* (1975). London: Hogarth Press.

Klein, M. (1946). Notes on some schizoid mechanisms. In: *Envy and Gratitude*, Volume 3, *The Writings of Melanie Klein* (1975). London: Hogarth Press.

Klein, M. (1955) The psychoanalytic play technique: its history and significance. In: *Envy and Gratitude*, Volume 3, *The Writings of Melanie Klein* (1975). London: Hogarth Press.

Klein, M. (1957). Envy and gratitude. In: *Envy and Gratitude*, Volume 3, *The Writings of Melanie Klein* (1975). London: Hogarth Press.

Klein, M. (1959). Our adult world and its roots in infancy. In: *Envy and Gratitude*, Volume 3, *The Writings of Melanie Klein* (1975). London: Hogarth Press.

Klein, M. (1963). On the sense of loneliness. In: *Envy and Gratitude*, Volume 3, *The Writings of Melanie Klein* (1975). London: Hogarth Press.

Kram, K., & McCollum, M. (1995). When women lead. Paper presented at ISPSO Symposium, London.

Lacan, J. (1977). *Ecrits: A Selection*. London: Tavistock.

Lawrence, W. G., & Robinson, P. (1975). An innovation and its implementation: issues of evaluation. Tavistock Institute of Human Relations: document no CASR 1069 (unpublished). (cf. Miller, E. (1993). *From Dependency to Autonomy: Studies in Organization and Change*. London, Free Association Books.)

Lawrence, W. G., Bain, A., & Gould, L. (1996). The fifth basic assumption. *Free Associations*, 6:1(7): 28–55.

Lawrence, W. G. (Ed.) (1998). *Social Dreaming @Work*. London: Karnac.

Lawrence, W. G. (Ed.) (2003). *Experiences in Social Dreaming*. London: Karnac.

Legum, C. (2001). The role of facilitators as mediators in transitional process: a South African case study. In: G. Amado & A. Ambrose (Eds.), *The Transitional Approach to Change* (pp. 197–226). London: Karnac.

Lewin, K. (1946). Action research and minority problems. *Journal of Social Issues*, 2(4): 34–46.

Lewin, K. (1947). Frontiers in group dynamics I. Concept, method and reality in social sciences; social equilibria and social change. *Human Relations*, 1: 5–41.

Litwin, G., Bray, J., & Lusk Brooke, K. (1996). *Mobilising the Organization*. Englewood Cliffs, NJ: Prentice Hall.

Locke, E. (2003). Leadership: starting at the top. In: C. Pearce & J. Conger (Eds.), *Shared Leadership: Reframing the Hows and Whys of Leadership* (pp. 271–284).Thousand Oaks, CA: Sage.

Loden, M. (1985). *Feminine Leadership*. New York: Random House.

MacIntyre, A. (1981). *After Virtue: A Study in Moral Theory*. London: Duckworth.

Main, M. (1996). Introduction to the special section on attachment and psychopathology: II: Overview of the field of attachment. *Journal of Consulting and Clinical Psychology*, 64: 237–243.

Mant, A. (1997). *Intelligent Leadership*. St Leonards, NSW: Allen and Unwin.

Marrow, A. J. (1969). *The Practical Theorist*. New York: Basic Books.

Martin, P. (1993). Feminist practice in organizations: implications for management. In: E. A. Fagenson (Ed.), *Women in Management* (pp. 274–296). Newbury Park: Sage.

Meltzer, D. (1983). *Dream-Life*. Strath Tay, Perthshire. Clunie Press.

Meltzer, D. & Harris Williams, M. (1988). *The Apprehension of Beauty*. Strath Tay, Perthshire: Clunie Press.

Menzies, I. (1959). The functioning of social systems as a defence against anxiety: a report on a study of the nursing service of a general hospital. *Human Relations, 13*: 95–121. Reprinted in Menzies Lyth, I., *Containing Anxiety in Institutions*, London: Free Association Books, 1988.

Menzies Lyth, I. (1990). A psychoanalytical perspective on social institutions. In: E. Trist & H. Murray (Eds.), *The Social Engagement of Social Science*, Volume 1: *The Socio-Psychological Perspective*, (pp. 463–475). London: Free Association Books.

Menzies Lyth, I. (1991). Changing organizations and individuals: psychoanalytic insights for improving organizational health. In: M. Kets de Vries (Ed.), *Organizations on the Couch* (pp. 361–378). San Francisco: Jossey-Bass.

Miller, E. J. (1990). Experiential learning in groups. I: The development of the Leicester Model. In: E. Trist & H. Murray (Eds.), *The Social Engagement of Social Science*, Volume 1: *The Socio-Psychological Perspective*. London: Free Association Books.

Miller, E. J. (1993). *From Dependency to Autonomy: Studies in Organization and Change*. London: Free Association Books.

Miller, E .J. (1997). Implications of the changing world of work. In: D. Kennard & N. Small (Eds.), *Living Together* (pp. 99–118). London: Quartet Books.

Miller, E. J. (1999). Dependency, alienation or partnership? The changing relatedness of the individual to the enterprise. In: R. French & R. Vince (Eds.), *Group Relations, Management and Organization* (pp. 98–111). Oxford: Oxford University Press.

Miller, E. J., & Rice, A. K. (1967). *Systems of Organization: Task and Sentient Systems and their Boundary Control*. London: Tavistock Publications.

Miller, E. J., & Gwynne, G. V. (1972). *A Life Apart: A Pilot Study of Residential Institutions for the Physically Handicapped and the Young Chronic Sick*. London: Tavistock Publications.

Milner, M. [J. Field, pseud.] (1934). *On Not Being Able to Paint*. 2nd edn. London: Heinemann.

Obholzer, A. (1995). Thinking creatively in context. Tavistock 75th anniversary paper. Unpublished.

Obholzer, A. (2001). The leader, the unconscious and the ,anagement of the organization. In: L. Gould, L. Stapely & M. Stein (Eds.), *The Systems Psychodynamics of Organizations* (pp. 197–216). New York: Karnac.

Obholzer, A. (2003). Personal communication.

Obholzer, A., & Roberts, V. Z. (1994). *The Unconscious at Work: Individual and Organizational Stress in the Human Services*. London: Routledge.

Oldfield, C. (2000). Working mothers' secrets. *The Sunday Times*, 2 July.

O'Neill, O. (2002). A *Question of Trust: the BBC Reith Lectures 2002*. Cambridge University Press.

OPUS (1980–1989). *Bulletin Nos. 1–29*. OPUS.

Ostroff, F. (1999). *The Horizontal Organization*. Oxford: Oxford University Press.

Owen, H. (1992). *Open Space Technology: A User's Guide*. Potomac, MD: Abbott.

Peters, T. (1997). *The Circle of Innovation*. London: Hodder and Stoughton.

Penn, P. (1982). Circular questioning *Family Process*, 21(3) 267–280.

Penn, P. (1985). Feed-forward: future questions, future maps. *Family Process*, 24(3): 399–410.

Platzer, M. (2003). American Electronics Association, Tech. Employment Update, March 19.

Pooley, J. (1994). A systemic study into the meanings of time and temporal constructs in family life. Unpublished Thesis.

Power, M. (1994). *The Audit Explosion*. London: Demos.

Prince, B. (2001). Career opportunity in the new economy: mobility versus role enhancement and organizational attachment. Paper presented at the 42nd Annual Western Academy of Management Conference, Sun Valley, Idaho; 6 April 2001.

Reed, B., & Bazalgette, J. (2003). *Organizational Role Analysis*. London: Grubb Institute.

Reynolds, C. (2000). Workplace mediation. In: M. Liebmann (Ed.), *Mediation in Context* (pp. 166–176). London & Philadelphia: Jessica Kingsley.

Rice, A. K. (1958)[1987]. *Productivity and Social Organization*. New York and London: Garland Publishing.

Rice, A. K., (1963). *The Enterprise and its Environment*. London: Tavistock Publications.

Rice A. K. (1965). *Learning for Leadership*, London: Tavistock.

Rifkin, J. (2001). Log off now. The *Guardian*, 26 May.

Roberts, V. (1994). The self-assigned impossible task. In: A. Obholzer & V. J. Roberts (Eds.), *The Unconscious at Work: Individual and Organizational Stress in the Human Services* (pp. 110–120). London: Routledge.

Schein, E. H. (1987). *The Clinical Perspective in Fieldwork. Sage University Papers Series on Qualitative Research Methods*, Volume 5. Thousand Oaks, CA: Sage.

Schein, E. H. (1988). *Process Consultation, Volume I: Its Role in Organization Development*, 2nd edn. Wokingham: Addison Wesley OD Series.

Schein, E. H. (1990). A general philosophy of helping: process consultation. *Sloan Management Review: Reprint Series, 31*(Spring, 3): 57–64.

Schon, D. (1971). *Beyond the Stable State*. New York: Random House.

Segal, H. (1991). *Dream, Phantasy and Art*. London: The New Library of Psychoanalysis 12, Routledge.

Sennett, R. (1998). *The Corrosion of Character: The Personal Consequences of Work in the New Capitalism*. W.W. Norton.

Stein, H. F. (2001). *Nothing Personal, Just Business, a Guided Journey into Organizational Darkness*. Westport: Quorum.

Stein, S., & Book, H. (2000). *The EQ Edge: Emotional Intelligence and Your Success*. Toronto, Canada: Stoddart Publishing.

Steiner, J. (1993). *Psychic Retreats*. Routledge.

Stokes, J. (1994). What is unconscious in organizations? In: R. Casemore, G. Dyos, A. Eden, K. Kellner, J. McAuley, & S. Moss (Eds.), *What Makes Consultancy Work: Understanding the Dynamics* (pp. 312–319). London: South Bank University Press.

Taffinder, P. (1998). *Big Change: A Route Map for Corporate Transformation*. Chichester: John Wiley.

Tomm, K. (1987). Interventive interviewing: Part II. Reflexive questioning as a means to enable self-healing. *Family Process, 26*: 167–183.

Tomm, K. (1988). Interventive interviewing Part III. Intending to ask lineal, circular, strategic or reflexive questions. *Family Process, 27*: 1–15.

Trist, E. L., & Murray, H. (Eds.) (1990). *The Social Engagement of Social Science: A Tavistock Anthology, Volume 1. The Socio-Psychological Perspective*. Philadelphia, PA: University of Pennsylvania Press.

Trist, E. L., & Murray, H. (Eds.) (1993). *The Social Engagement of Social Science: A Tavistock Anthology, Volume 2. The Socio-Technical Perspective*, Philadelphia, PA: University of Pennsylvania Books.

Turquet, P. M. (1974). Leadership: the individual and the group. In: G. S. Gibbard, J. J. Harstman & R. D. Mann (Eds.), *Analysis of Groups* (pp. 349–386).San Francisco: Jossey-Bass.

Turquet, P. M. (1975). Threats to identity in the large group. In: L. Kreeger (Ed.), *The Large Group: Dynamics and Therapy* (pp. 87–144). London: Maresfield Reprints.

Wajcman, J. (1998). *Managing Like a Man: Women and Men in Corporate Management*. Cambridge: Polity Press.

Watson, S. (2002). Complexity and the transhuman, *Organizational and Social Dynamics, 2*(2): 245–263.

Winnicott, D. W. (1951)[1978]. Transitional objects and transitional phenomena. In: *Through Paediatrics to Psycho-Analysis*. London: Hogarth Press.

Winnicott, D. W. (1964). *The Child the Family and the Outside World*. Harmondsworth: Penguin Books

Winnicott, D. W. (1965). *The Maturational Processes and the Facilitating Environment*. New York: International Universities Press.

INDEX

Abadi, S., 127, 145, 231
Ackroyd, S., 134, 231
action research, 206, 221, 223
Andersen, T., 215, 231
Argyris, C., 188, 231
Armstrong, D., 1, 11, 27, 62, 66–67,
    81, 125, 132, 142–143, 145, 175,
    182, 192, 231, 235
attachment theory, 171, 223 *see also*:
    secure base
authority and power, 37, 62, 200,
    223

bad object, 225
Bain, A., 8, 144, 159–160, 224, 236
Baker-Miller, J., 55, 231
Banister, P., 221, 232
basic assumption, 8, 27, 40, 42–43,
    46, 54, 62, 144, 159, 206, 223,
    229
  dependence, 27, 224
  fight–flight, 27, 42, 76, 173–174,
    224

pairing, 8, 27, 42, 54, 76, 144, 206,
    224
Bateson, G., 4, 232
Bazalgette, J., 143, 145, 174, 235, 238
Beck, U., 131, 232
Bennis, W. G., 195, 232
Bion, W. R., 4, 8, 21, 26–27, 39–40,
    42, 46, 54, 62, 78, 111–113, 144,
    173, 180, 223–225, 229, 232
Book, H., 55, 239
Bowlby, J., 181, 223, 228, 232
Bray, J., 54, 236
Bridges, W., 163, 232
Britton, R., 113, 232
Brooks, L., 53, 232
Brunning, H., 221, 235
Burman, E., 221, 232
Burns, P., 51, 232

Campbell, D., 4, 215–216, 232
Carr, N., 156, 232
Castells, M., 60, 129, 132, 232
Caulkin, S., 60, 232

Civin, M., 59, 232
Clancy, J., 163, 232
Clark, G., 79, 235
Coffey, E., 49, 52, 232
Cole, C., 221, 235
"Communiversity", 63–66
complexity theory, 224
container–contained, 26, 85, 133,
    142, 149, 224
containment, 7, 32, 41, 48, 65–66, 72,
    75, 78, 80–81, 85, 115–116, 126,
    127, 145, 149, 152, 157, 163, 185,
    193, 202, 207, 210, 228
Cooper, A., 60, 125–127, 130–131,
    232, 234
Covey, S., 55, 233
creativity, 8–9, 25, 31, 33, 41, 46, 48,
    50, 58, 61, 63, 66, 75, 81, 83,
    85–87, 94, 100, 103, 107–118,
    120–122, 126, 134, 138, 142–143,
    149, 152, 155, 158, 160, 161, 173,
    181, 191, 193, 200, 206, 209–210,
    217, 219, 221, 225
Cronen, V., 176, 233
Cummins, A.-M., 131, 233

Damasio, A., 12, 233
Dartington, T., 60, 125–127, 133, 233
defence(s), 182, 184
    against anxiety, 20, 23, 40, 88–89,
        94, 102, 113, 160, 174, 196–197
        224, 229
    social system as, 91–92, 96, 132,
        229
    against envious attack, 78
    against loss of identification, 159
    boredom as a, 156
    the acknowledgement of risk, 26
Denis, J. L., 68, 233
Dentico, J. P., 68, 233
depressive position, 42, 45, 64, 86,
    103, 109–111, 113–115 224, 228
    see also: paranoid–schizoid
    position
Doyle, J., 50, 54, 233
Draper, R., 4, 215–216, 232–233

Drucker, P., 54, 223
Dunant, S., 134, 233

ecological perspective, 5, 22, 224
emotional intelligence, 13, 189
emotions in organizations, 11–27,
    32, 36, 55, 67–69, 71, 73, 75, 77,
    79, 85–86, 109, 115–116, 120,
    122, 143, 154, 156–157, 162–163,
    179, 181, 183, 186, 201, 206, 211,
    228–229
enactment, 17, 19–20, 229 see also:
    inactment
envy, 12, 15, 19, 58, 64, 89, 118,
    120–122, 153, 225
Equal Opportunities Commission,
    51, 233
Erikson, E. H., 225, 233

failed dependency, 133, 168, 225
Findlay, Z., 198, 233
Flores, F., 134, 233
followership, 31, 33–35, 38, 43–44,
    46, 48, 93, 94, 192 see also: lead-
    ership
force field analysis, 91, 225
Fox, M., 151, 233
Freud, S., 43, 233
Fukayama, F., 54, 233

generativity, 78, 225
Giddens, A., 5, 131, 233–234
Gilmore, T., 60, 234
globalization, xvi, 5, 127, 137, 155
Glouberman, S., 212, 234
Goleman, D., 13, 189, 234
good object(s), 113, 225, 228
Gould, L. J., 8, 27, 33, 144, 159–160,
    224, 234, 236–237
Gower, M., 216, 233
Gray, J., 134, 233
Gregory, M., 68, 234
Gribben, R., 54, 234
group process, 41, 43
    large, 226
group-relations model, 4, 8, 138,
    200, 207, 219, 221, 225

Guest, D., 51, 234
Gutmann, D., 159, 234
Gwynne, G. V., 96, 237

Habermas, J., 131, 234
Hardy, D., 118, 234
Harris Williams, M., 112, 236
Hayes, N., 4, 234
Heifetz, R. A., 79, 234
Helgesen, S., 55, 234
Hetherington, R., 130, 234
Hieker, C., 216, 234
Hipple, J., 118, 234
Hirschhorn, L., 50, 59–60, 66, 71, 81,
    147, 149, 234
Hite, S., 53, 58, 235
Hoggett, P., 129, 235
holding, 79, 225
Huffington, C., 1, 4, 31, 49, 52,
    215–216, 221, 235, 232–233
Hutton, J., 143, 145, 235

idealization/idealized, 58, 72, 89,
    115, 182, 226
identification, 8, 159, 226
    projective, 47, 74, 92, 102, 105,
    197, 226
inactment, 20, 224–225, 229
inner world, 27, 37–38, 114, 186, 226
input-conversion-export model, 50,
    143, 226
interpretation, 45, 147, 226

James, K., 67, 79, 235
Jaques, E., 17, 20–23, 40, 43, 78,
    88–89, 92, 235
jealousy, 225

Kabacoff, R., 56, 235
Khaleelee, O., 133, 235
Klein, M., 42, 88. 103, 108–109,
    112–114, 118, 186, 224, 227, 235
Kram, K., 57, 235

Lacan, J., 66, 236
Lamothe, L., 68, 233

Langley, A., 68, 233
Laurie, D. L., 79, 234
Lawrence, W. G., 6, 8, 97, 144,
    159–160, 217, 219, 224, 228,
    236
leaders/leadership, 1, 3, 7, 9, 12, 14,
    16, 19, 29, 31, 33–34, 36–39,
    41–50, 85, 108–109, 116–117,
    121, 126, 136, 139, 144, 146, 155,
    163, 167, 171, 175, 184, 188,
    191–192, 202, 207, 210–211, 213,
    219, 223, 227 see also: follower-
    ship
    distributed, 32, 50, 67–69, 71–75,
    77–81
    -followership interaction, 35, 41,
    46–47, 49
    horizontal, 32
    vertical, 32
    women, 32, 49, 52–66
learning organization, 2, 55, 62, 65,
    68, 77, 120, 130, 152, 155, 160,
    212, 226
Legum, C., 194, 201–203, 236
Leicester Conference, 219, 226
Lewin, K., 65, 91, 219, 221, 223, 225,
    236
Litwin, G., 54, 236
Locke, E., 69, 236
Loden, M., 56, 236
Lusk Brooke, K., 54, 236

MacIntyre, A., 26, 236
Main, M., 180, 236
manic–depressive response, 110,
    114–117, 122
Mant, A., 55, 236
Marrow, A. J., 219, 236
Martin, P., 55, 236
McCollum, M., 57, 235
Meltzer, D., 111–112, 236
Me-ness, 144, 159, 206, 224
Menzies, I., 23, 78, 88–89, 90, 92, 96,
    237
Menzies Lyth, I., 23, 40, 161, 237
Michalski, J., 118, 234

Miller, E. J., 4, 27, 34–35, 59, 96–97, 133, 135, 143, 168, 227, 235, 237
Miller, S., 31, 33
Milner, M., 108, 237
Murray, H., 2, 4, 239

narcissism, 146, 227
National Health Service (NHS), xvii–xviii, 2, 37, 130, 137
network(s), 127–130, 132, 142, 144–146, 149, 175, 207, 212

Obholzer, A., 4, 10, 24, 27, 31, 33–34, 37, 48, 54, 64, 75, 121, 180, 220, 237–238
Oedipus complex, 227
Oldfield, C., 54, 238
O'Neill, O., 131, 238
Oneness, 8, 144, 224
OPUS, 133, 238
organization and enterprise, 7, 9, 22, 26, 32, 35, 37, 48, 61–66, 72–73, 80–81, 108, 126, 147, 227
organization as system, 13–14, 20, 128, 211, 215, 227
organizational dynamics, 8, 10, 19–20, 27, 39, 68, 82, 92, 111, 140, 168–169, 172, 178–179, 200
organizational object, 22, 24, 26–27
osmotic boundary-keeping function, 37, 227
Ostroff, F., 134, 238
Owen, H., 212, 238

paranoid–schizoid position, 42, 103, 108, 113–117, 122, 225–228
paranoid-schizoid response, 115–117, 122
Parker, L., 221, 232
Pearce, W., 176, 233
Penn, P., 216, 238
persecutory anxiety, 89, 228
person–role–system model, 32, 59, 210–211, 227
Peters, H., 56, 235
Peters, T., 51, 238

phantasy/phantasies, 12, 19, 23, 108, 227
    oedipal, 17, 19, 227
Platzer, M., 156, 238
Pooley, J., 167, 169, 171, 179, 238
Porter, R., 134, 233
Power, M., 38, 131, 238
primary process, 27, 228
primary task, 7, 32, 34–35, 37–39, 40, 42, 47, 49, 62, 86, 89, 92, 96–98, 100–101, 103–104, 106, 110–111, 144, 172–173, 228
Prince, B., 163, 238
process consultancy, 103–105, 193–197, 200, 213, 217–218, 221–222, 228
pro-tainment, 7, 32, 80, 210, 228
psychotic anxiety, 20, 88, 228

Reed, B., 174, 238
reframing technique, 59, 143, 228
resistance [to change], 9, 18, 27, 36, 38, 44–45, 87–88, 90, 95–98, 100–101, 103, 106, 115, 117–118, 137–139, 142, 161, 185, 188, 197, 200, 213, 228
    psychoanalytic theory of, 88–89, 91–92
Reynolds, C., 193–194, 198, 233, 238
Rice, A. K., 4, 34–35, 59, 117–118, 143, 219, 228, 237–238
Rifkin, J., 135, 238
rivalry, 146, 153, 225
    group, 121
    sibling, 39
Roberts, V. Z., 4, 10, 24, 27, 34, 37, 121, 184, 220, 238
Robinson, P., 97, 228, 236

Schein, E. H., 103, 194–195, 221, 228, 238–239
Schon, D., 132, 239
secure base, 181, 228
Segal, H., 109, 186, 239
selected fact, 112, 229
Sennett, R., 158, 239

Smith, P., 130, 234
Stapley, L. F., 27, 33, 234
Stein, H. F., 139, 239
Stein, M., 27, 33, 234
Stein, S., 55, 239
Steiner, J., 36, 239
Stokes, J., 58, 219, 239
superego, 141, 229
sycophant/saboteur responses, 85, 87–106, 222
system(s), 4, 13–14, 19, 35, 37, 39, 41, 46, 50, 61, 76, 80, 110, 117–118, 120, 131, 134, 136, 138–139, 145, 148, 152–156, 161, 168, 172, 174, 176, 179, 184, 187, 189, 196–197, 211, 223, 227, 229
   closed, 138–139
   defensive, 188
   delusional, 34
   family, 110
   health, 195, 200, 202
   mental, 179
   open, 4, 7, 125, 142, 195, 200, 202, 212, 226
   psychodynamics, 27, 33, 142
   psychotherapy, 215–216
   theory, 221–222, 224

Taffinder, P., 50, 239
Tavistock and Portman NHS Trust, ix, xi–xiii, xviii, xx, 2, 64

Tavistock Clinic, xi, xiii–xiv, xvi, xx, 2, 4, 10, 23
Tavistock Consultancy Service (TCS), xi–xiii, xv, xvii–xviii, 1–3, 10, 192–193, 196, 198, 205, 213, 217–218 220, 225
Tavistock Institute of Human Relations, 2, 4, 23, 219, 225–226
Taylor, M., 221, 232
Thompson, P., 134, 231
Thomson, P., 49, 52, 232
Tindall, C., 221, 232
Tomm, K., 176, 216, 233, 239
transference/counter-transference, 15, 154, 168, 229
   institutional/organizational, 6, 168, 226
Trist, E. L., 2, 4, 239
Turquet, P. M., 46, 48, 60, 144, 224, 226, 239

valency, 39, 40, 42, 54, 76, 180, 229

Wajcman, J., 53, 58, 239
Watson, S., 145, 239
Wilford, G., 130, 234
Wilson, S., 118, 234
Winnicott, D. W., 108, 183, 240
work group, 6, 27, 32, 42, 46, 62, 125, 144, 229
work–life balance, 5, 56, 159, 173, 196